Teaching Religious Education

Second Edition

Also available from Bloomsbury

Does Religious Education Work?, James C. Conroy

MasterClass in Religious Education, Liam Gearon

New Perspectives on Young Children's Moral Education, Tony Eaude

Reflective Teaching in Schools, Andrew Pollard

Religious Education, L. Philip Barnes and Andrew Davis, edited by J. Mark Halstead

Forthcoming from Bloomsbury

Mastering Primary Religious Education, Maria James and Julian Stern

Teaching Religious Education

Researchers in the Classroom

Second Edition

Julian Stern

Bloomsbury Academic
An imprint of Bloomsbury Publishing Plc

B L O O M S B U R Y
LONDON · OXFORD · NEW YORK · NEW DELHI · SYDNEY

Bloomsbury Academic

An imprint of Bloomsbury Publishing Plc

50 Bedford Square   1385 Broadway
London   New York
WC1B 3DP   NY 10018
UK   USA

www.bloomsbury.com

BLOOMSBURY and the Diana logo are trademarks of Bloomsbury Publishing Plc

First edition published 2006
Second edition published 2018

British Library Cataloguing-in-Publication Data
A catalogue record for this book is available from the British Library.

ISBN: HB: 978-1-3500-3710-6
         PB: 978-1-3500-3709-0
       ePDF: 978-1-3500-3712-0
       ePub: 978-1-3500-3711-3

Library of Congress Cataloging-in-Publication Data
A catalog record for this book is available from the Library of Congress.

Cover image © Cory Eastman / GettyImages

Typeset by Integra Software Services Pvt. Ltd.
Printed and bound in Great Britain

To find out more about our authors and books visit www.bloomsbury.com. Here you will find extracts, author interviews, details of forthcoming events and the option to sign up for our newsletters.

Contents

Preface to the Second Edition

This is an updated, expanded, edition of my book for teachers of RE who see themselves and the children and young people in school as curiosity-driven researchers. It is a book for and about teaching and learning RE. In addition to revising the eight chapters of the first edition, there are six additional chapters on the real lives of teachers and pupils; RE around the world; spirituality; thinking about philosophy and truth; ethics, rights, values, and virtues (incorporating a chapter from the first edition); and creativity. This second edition was stimulated by the continuation of the Westhill seminars (five of which I attended – after the six seminars that formed the basis of the first edition), and by the continuing growth of RE research and the persistent need to support teachers with more than cookie cutter 'how to' guides and lesson plans. It was also stimulated by my own increasing work with and understanding of RE outside the UK, notably in Australia, Canada, Finland, Germany, Israel, Latvia, the Netherlands, Norway, Russia, South Africa, Sweden, Turkey, and the United States. I am all too aware of the different ways in which RE exists in these and other countries. Even the name 'RE' will have quite different implications in different contexts – and it is a contested name within the UK too. But RE teachers find things to talk about with colleagues in other countries, and those writing for teachers should find ways of addressing an international audience. So, although the second edition still has its roots in the UK, and has retained much of the material that proved popular in the previous edition, it is now, I hope, a book that supports RE teaching internationally.

For those teaching RE, wherever you are based, I hope that this book will familiarize you with research in RE from around the world, enable you and your pupils to become curiosity-driven researchers, and give you confidence to have a curiosity-driven pedagogy.

I should mention that there are, of course, other professionals in schools – school counsellors, teaching assistants, therapists, and many more – and they also need to understand the work of RE, in order to understand their own roles. In the UK, teaching assistants often have responsibility for RE in primary schools. In the United States, counsellors will often deal with religious issues, as teachers are nervous of doing so, at least in publicly funded schools. And in many other countries those with religious roles (chaplains or senior members of religious organisations) may have key roles in RE. Although I will not write at length about these other professionals in schools, I hope that the term 'teacher' can be read as inclusively as possible, to incorporate all those professionals who help pupils learn in school.

Spellings of technical terms throughout this book are taken where possible from the QCA glossary of terms in RE (SCAA 1994) or from the *Oxford Dictionary of World Religions* (Bowker 1997). References to websites were appropriate and accurate at the time of writing, but these things change. Search engines can usually find good alternatives.

Acknowledgements

The Westhill Endowment Trust sponsored the series of seminars on which the first edition of this book is based, and additional series of seminars on which much of this second edition is based. Many thanks should go to all the trustees, both for sponsoring and for helping organize the series. Lat Blaylock of RE Today S᠁ was the chief organizer of several series of seminars and of the arrangements for the publication of the first edition: his wisdom and knowledge of the world of RE is invaluable. Many of the presenters and participants in the seminars will, I hope, find themselves in the book. I hope I have not misrepresented or ignored too many of their views, and thank them anyway for their ideas and good company. (Throughout the book, if a person's work in RE is referred to, without any reference to a publication, the source of their wisdom will be what they said at one of the Westhill seminars.) Pupils in a number of schools contributed to this book and are quoted from various research projects and from an RE festival database (*old.natre.org.uk/db/*). The researchers in those schools agreed not to name pupils, but I hope they recognize themselves: readers will recognize their insight and authority, and thank them for that. As the 8-year-old is quoted in Chapter 2 as saying, 'We're sort of teaching the grown-ups.' Indeed. Others who helped in the various stages of writing the first and second editions include Lat, once more, and Mike Bottery, Cheryl Hunt, Maria James, Pam Rauchwerger, and Marie Stern. Colleagues in the International Seminar on Religious Education and Values (*www.isrev.org*) have helped me understand RE around the world (and in the UK), for which I am immensely grateful. I'd like to thank John Hull in particular for his support and encouragement. Editorial staff at Continuum and Bloomsbury have been consistently helpful. All the faults in the book remain my own.

Julian Stern, March 2017

j.stern@yorksj.ac.uk

Chapter 1
Introduction: Inclusive RE:search

I have enjoyed all my RE lessons, religion is not as boring as you may think, it can be as interesting as you make it to be. I have learnt and understood other people's religions, which have helped me understand things in life. I have learnt about the world, and how we are not all equal. Plus lots more.

(a 13-year-old)

How did we get here?

The idea for the book started back in 2001, with a seminar funded by the St Gabriel's Trust on research in RE. Following that, the CEM (the UK-based Christian Education Movement, now Christian Education, or CE, *www.christianeducation.org.uk/*) Research Committee thought it would be a good idea to bring together RE professionals in schools, advisory services, and universities in a series of meetings, to exchange ideas on what was going on in RE classrooms and what was going on in RE research. Over a year was spent working out what areas of research were going on in RE and how to divide up the meetings, geographically and by topic. Thanks to the generosity of the Westhill Trust, a series of six meetings subsequently took place during 2004 and 2005, the *Westhill Trust Seminars*. A total of seventy-three people attended one or more of those meetings, over thirty of whom were practising classroom teachers. The topics were RE and sacred text, dialogue, inclusion, pedagogy, human rights and citizenship, and ethnography. All the meetings included presentations by key researchers (based in schools, advisory services, and universities) and contributions by, and discussions with, all the participants. I attended and made notes on every presentation and discussion, and the notes were later sent around all the participants, so that they were happy with what was described of the meetings. In addition to this book, a number of other publications related to the seminars have been written (e.g. Blaylock 2004a; Holt 2004; Johnson and Stern 2005; Stern 2007a, 2007b, 2010, 2011). It is to the enormous credit of the Westhill Trust that the first edition of this book was distributed free to all newly qualified RE teachers in the UK for several years after it was published. The trust continued to support seminars, and an account of the first eleven seminars, that is, the six seminars leading to the first edition of this book and five subsequent seminars also sponsored by the Westhill Trust, was provided as a major element in the national RE CPD Handbook (*re-handbook.org. uk/section/approaches*). All eleven Westhill seminars appear, in one form or another, in this second edition – with new chapters on the real lives of teachers and pupils, thinking about philosophy and truth, and creativity, inspired by the later Westhill seminars, along with chapters on spirituality, ethics morality and virtues, and RE around the world.

The relationship between RE and research has importance well beyond the Westhill seminars of course, and the whole world of RE research has grown and developed nationally and internationally. But the influence of those Westhill seminars was researched and published (Stern 2014a), in order to see what lessons can be learned. The results of that research have informed the writing of this second edition. But before anything else, we should get back to the basics of RE and research, starting with the two obvious questions: 'What is research?' and 'What is RE?'

What is research?

Research is connected to the search for understanding and perhaps even truth (a good tradition of that in religions, of course) and is identified as searching for understanding in particular ways. One definition of research comes from the Higher Education Funding Council for England, the largest funders of research in the UK, so worth listening to. It says that 'research is defined as a process of investigation leading to new insights, effectively shared', and 'it excludes routine testing and routine analysis' (Hefce 2011, p. 48). So research involves originality ('new insights') and a systematic process of investigation – the investigation is not just a collection of a random set of information but is thought-through and set in a wider context, which can usually be called a theory. The theory may be a theory of how to collect data (a 'methodology') or a theory about how the world works (a 'social' or 'scientific' theory). Research also involves 'sharing' those insights – with others able to comment on what you say. So if you have 'finding out' that is original, careful and systematic, and that is shared effectively, then you probably have research. So, despite all these grand-sounding phrases, it is worth saying that research is something quite ordinary. It is something we expect of pupils in our schools, for example. (I use the term 'pupils' in this book to cover all the children and young people in schools.) How can pupils be educated without their being researchers? The only learning that could not be covered by the definition of research given here would be learning that is wholly unoriginal or routine, or that does not involve systematic investigation, or that is not shared with anyone. Would teachers be happy with education that did not involve their pupils in research? Would teachers themselves be happy with a life in teaching that did not involve research?

Good examples of activities that are very close to research, but that are understandably considered rather problematic by teachers, are the preparations for audits and inspections (such as Ofsted inspections in the UK) or the achievement of various 'charter marks' and other forms of school accreditation. These are very close to research, because information is systematically collected, and it is carefully described with evidence provided to back up each piece of information. Sometimes, the processes – the ways of collecting data and the ways of analysing data – are 'routine' rather than original, and often the results (the 'insights') are not new or are only new to the inspectors/auditors (but not those in the school), and are not open to review by others. So research still has its boundaries. I have heard professional researchers say that children are rarely able to be original. I wonder if they have met a 7-year-old child, as children at that age seem to me to be bursting with originality. (Schooling can sometimes knock all that originality out of them, but that's another story!) In my own research, I take as much pride and pleasure in quoting children as I do in quoting professional adult researchers.

This book therefore includes many ways in which pupils and teachers can investigate, come up with new insights, and share those insights. It is presented as the best way to engage with RE, because RE is such a rich and complex area of study that a 'routine' exchange of information can never be enough. There is more theory and critical evaluation than is commonly found in books for teachers, and that is commonly found in a great many school audits and inspections. That's where curiosity gets you.

What is RE?

The RE described in this book is a subject in a particular place and time. RE is probably the most 'ecological' subject on any curriculum: it changes and adapts to different times and places. Most of what I studied as a child in England was similar to the subjects I taught as an adult, but RE had changed almost beyond recognition. It had become multi-religious and much more exploratory (including exploring non-religious ways of life), in contrast to the rather factual study of Christianity that I had reluctantly sat through as a child. 'Why do I have to do RE?', I grumpily asked my RE teacher when I was eleven. I know that I asked that, because not so long ago I gave a talk to teachers and advisors, and my old RE teacher, now an advisor, came up to me in the coffee break and told me that she'd taught me when she was in her first year of teaching. Now, much less grumpily, I still ask why we have RE on the curriculum – and I can come up with a number of good answers, as can my old teacher. (At the time, she said she had 'mumbled something about learning about people', and moved on.) But the RE was different then to what it is now, and it is different in almost every country around the world. There is more on that in Chapter 4. The reason for saying how varied and 'ecological' RE is, is that whatever is said about RE will *change* from place to place and time to time. A number of school subjects like to think of themselves as more universal: the same in all places and, other than being updated by new discoveries, the same subject at all times. RE has never been like that. Perhaps other subjects are changeable too, but RE seems the most variable. One religion or many? Non-religious ways of life or just religions? Children taught amongst children of the same religion or mixed? Religious groups involved in creating the curriculum or not? Attempting to bring people into religion or not? Connecting religion to the personal lives of children or studying religions using the methods of the social sciences? Incorporating moral education or an alternative to it? Compulsory or voluntary, and/ or with a parental opt-out? Is the subject even called RE, or is it 'religious instruction', 'religion education', 'religious and moral education', 'religious studies', 'worldviews education', 'religious literacy', 'theology and philosophy', 'philosophy and ethics', 'beliefs and values', 'sophology', or something else?

What does *this* book mean by RE, then? It is the RE that is taken as 'mainstream' in most contemporary education debates in England and Wales. (England and Wales share much in their approaches to RE, whereas the other parts of the UK – Scotland and Northern Ireland – have their own, different, approaches.) Broadly, the RE most visible in this book is as described in the National Framework for RE in England (QCA 2004), the Review of Religious Education in England (REC 2013), and in most of the locally agreed syllabuses for RE (available from *www.REOnline.org.uk*). However, I hope to treat seriously – and am certainly open to the many other forms of RE that are used around the world. The English and Welsh RE that is central to the book, though, is a subject that is non-confessional (i.e. it should not try to convert pupils to any particular religion, and it is open to pupils of all religions and none), multi-religious (i.e. it should involve learning about a number of religions), and respectful of non-religious ways of life (i.e. it is not just about religions). Those who have studied the history of RE in England and Wales, or who have worked with RE specialists in other countries around the world, will know how distinctive, even 'odd', is that version of the subject. Indeed, there are those currently working in England and Wales who would prefer a more confessional RE (as in Thompson 2004a, 2004b), a single-religion RE, or an RE that rejects the study of non-religious ways of life (Birmingham City Council 2007), just as there are those who would ban RE or replace it with moral or personal or citizenship education. Recognizing the existence of these debates is important; engaging in all of them, in this short book, would be impossible. It is hoped, nevertheless, that the accounts of RE and research throughout the book do speak to all those interested in every kind of RE. And there is an activity that all can complete, exploring the 'value' of RE in your school.

RE of the kind that is central to this book is, by its nature, inclusive. It includes pupils and their communities; it includes cultures and belief systems from around the world and from all of human history. It includes the non-religious and the anti-religious, as well as those passionate about their religion. This book shows how RE includes research. As this involves 'search' in RE, it can be called RE:search. Since the first edition of this book was published, Freathy and colleagues have developed a systematic approach to teaching RE that, like this book, puts research at its centre

Activity 1.1: The value of RE

In any organization there are different parts. For example, in a school, there are different subjects. Forget about the things that could be sold in the shops (such as furniture), and think instead about the value of each subject. Why is one more valuable than another? To what extent is the value intrinsic to the subject (the value of the subject in itself, for example, in helping pupils develop their own ideas), and to what extent is the value extrinsic to the subject (the value of the subject for other purposes, for example, in helping qualify pupils for a job)?

If all subjects in school were, in total, worth exactly 1,000 units, how much would each subject be worth, and why? Pupils and teachers might work on this, preferably in small groups. The list of subjects below is based on a typical English curriculum for pupils aged 11–14 (DfE 2013), but of course could be adapted to suit other curricula.

Once individual pupils or groups have filled in the values and the reasons for attributing those values, these responses can be combined into a whole-class or whole-school account.

More sophisticated analysis can be achieved if other characteristics are included on the response sheet, such as the age and gender of the respondent, and other social or religious characteristics. It could be used, for example, to analyse whether religiously active pupils set a higher value on RE, as long as responses were suitably anonymous to avoid ethical research problems of requiring responses on issues that pupils may wish to keep private.

Subject	Value	Why this value? (intrinsic and extrinsic values)
Art		
Citizenship		
Computing		
Design and technology		
English		
Geography		
History		
Maths		
Modern foreign languages		
Music		
Personal and social education		
RE		
Science		
Total value:	1,000 units	

A more sophisticated use of the activity might involve more 'modelling', where one variable is changed in order to see the impact on other variables. For example:

- If RE were abolished, which other subjects might increase their 'value' in order to compensate for this loss, and how would they change?
- If RE were to become the study of a single religion, what 'value' would it lose or gain?

and, like this book, uses punctuation in the middle of 'research', albeit to make 'RE-search' and 'RE-searcher' (Freathy et al. 2015; Freathy 2016) rather than RE:search. I am encouraged by their work to persist in my own promotion of the importance of research in RE. Pupils can be researchers, teachers can be researchers, and all can be in conversation with the people who have 'research' in their official job titles. Amongst the key writers about research in RE have been Michael Grimmitt, whose *Pedagogies of Religious Education* (Grimmitt 2000) brings together research on the teaching of RE from a wide range of writers in the field, Bob Jackson (e.g. in Jackson 2004), who writes about the development of both empirical and non-empirical research in RE, and Francis and Kay (e.g. Francis et al. 1996, or Kay and Francis 2000), who write books to support distance learning research in RE. The bringing together of RE and research is therefore well established, and exciting for RE teachers and researchers and, most of all, pupils. For RE to thrive, pupils and teachers must be involved and active. The thirteenth-century Sufi Muslim poet, Rumi, was rather critical of 'school learning', but provided the cure to some of its limitations, in the poem *Two Kinds of Intelligence* (Rumi 1995, p. 178). There he contrasts 'acquired' intelligence that flows into a schoolchild from books and teachers with the intelligence that comes from within, from the heart or soul, that flows outwards: a fountain continually flowing. The latter intelligence is described by Rumi as God-given. Whatever view people take on the source of the intelligence, it helps to promote the idea of RE being research-based and involving pupils as they are and can be, rather than passive and merely fact-driven. Of course, Rumi was not denying the importance of the first kind of intelligence either. The flow must be in both directions. That is what this book is attempting to achieve.

Teaching RE: Researchers in the classroom

The title of the book brings out two questions:

- First, how can RE improve further and bridge the gap between its own self-image as a vital and vibrant subject and the image of it portrayed by some inspectors and even some pupils, parents, and teachers as something of a backwater? An answer may be for RE as a school subject to engage more in research. That includes research undertaken by professional academics *and* research undertaken by RE teachers and pupils. Along with the accounts of RE and research in each chapter, there are thirty-three activities spread through the book: thirty-three ways in which teachers can use research in their classrooms.

- Second, how can research hope to understand the complex and relatively impenetrable world of school RE? Schools are a challenge to researchers (as described in McDonald 1989), just as religion is a challenge to researchers (as described in McCutcheon 1999), so RE presents even more problems (as described in Conroy et al. 2013). An answer may be for professional academic researchers to see pupils, their families, and schools as *co-researchers* rather than as *subjects* of research. Researchers can build in to their research a commitment to the improvement of people's lives, and to the improvement of RE and schooling more generally. This is the basis for research, such as that of Rudduck et al. 1996; MacBeath 1999; Flutter and Rudduck 2004, that attempts to give voice to pupils and teachers.

This book therefore uses some of the common themes in contemporary RE and sits them alongside some of the common themes in contemporary research. It is not a comprehensive survey of research in RE; it is a selection of some important topics; it is not an attempt to say that RE teaching and research are one and the same thing; and it is not an attempt to get busy, harassed, underfunded RE teachers to do yet another 'something else' that is research (the picture of research given at one point in Conroy et al. 2013, pp. 178–179). My description of teaching and research is a description of considerable overlap and considerable complementarity, an enlivening and a justification of both teaching (as curiosity-driven, learning-driven) and research (as 'voicing', as learning-driven) (see also Baumfield 2014: *To Teach Is To Learn*). Bringing together RE and research leads to an argument, in Chapter 13, for the value of sincerity in RE research. Sincerity is a quality that should help RE and research develop further in the future. It is not the answer to all the problems of RE and of research, but it is a valuable principle rarely addressed in the literature.

Chapter 2
Dialogue Within and Between

It's like we're sort of teaching the grown ups.
(an 8-year-old)

Introduction

Dialogue has been central to religious and educational traditions for thousands of years, yet many people associate religion with authoritative monologue (such as in stereotypes of endless sermonizing), so the importance of dialogue needs stressing. One of the great defenders of educational dialogue was Socrates. Many write about Socratic methods, with Socrates having philosophized through dialogue or argument. Socrates even went to the lengths of refusing to write things down, as that would restrict his thinking and teaching. It is fascinating in today's literacy-obsessed society to think that this refusal to write was the basis of the criminal charges brought against Socrates for 'corrupting the youth of Athens'. In religion, many write – or, better still, talk – about the Buddha's dialogues or Jesus' arguments, or about the many dialogic forms in Hindu traditions, notably the Bhagavad Gita. Religious dialogues include dialogue between religions, as well as within religions. Early Christian dialogue crossed Jewish and non-Jewish boundaries, Sikh dialogue worked across Hindu and Muslim traditions (both within and beyond both, as Hindu and Muslim writers are recognized in the Guru Granth Sahib, whilst Sikhism asserts itself as a quite distinct religion), and the Sufi Muslim poet Rumi wrote of the state of heightened awareness through *dhikr* ('remembrance' or 'listening') when 'I belong to the beloved' and am 'not Christian or Jew or Muslim, not Hindu,/Buddhist, sufi, or zen' (Rumi 1995, p. 32). The Bahá'í tradition recognizes the teachings of Zoroaster, the Buddha, Jesus, and Muhammad (pbuh), as well as Baha'u'llah. In these and countless other ways, talking and listening within and across religions have been central to how people have lived. In the twentieth century, the great religious philosopher Martin Buber described living itself in terms of dialogue as 'all real living is meeting', whilst also, helpfully, warning against the temptation of 'monologue disguised as dialogue' (Buber 2002, pp. 22 and 25).

RE can and often does reflect the same dialogic approach, especially when the educational and religious traditions come together in a multi-faith RE, the most widespread tradition in English and Welsh RE since the 1970s. Ninian Smart was perhaps the most influential person in the growth of multi-faith RE, and one of his first books was a description of a dialogue between a Christian, Jew, Muslim, Hindu, Ceylon Buddhist, and Japanese Buddhist. 'The demand for fairness is one reason for the dialogue form', says Smart (Smart 1960, p. 13).

> The dialogue form also emphasizes anew the point that where there is discussion, there reasons are found. The possibility of argument implies that there are criteria of truth, however vague. Indeed, the man [*sic*] who refuses to argue at all is guilty of slaying truth: both the true and the false perish, and he is reduced to mere expressions of feeling. *(Smart 1960, p. 14)*

Interfaith dialogue, and dialogue beyond religions, is now built in to many RE syllabuses, and a 2013 review noted that RE 'should develop in pupils an aptitude for dialogue so that they can participate positively in our society with its diverse religions and worldviews' (REC 2013, p. 14). That could be interpreted as rather glib, but the review and other such documents also stress that interfaith dialogue recognizes conflicts as well as collaboration, both within and between religions and beliefs, religious and non-religious.

Such a strong and vibrant tradition is clearly ready for detailed work on dialogue in RE, as represented in the rest of this chapter, which describes some of the leading classroom-based research on dialogic approaches to RE. Research on dialogue is distinctive in that the research itself may directly help improve RE, and yet it also complements a wide range of other research in RE such as Wright's work on religious literacy (Wright 1993, 1997 and much else since) or Baumfield on thinking skills (e.g. in Baumfield 2002, 2003).

Global dialogue

Bob Jackson, in a Westhill seminar, described the tremendous amount of interest across Europe – and beyond – in addressing religious diversity in school education, and this is related to the aims of RE as understood in England and Wales. Those aims include first-order aims of increasing knowledge and understanding, and relating new learning to one's own experience – whichever way around these go. Many new RE teachers see some of the second-order aims as first-order aims, but for Jackson, these are importantly second-order aims: increasing tolerance and respect, and promoting social cohesion and good citizenship. Such aims are not just the province of RE. Those second-order aims are particularly influential in Europe, especially with respect to social cohesion, since the various terrible events that include the terrorist attack on 11 September 2001 in the United States, the Afghanistan and Iraq wars, and events in Bali, Casablanca, Jakarta, Madrid, London, Paris, and Nice – including activity by far-right organizations for several years.

It is the reaction to these events that has stimulated projects such as that of the Council of Europe (made up of forty-five states, with information at *www. coe.int/*), called *Intercultural Education and the Challenge of Religious Diversity and Dialogue*. The Council of Europe includes states with a very wide range of approaches to RE (from very little, in France, to confessional RE in many countries), but the project was about intercultural education regardless of the state of RE and promoted 'education for democratic citizenship', which 'is a factor for social cohesion, mutual understanding, intercultural and inter-religious dialogue, and solidarity' (Council of Europe Committee of Ministers 2008, p. 1). Work on UK RE feeds into more general intercultural education, then. Similarly, the UN-sponsored Oslo Coalition on Freedom of Religion or Belief set up the *Teaching for Tolerance* project, based at Oslo University. It is an international project, including states from the Islamic world such as Nigeria (50 per cent of whose population are Muslim and 40 per cent Christian, according to *www.wikipedia.org*, quoting *www.state.gov/* and *www.cia.gov/*). Avest et al. (2009) is perhaps the largest collection of classroom research on dialogue in RE across Europe (and the sixteenth book in a series on religious diversity and education in Europe from the REDCo and ENRECA projects on religion and education). The editors describe their 'dialogical methodology'. The research itself, as well as the topic of the research, used dialogue. There are studies from a range of European countries, some familiar to RE researchers (the UK, Germany, the Netherlands, and Norway), and some far less well represented in the literature (Estonia, France, Russia, and Spain). The team 'were pleasantly surprised to find in the course of our surveys that the majority of respondents in all the countries studied showed themselves open to and accepting of religious and cultural heterogeneity, and stated that peaceful coexistence between people of different religious backgrounds was easily achievable', but that 'prejudices against specific cultures and religions … [were also] prevalent, as was the firm conviction among a significant minority that religion in itself constituted an obstacle to peaceful coexistence' (Avest et al. 2009, pp. 7–8). In order to build on the openness and to work with and overcome the prejudices, the book describes and is an example of the value of 'how classroom interaction unfolds in reality, and which forms of dialogue, under which circumstances, are conducive to this development' (Avest et al. 2009, p. 8). Some of my own favourite contributions are those set in Estonia, France, Hamburg in Germany, and Russia. Olga Schihalejev describes the challenges of students adapting to more student-centred approaches to schooling in Estonia, with one young person saying, 'I have learned to think in RE lessons', and continuing, '[n]ot that I was not able to do it before but in these lessons I felt the creaking of my brain and I liked it' (Schihalejev, in Avest et al. 2009, p. 78). Enjoying the 'creaking of our brains' could well be a rallying call for RE teachers across the world. Bérengère Massignon and Séverine Mathieu describe the changes in France in recent years, with public schools now dealing with religions far more than was previously seen as acceptable.

Increased teaching of what are referred to as 'religious facts' (or what in the UK might be referred to as 'learning about religion') was not based on increasing interest in religion but on increasing ignorance of the religious ideas informing literature, history, and society, along with a concern for promoting inter-religious dialogue in France. Although some of those who are working in contexts where RE has a much stronger history will be surprised to hear phrases like 'the teacher is supposed to be "blind to religion"' (in Avest et al. 2009, p. 100), and 'Here I am neither Christian nor Muslim nor Jewish, I am your teacher' (in Avest et al. 2009, p. 102), in the French context, this is how teachers are dealing with the tension between the need to teach about religion and the ideology of *laïcité* (see also Gaudin 2017). The authors summarize their position in a statement that could apply to the whole book:

> Dialogue and conflict are intertwined and complementary notions: dialogue in the classroom about religious issues may lead to conflicts among pupils; these conflicts may then be the opportunity to develop a deep and stimulating dialogue regulated by the teacher, whose aim is to remove the ambiguities and to diffuse the stereotypes which are underlying these conflicts. Thus, conflict should not be seen as the opposite and negative word to dialogue: conflicts can prove to be fruitful as far as they are handled in the appropriate way by the teacher. (*in Avest et al. 2009, p. 103*)

In this way, the authors claim, teaching about religion in French schools can help pupils 'build their own personality', and therefore learn 'from' as well as 'about' religion (in Avest et al 2009, p. 108).

The Hamburg chapter is written by Thorsten Knauth, who reaches back to the philosophies of Martin Buber and Emmanuel Levinas to explore the existential significance of dialogue, and Knauth also criticizes the idea of dialogue and conflict as unquestioned opposites, as true dialogue itself 'relies on different, partly conflicting perspectives' (in Avest et al. 2009, pp. 111–112). This also reflects the research of Wolfram Weisse (e.g. in Jackson 2003, 2004, chapter 7, and in Avest et al. 2009), who has also researched in Hamburg and in South Africa. There is both intercultural and inter-religious learning, and learning about those without religion. There are existential, ethical, social, and environmental issues to be considered. It is important to allow for individual expression, not labelling students by religion, as students from different backgrounds are learning to listen to others, and to reflect and criticize, grounded in human rights theory. This approach once again treats conflict as *normal* and not to be avoided. Indeed, conflict is seen as 'the practical test of living together' (in Avest et al. 2009, p. 112). Fedor Kozyrev's chapter on research in St Petersburg also makes good use of theorists of dialogue. This includes discussion of Bakhtin's views on *heteroglossia* or 'polyphonic', many-voiced, places – in Bakhtin's writings, in the novel, and for Kozyrev, as for me, in classrooms (Kozyrev 2011, and in Stern 2007a, p. 41). Linked to the psychologist Vygotsky, Bakhtin's views have been promoted in the UK by philosophers such as Wegerif (2008), and they in turn built on eighteenth- and nineteenth-century educational writers such as

Rousseau and Tolstoy. In contemporary Russia, it is tremendously refreshing to see that 'the notorious conflict-generating potential of religion cannot be considered as an obstacle to introducing religion in schools', but, rather, it 'proves ... that religious topics may be used as a rich educational source' (in Avest et al. 2009, p. 215). The examples from such a range of national contexts, complemented by classroom-based research, are most impressive. The more research on the reality of dialogue in classrooms around the world, the better.

Within the UK, dialogic intercultural education is happening in citizenship as well as RE. RE professionals in the UK, according to Jackson, need to engage with citizenship education – which includes knowledge and understanding, and appreciation of the 'diversity of national, regional, religious and ethnic identities in UK and the need for mutual respect and understanding'. This is quoted from a UK RE document (QCA 2004), which goes on to say that RE provides opportunities to promote 'education for racial equality and community cohesion through studying the damaging effects of xenophobia and racial stereotyping, the impact of conflict in religion and the promotion of respect, understanding and co-operation through dialogue between people of different faiths and beliefs'. The connections between RE and multiculturalism go back over the decades, as do criticisms of the connections. For example, some specialists in antiracist education have criticized RE for seeing cultures as closed systems, for a rather superficial treatment of cultures ('saris, samosas, and steelbands', as highlighted by Troyna 1983), and for an emphasis on the exotic more than the everyday. Minority cultures were often contrasted with the national or majority culture, as long as there was no 'threat'. This meant that there was a lack of attention to power issues in multicultural education.

Some antiracist educators in the 1990s responded to the early critique of multiculturalism by suggesting a more sophisticated approach to cultural analysis in schools. This work was paralleled independently by Jackson and colleagues through their ethnographic research on religious diversity and Jackson's development of this into an interpretive approach to RE (Jackson 1997). Gerd Baumann's work (Baumann 1996, 1999) is a good example of the 'new multiculturalism'. Baumann completed fieldwork in London on cultural discourse, suggesting that there was a 'dominant discourse' that treats cultures as separate and homogeneous (e.g. 'the Sikh community' as a unified whole): this separation creates a superficial view of the issues. In contrast to the dominant discourse is a 'demotic discourse': the process of making new culture through interaction – as Ipgrave found in her early research on children in dialogue (e.g. Ipgrave 1999). 'Culture' can in this way be seen as a possession of an ethnic or religious community, and also as a dynamic process relying on personal agency. Culture should therefore be seen as a process, including individuals making choices, and individuals drawing on their own families' and other cultural resources and sources of spirituality, as also described by Smith (2005). People must not be labelled in the way the media sometimes labels, such as 'Muslim = terrorist'. Pedagogical ideas on dialogue challenge precisely such fixed views of culture.

The 'new multiculturalism' of the 1990s included antiracist multicultural education (Leicester 1992), reflexive multiculturalism (Rattansi, in Donald and Rattansi 1992), and critical multiculturalism (May 1999). These combine antiracist and cultural concerns, rejecting closed views of cultures and antiracist fears of cultural difference as a source of division. At the same time, Jackson's interpretive approach looked at people in their contexts, covering the *representation* of religions and 'cultures' showing their diversity (individuals, groups, traditions), *interpretation* (comparing and contrasting familiar and unfamiliar concepts), and *reflexivity* (pupils relating learning to their own views). The *Bridges to Religions* materials for 5–7-year-olds (written by Margaret Barratt, e.g. Barratt 1994a, 1994b, 1994c) attempt to introduce children to other children in the books, as steps towards dialogue. Children reading, and those quoted in the books, are in a kind of preparatory dialogue, rather than a face-to-face dialogue. The source material is ethnographic studies of children in family and school, as also described in Chapter 9. Children in class compare and contrast their concepts, experiences, and beliefs. Texts deal with similarity and difference, and diversity of views of children in the class is recognized. In these ways, taking account of the real experiences of children, the books take out 'the exotic' from RE. The importance of context is emphasized, as are different elements of individual identity that can be expressed in different social contexts. For example, different dress codes can be discussed, compared, and contrasted (as in French debates over the wearing of religious dress and symbols), and cultural change over generations can be shown in order to break down stereotypes (as with an 'English'-style birthday party given a 'South Asian' slant).

Activity 2.1: What more can we do?

A simple and profound research question involves asking pupils, 'What more can we do to promote religious harmony?' Similar, and similarly profound, questions might be 'What more can we do to promote racial harmony?' or 'What more can we do to promote social harmony?'

   This research task can be completed with individual pupils responding on paper to the open-ended question, followed up with groups of pupils creating plans for enacting their ideas. They might create pictures, dramas, or videos to explain their views, like those respondents used in Burke and Grosvenor 2003 on *The School I'd Like*.

Other dialogue work includes that of Leganger-Krogstad (e.g. in Jackson 2003, 2004, chapter 7) in the context of Finnmark, Norway's most Northerly county. This project involved pupil research on their own local knowledge, which was used for analysis and reflection. They then moved outwards from the local to the national to the global. Themes included connections, self-other, inside-outside, and past-future. The work explored the practice of plurality and identity, with pupils involved in selecting topics and methods, and developing competence to handle cultural material. Leganger-Krogstad refers to this ability to handle diverse cultural material as 'metacultural competence'. She goes on to study religious practice and the environment, involving a large number of items: cultural landscape, architecture, historical signs, monuments, music, art, symbols, traditions, language and use of names, sacred texts, narratives and songs, institutions and values, clothing, food, days and hours, rites, rituals, customs, behaviours, events, discussions in the media, attitudes to the natural environment, membership, and leadership. Exploring nature in Northern Norway involved exploring the experience of nature in time and space, using a camera to record the midnight sun. When Leganger-Krogstad moved to Oslo, she started working on exploring the city environment, with trainee teachers exploring the city, visiting mosques and a Lutheran Christian churchyard.

Julia Ipgrave (Ipgrave 1999, 2001, 2003, 2004, 2009, 2012) makes an important contribution to dialogue by discussing conditions for dialogue, acknowledging plurality within the school, and being positive about that plurality. She discussed this at a Westhill seminar. There are different levels of dialogue: primary (acceptance of plurality), secondary (openness to difference), and tertiary (pupil interaction). Use is made of children's religious language, and providing opportunities for structured dialogue. Children negotiate their viewpoints. The project developed from phase 1 in one school, through phase 2 between schools in a single city, to phase 3, which is the e-bridges project making use of email dialogue. *Building e-bridges* (Ipgrave 2003) uses email in three dialogic stages: the dialogue of life (getting to know each other, building friendship), the dialogue of experience (finding out about each other's practices), the dialogue of action (debating moral issues, exploring issues of justice and social concern), and questions of faith (reflecting on 'big' questions and comparing different viewpoints).

Most primary school pupils say they share parental beliefs. However, the research showed some openness to the beliefs of peers, highlighting issues of agency, and of exploring religious language using one's own experience of religious plurality – including peer relationships. Pupils are searching for integration and coherence, and make their own current religious identity in dialogue with others, meanwhile negotiating new meanings.

Activity 2.2: Dialogue now

What opportunities are there in the curriculum for pupils to be in a meaningful dialogue with other pupils? This is a more challenging research question than it seems. Pupils clearly talk with other pupils and discuss both personal and school-related issues. However, the degree and level of dialogue relevant to the *curriculum* has rarely been studied. Pupils working together, even in what is called 'group work', often only take part in the 'dialogue of life', and rarely take part in the other forms of dialogue.

A way of completing this research is to ask pupils to describe as many examples as possible of each of the four types of dialogue, with respect to RE, that they have taken part in over the past year. They will need quite detailed descriptions of those types of dialogue, taken initially from this chapter and also from Ipgrave 2003, p.

11 onwards. The descriptions here are given in the form of questions. Pupils may need reminding that dialogue does not only involve two people talking but asking questions and also listening to answers.

- The dialogue of life: getting to know each other, building friendship. What do you like doing in your spare time? What are you especially good at? This kind of dialogue may include reference to all kinds of everyday activities, as well as to religion.
- The dialogue of experience: finding out about each other's practices. Occasions and places, comparing experiences. How do you welcome a new baby into your family or community? What are the times of the year special for you, and how do you celebrate? Do you pray, and if you do, how do you pray? What do you think happens when you die?
- The dialogue of action: debating moral issues, exploring issues of justice and social concern. Is it ever okay to kill a living creature?
- Questions of faith, that is 'theological' dialogue about religion, whether for or against: reflecting on 'big' questions and expressing views. Comparing different viewpoints, such as do you believe in angels, and if so, what do they do?

There is a distinction between research into what opportunities pupils have for each of these four kinds of dialogue and having the dialogue itself. Once the initial research has been completed, pupils and their teachers might work together to plan for opportunities to promote all four types of dialogue, in the years to come.

There are three themes arising from this very wide-ranging research, relating to the word 'all', to time, and to teacher dialogue.

- One of the participants in Ipgrave's dialogue research noted that it revealed the narrowness of many children's understanding of diversity. For example, some Muslim pupils thought that all 'white' children were Christian (as also described in Smith 2005). It made her think about RE syllabuses, and how far they promote diversity within faiths: perhaps not enough. Dealing with this issue, as the Warwick approach attempts to do, involves getting rid of the 'all' from the discussion of religions. It is rarely true to say 'all Christians …' or 'all Hindus …', and RE teachers could helpfully avoid the word 'all' altogether.
- In addition to contemporary dialogue amongst pupils, there are many opportunities for inter-generational dialogue. Schooling in general has been described as 'a continuing personal exchange between two generations' (Macmurray 1946a), and in RE, children might be involved, for example, in interviewing members of their grandparents' generation, in order to understand a 'tradition' – not a passive 'receiving' of tradition, but as active participants in a tradition. By 'traditions', I just mean ways of living that have persisted over time, a 'collage' as Parker describes it (Parker et al. 2015, p. 339), although I recognize it can be used to mean a fixed and unchangeable orthodoxy. Beyond the living

generations, texts, sacred and secular, may allow for a form of dialogue across time, as described in Chapter 7 of this book.

- RE teachers themselves can be in dialogue with one another, and this will help in their own training, a critical issue for RE – a subject which, in the UK, has a lower proportion of specialist-trained teachers in secondary schools than almost any other subject (as described by Gates 1994, and often since then). This should be a true dialogue between teachers, rather than the promotion of a 'body of knowledge' about religions. Some of the possible processes are described in Blaylock (2000a), which reported on research with teachers having other specialisms but working in RE.

Activity 2.3: Inside out

This activity is adapted from Stern 2003a, which was about communication and dialogue with parents. If it is to be considered a research task, then the dialogue can be recorded and analysed using the same categories as used in Activity 2.2.

From within a school/institution, communicate with an 'outside' group, justifying an aspect of that school. For example, following on from Activity 1.1, a class might write to a parent or to a religious community about why RE is valuable.

From outside a school/institution, communicate with an 'inside' group, justifying what is being done, as an outsider, for the issue covered by the school. For example, a parent or religious community might write to a school saying what they contribute to RE.

The work will only make sense if teachers and pupils really want to tell parents and others about what they are doing and if the outsiders really want to know what teachers and pupils are doing.

Here is a writing frame for the initial task, to be completed collectively by teachers and pupils, although it should of course be adapted to suit the circumstances and technologies to be used.

Dear Parent/Carer

In Religious Education, we have been studying . . .

You may have [seen, read about, heard about] . . .

We enjoy teaching and learning about these topics because . . .

The most important reason for studying these topics, though, is to be able to . . ., and also to understand . . . and . . .

This will be useful when [or because] . . .

It would be good to hear about anything that interests you about Religious Education. If you have any ideas, or any information that is useful, do let me know. You could fill in the slip, below.

To: . . . Date: . . .

When I/we did Religious Education in school, and since leaving school at home or at work, my/our favourite topics and activities were/are . . .

I/we have these ideas or resources that might be useful for Religious Education: . . .

Name of parent/carer: . . .

Dialogue and children's voices

Ipgrave's work on dialogue helps to give voice to children's own lives, and these voices are themselves highlighted in this section, with quotations and paraphrases, and comments after each quotation. For example, a boy aged 10–11, self-identified as Rastafarian, described himself in this way:

> quite a lot of my friends only believe … I say to them, 'Do you believe in Jesus?'. They go, 'No' … But when they ask me, I say, 'Yes, I believe there's only one God'. And they ask me, 'What colour do you think he is?'. And most people my colour will say he's black, but I think he's all mixed colours – black, white, Asian – blue, pink. I think he's every single colour in the world. I don't just think he's one particular colour. Because, even though you have only one God, God must be like everyone's colour because to me I think he's everyone's God, because in my religion I think there's only one God and he's everyone's God, so he's got to be everyone's different colour. He can't just be black and be everyone's God.

The pupil here is recognizing both diversity and that there is only one God: his description is ambiguous, in the positive sense that it is rich with multiple meanings. It is important to note that children at this age are already talking about religion and are reconciling diversity with their beliefs. A younger child (aged 8) said as follows:

> But you know, if more of us would be able to get along better it would boost the chance of even more people getting along better, and if the kids do it then the grown ups might try and do it too, so it's like we're sort of teaching the grown ups.

What interesting ideals are being expressed here. They illustrate the need for voicing children, if only to understand how mature they can be, when not simply trying to guess the 'right answers'. The following quotations are from a conversation between a number of pupils aged 10:

> I think there's only one [God] and he's called different things
> I was going to say that!
> We can't actually say that because we've got so many gods.
> Yeah but they could be called – em …
> You have to believe in all of them because all of them have got something
>   different, like special …
> Yeah, because – look, they can all – God can …
> Do lots of things
> Change into different – like different features. Like he can be in you
> He can come into anybody.
> He can change into anything.

Here, children themselves are working through dialogue to develop their own theologies, and Ipgrave's e-bridges work has tried to encourage such dialogue, with the email dialogue growing out of more general dialogue work. One activity tried in the e-bridges project is sentence starters, such as 'A Muslim is someone who ...'. This was responded to by the children in many varied ways, including formal religious behaviours (goes to the mosque to pray, prays to God, reads the Qur'an, wears a topi, fasts at Ramadan), behaviour exhibiting moral characteristics (doesn't backbite, doesn't swear, is honest), and beliefs (believes in Allah, Muhammad, pbuh, is his prophet, believes in one God, believes in the Qur'an). All these types of response overlap with each other, and pupil explanations of their statements provide good stimulus for further dialogue. Examples of responses can also be put on cards, with these cards used for further dialogue work, and, if pre-prepared, sorted by the pupils, for example, into beliefs and other characteristics, things unique to Muslims or shared by others. Another practical interpretive kind of work involves asking pupils who have worked on holy books to come to agreement, in pairs or groups, on which of the following statements come from holy books, and why: my cat likes to lie in the sun; God has done great things for us; love each other; it was Sara's birthday last Monday; do not worry about what will happen tomorrow; work honestly and give money to the poor; my favourite food is chips; don't be happy, be sad; our school is in Leicester; all human beings belong together; keep all your money and things for yourself; giraffes can be six metres tall; do not quarrel with each other but make friends; keep your body clean. Children as young as 6 can use these statements as the basis of further dialogue.

Starting points for dialogue suggested by pupils aged 8–9, from Ipgrave's project, were based on the moral issue of whether or not people should be allowed to hunt and kill tigers. Statements included: no you cannot because we have to save them; yes you should kill them all as they killed my grandson; no they are God's lovely creatures; yes they might eat all my children; no don't kill them as tourists pay money to come to India to see them: just give them more land. This proved a good basis for discussion, with pupils saying: we're the same though because God made us and God made tigers and we're animals too really; we're the same because God made people to look after animals and he made animals to help people; tigers are more precious because there are lots of people but tigers are in danger of becoming extinct; people can die before they should, in accidents, or they could be ill and people are in danger, too.

Children aged 10–11 formulated their own questions for Christian visitors, working out questions in groups, with the questions given to the visitors in advance:

In my religion, Islam, we have to respect our Holy Book, the Qur'an, because it has God's name in it – so we have to put it higher than our feet. Why don't Christians do the same with their Bible?

What do you think about Christians that don't go to church? Do you think the world would be a better place if they did?

Do you feel sad at Christmas because most people think about presents and food and TV instead of thinking about God and Jesus?

I am a Muslim and I believe that when people die they are judged by God. Do
   you believe that?

What makes Christians believe that Jesus was the Son of God? What evidence is
   there that he was?

The quality and range of the questions indicate the amount and depth of dialogue
work the children had completed over the years. Interfaith issues and negotiations
between different religious points of view, and getting children used to that, are
well illustrated by such work. To extend the work, children can be given a number
of problems and asked to solve them. For example, pupils aged 10 and upwards
might be asked to design a multi-faith prayer room for a hospital serving Buddhists,
Muslims, Christians, Hindus, and Jews, or they might be asked to plan a menu for
a leavers' party for children from Christian, Hindu, and Sikh backgrounds who are
about to leave their primary school.

   Another challenging question from Ipgrave's work, set for children aged 7–8,
was 'Why is it okay to kick a football but not okay to kick a cat?' Some children
said: a football is a toy but a cat isn't; you can't put a cat in a cupboard or throw
it away when you don't want it; a football belongs to you but a cat doesn't; a cat
belongs to God; a cat will get hurt; a football won't say 'ouch'; a football can't be
hurt – it can go flat but it can't feel it; cats are like us – we are animals; you have to
look after animals; God says we must be kind to animals; cats are our brothers and
sisters: it's Brother Cat but it's not Brother Ball. This work might have arisen out of
prior study of ethics or of creation, or work on sacred texts. It might overlap with
work in science, personal and social education, and RE. The dialogue is of value in
itself, and it reveals children's moral thinking in a way that is valuable for all adults.
Too often, it is assumed that pupils need to be taught morals, rather than that they
already have sophisticated moral positions, even at a young age, to be investigated
and further developed.

   How then can teachers plan for more and better dialogue in RE? There are several
issues to keep in mind, according to Ipgrave and others involved in the e-bridges
work:

- There is a need to let the children respond at their own level, having built up
  a real rapport. In order to build up a rapport, pupils can use 'chat' at first, and
  not leap straight into RE issues.

- It is also useful for children to find things out for themselves, in addition to the
  agreed questions, so they have an opportunity to become more independent
  learners.

- Children will generally have had first-hand experiences at a young age that can be
  the basis of a great deal of future learning, and teachers should have confidence
  in the tendency of children to be very open-minded, especially on email.

- Shy children could come out of themselves in the email dialogues. In
  addition, children can often discuss on email things they would not be likely
  to discuss face-to-face, so that community cohesion becomes a central issue.

Pupils said that as a result of the project they 'have learned that other schools have a lot of different religions'. 'The project made Christians seem like real people', 'Islamic children are as normal as they are' (from a teacher), and 'I used to think our religions were really different, but they're not'. These are all illustrations of Jackson's 'second-order aims' of the e-bridges project.

The email project included blocks of exchanges (rather than a 'trickle' of correspondence), with planning completed around subjects (RE and citizenship), themes, and questions. A dialogue grid of this form was used:

	September	November	January	April
RE topic				
Stage of dialogue (introduction, sharing experience, ethical debate, questions of faith)				
Questions				
RE expectations				
Citizenship				

An example of a completed dialogue grid:

	September	November	January	April
RE topic		Celebrations	Creation and the natural world	Islam
Stage of dialogue (introduction, sharing experience, ethical debate, questions of faith)	Introduction	Sharing experience	Ethical debate	Questions of faith
Questions	What are your favourite subjects at school? What do you like doing in your spare time? Is there anything you're especially good at?	Are there any days or times of year that are particularly special for you? Why are they special? How do you celebrate them?	Is it ever alright to kill a living creature? If it is, under what circumstances? If not, why not?	Do you believe in angels? If not, why not? If so, what are they? What do they do?

	September	November	January	April
RE expectations	Compare their own and other people's experiences.	Respond to others' experiences. Compare experiences. Make links between beliefs and festivals.	Think about own and others' ideas of right and wrong. Make links between values and behaviour. Consider different points of view when discussing matters of right and wrong.	Describe some religious beliefs. Use religious language to discuss religious beliefs. Explain how some beliefs are shared and how religious symbols are differently used. Compare ideas about difficult questions.
Citizenship	To recognize their worth as individuals. To identify positive achievements. To think about the lives of other people.	To think about lives of other people. To be aware of cultural and religious differences between people.	To write about opinions and explain views. To debate topical issues. To consider moral dilemmas.	To reflect on spiritual issues. To be aware of religious differences.

Ipgrave's work started in one school, and has continuously developed – including her working paper (Ipgrave 2001), the book for teachers (Ipgrave 2003), and a research report on interfaith dialogue (Ipgrave 2009). Through this work, she sees children as presenting themselves and learning to relate in three ways, each of which corresponds to the levels of dialogue: as a friend or 'pal', related to the 'dialogue of life'; as a member of a faith or cultural community and tradition, related to the 'dialogue of experience' (which brings in issues of the description of religions and the ambiguity of 'secularisation', as explored by Smith 2005 and Davie 1994, 2015); and as a thinker, related to the 'dialogue of action' (stimulated by phrases like 'Have you any comments', 'I hope to hear your comments', or 'I am surprised that …').

Activity 2.4: Friendship, membership, and thought

For each of these ways of presenting oneself, a 'circles of importance' activity can be completed. This activity involves drawing a set of concentric circles and putting the 'self' in the middle, and the things closest to the 'self' in the inner circle, the next most important in the ring created by the next circle, and so on to the outer circles. The choice of membership and thought as themes comes from Davie (1994, 2015) and others who have written about 'believing and belonging'. The choice of friendship comes from a concern with the nature of self and friendship, as described by Macmurray 1992 (see also Stern 2002, 2012).

- For the 'friendship' version of circles of importance, the title will be 'me and the people closest to me'. Previous research using this technique indicates that at different ages, there is often a very different balance of friends and family in the 'inner circle'. The use of this research tool is described in Smith (2005), with one quoted as saying, 'I've put as closest God ... because He is everywhere ... [then] my mum, my dog, my baby sister', whilst another report indicated that 'the PS2 or Xbox was sometimes listed as a significant member of the household in network diagrams' (Smith 2005, pp. 20 and 59). However, when the title used is 'In school, who are you closest to?' without any mention of the word 'friend' and without mention of homes, then younger and older children, and adults, tend to have similar patterns of closeness, and mix the generations easily (Stern 2012).
- For the 'membership' version, the title will be 'To what do I belong?' Previous research suggests that the venue of the research itself affects the results: within a school, school membership is likely to be more 'central' than it would be for the same people completing the activity in their homes.
- For the 'thinking' version, the title will be 'What beliefs and ideas are most important to me?' Previous research suggests, as did the work on moral issues described above, that young people have very complex and sophisticated moral systems.

Following each of the activities, pupils can discuss with each other (and with their 'dialogue' friends, if involved in e-bridges work, for example) why different people and memberships and ideas are so important.

Conclusion

Activity 2.4 brings us back to the start of this chapter. It is the foundation for good dialogue with other pupils. Giving pupils a voice is important for schools (as described in Ranson 2000; Flutter and Rudduck 2004; Stern 2015) and important for research (as described in O'Hanlon 2003). The nature and use of that voice is vital for RE and for life. When Smith writes about the beliefs, practices, and memberships of children aged 9–11, one of his conclusions is a message of hope with respect to complex issues of freedom of thought, conscience and religion, and diversity, conflict, and segregation:

Perhaps the most hopeful note from this research is that we have discovered children who, in their everyday lives, are deeply engaged with these issues, aware of many of the opportunities and problems and already taking steps to work things out for themselves. (Smith 2005, p. 69, the final words of the book)

That hope links dialogue in RE with research in RE and with hope for the future of humanity. Including pupils in dialogue is what is allowed by RE and increasingly required of research. Teachers and pupils in school can in this way come to understand their own, and others' real lives, and that is therefore the subject of the following chapter.

Chapter 3
The Real Lives of Teachers and Pupils in RE

I am nothing.
(Rudge 1998)

Introduction

This chapter explores the lived experience of pupils and of teachers in RE classrooms. How is the subject understood and 'felt' by those involved in it? Teachers and pupils may have very different views of the subject, but they are all too rarely asked what they think – with writers about RE more often concentrating on what 'should' happen in the subject or what curriculum policies say is happening. However, there has been some work on how pupils and teachers experience RE. Conroy et al. 2013 is an excellent recent example of exploring how RE is experienced, RE's 'inscape' (the 'inner landscape' of poet Gerard Manley Hopkins). This chapter both accounts for such work and provides ways in which more people can explore this vital and illuminating topic. And by 'real lives', I do not mean to address pupils' and teachers' private lives, except in so far as they are present in the RE classroom. Classrooms are complex enough to understand without also trying to grasp the whole of childhood and adulthood. Yet RE classrooms are distinctive in dealing with many issues that are considered intensely private – not only religion itself but life and death and all that happens in between (and beyond). So RE has to come clean and admit that it touches on issues that are awkward, personal, and generally private. Some people – especially new teachers – find this worrying. For me, with many years of experience, it remains worrying, but it is also one of the best reasons for teaching RE.

RE with all the sensitive, difficult, bits taken out is like the blandest of food or music that has no dissonance in it. Young people of every generation find a kind of music that their parents' generation hates. 'Turn that music down!' or 'that's not music; it's just noise!' has been said by parents throughout the ages. The pianist-composer Franz Liszt (1811–1886) was innovative in introducing the 'tritone' in his compositions. The tritone (three whole tones, e.g. from C to F#) was known as

the 'devil's interval' because it was considered so unpleasantly dissonant up to that point. Liszt's predecessors and contemporaries would all have found it shocking (and Liszt himself used it to represent hell), yet today it is considered perfectly acceptable ('consonant') and appears in such pleasant music as the theme tune to *The Simpsons*. The same is true of RE. If you take all the sensitive bits out, then it will be bland and you will miss out on the possibility of discussing issues that may be shocking at the moment (especially for older people), but will become mainstream in the future. A good example is sexuality. When I was at school, sex was taught, but I can't think of sex education lessons without thinking of a drawing of a cross-section of a rat, which was used to describe the mechanics of sex. Today, sex education is more confident in discussing sexuality – including a range of different sexualities. Somewhat to my surprise, research recently found that RE was also a place where sexuality was discussed – more than in other lessons. Helen Sauntson (e.g. Sauntson 2013) researched young women in school who self-identified as lesbian. She found that being gay or lesbian was barely discussed in English lessons even when studying authors (such as Oscar Wilde or Carol Ann Duffy) who are well known as being gay or lesbian and/or who write on the subject. Yet those same young women reported that such discussions were most likely to take place in RE lessons. I was delighted to learn that RE had – in this research – been open to such sensitive issues, and more open than some other school subjects.

A similar sensitive, private, issue that is addressed by RE is that of death. Even the most conventional and 'fact-based' RE lessons are likely to have something about what religions say happens when people die. Such lessons will be likely to raise sensitive issues and will challenge pupils and teachers alike. I remember discussing with a group of primary teachers the Bible account of David killing Goliath. I was discussing how Jewish interpretations of the narrative tend to emphasize the political dimension of the story (the battle was won because David was a Jew and Jews had G-d on their side), whilst Christian interpretations of the narrative more often emphasize the individual dimension of the story (a small but 'plucky' person beating a larger opponent). However, one teacher said that she couldn't possibly use that narrative with her children. I asked why. She said that it was because the account was immoral and a bad example for children: David killed Goliath and was not punished for it. I admire that teacher's sensitivity, as we all too often see historic battles as impersonal and not 'really' violent. But I remain troubled by the idea of taking all the unpunished killing out of RE lessons. For a start, the Bible would be a very short book indeed, as would other sacred texts. And RE can be the place where death – and killing, punished or not – can be sensitively discussed. In my own research I find children, as young as seven (the youngest age group I have researched), can discuss death freely and with subtlety. To edit the topic out of RE lessons is to miss a golden opportunity.

An activity that explores some of the toughest challenges that can be tackled in RE is one that imagines there is a 'religion police'. Sadly, this is all too real in a number of countries, and there are elements of criminalizing religious practices in many countries. But what if religion and religious practices of all kinds were simply banned?

Activity 3.1: The religion police

Ask pupils to imagine that religion has been made illegal, and they have all been recruited, for one week only, to the 'religion police'.

Working initially in class time, and then completing the work for homework, they must identify all evidence they can of religion, over seven days. Evidence might include religious symbols worn by people (whether worn for religious reasons or simply as jewellery), religious buildings, signs and writing on shops (such as 'ideal for Christmas', or 'Halal meat'), conversations in which people use religious terms (including 'bless you'), television programmes mentioning religion, art work including religious symbolism, or music with religious lyrics.

Pupils engage imaginatively in the activity, many showing a frightening affinity for police work of this kind and/or for well-organized resistance fighting, and RE teachers are more likely to fear the completion than the absence of the homework.

Extended work may be completed on more 'real' situations. For example, there have been bans on religious dress, by some UK schools who have inflexible uniform rules, and by all French schools. In contrast, pupils may also look at the opposite situation, such as the legal requirement for UK school to start every day with 'collective worship' (see, for example, Cush 1994).

It matters what pupils bring

RE can easily ignore what pupils bring to classrooms. I don't mean the child in a school I worked with who, for a 'show and tell' session, brought in a dead cat he had found in the road. That really needed to be ignored. It is the lived experience, the understanding, the knowledge that pupils can bring in to classrooms, just for it all to be ignored. Few pupils are completely ignored; few are so shy or invisible that teachers simply don't notice them. (There are a few children in this category, but most teachers recognize the risk of missing out the 'quiet ones', if only because parents consultation evenings are so painful if you have nothing at all to say about one of your pupils.) But there are aspects of many – perhaps most – children that are ignored by some of the best teachers. This may be related to the language used or the divisions or hierarchies in the school. Some of the best known research on these issues is that of the sociologist Basil Bernstein (1975). He described the language 'codes' that children bring in to school. 'Restricted' codes are ways of speaking and writing that use forms of language that will be understandable within a particular group (typically, the child's own family, friends, and community) and that therefore do not need to explain all the assumptions behind the language. 'Elaborated' codes are ways of speaking and writing that are more explicit and thoroughly explanatory. Having 'restricted' codes does not mean being limited in what you can say. In some senses, 'restricted' codes might be described as more poetic, and 'elaborated' codes as more prosaic. The poet T S Eliot described poetry as 'writing with a lot of silence on the page', and the same can be said of 'restricted' codes: there's a lot left unsaid. Some dramatists use 'restricted' codes as markers of their own style: playwrights such as Harold Pinter or Samuel Beckett, or contemporary writers for television such as Sally Wainwright (*www.imdb.com/name/nm0906550/*). Others use more 'elaborated' language codes, explaining things more fully as they go along. Shakespeare is in this category, not least because he tended to write his stage directions into characters' speeches, in order to ensure the actors did as he wanted them to do. (Shakespeare and his contemporaries use few separate stage directions or descriptions of scenes or 'blocking', so the characters' speeches have to provide this guidance.) But it matters, more than we might think, what language codes the children bring to school.

Bernstein's research on language codes included giving children a strip cartoon with no words and asking them to describe what happens in the story. What he found important, and very significant for schooling, was that working-class children were more likely to use 'restricted' language codes, whilst middle-class children were more likely to be able to use both 'restricted' and 'elaborated' codes. On its own, this would not affect schooling. However, teachers in school, and the typical activities carried out in school, use and benefit from the use of more 'elaborated' codes. So the language codes the children bring in to school give advantages to some, disadvantages to others. Few teachers would realize they were doing this, and, before Bernstein's research, few educationalists even realized such differences existed. Rather than blaming working-class children or their families or communities for their lower average achievement, Bernstein's research suggested that it was just as much – or, rather, more – the responsibility of schools and teachers. And the skills of using 'elaborated' codes could, in any case, be taught, so there are ways of overcoming class differentials in schools. That is a much more positive account than had previously been given of how social class might affect achievement. But almost half a century later, there is still a significant gap between the average achievements of working- and middle-class children in the UK and many other countries. There may be more complex issues at work, as some critics of Bernstein have pointed out (as in standard sociology textbooks such as Haralambos et al. 2013, pp. 694–695), but understanding pupil and teacher language is undoubtedly helpful: if teachers and pupils become more aware of language (including language codes), they can also take more control over their own destinies. A good reason to see all in schools as researchers.

In addition to language codes, Bernstein's later work included an understanding of 'classification' and 'framing', which is taken up again in Chapter 5. Other aspects of social class were researched by Stephen Ball (1981), who described how pupils search for dignity at school: if they don't get it from their teachers, they are likely to try to get it from their peers by misbehaving. His research, and that of a number of other sociologists of education, helped teachers understand that pupils will often decide that it is better (for them) to be seen as 'bad' by teachers (and therefore 'good' by their peers) than to be seen as 'stupid' by teachers. The more that teachers make pupils feel bad about themselves, the more likely the pupils are to find their dignity some other way – notably through misbehaving. Some teachers may read this and think that the solution is to praise all pupils indiscriminately. However, that doesn't work either. Pupils can tell if teachers are being insincere in their praise. Benjamin (2002) writes of three ways in which teachers talk to pupils about success in secondary schools, all of which are recognized by the pupils interviewed by the researcher. There is 'normal' success (getting high grades), there is 'really disabled' success (the genuine success of people who have very significant limitations on their achievement, so that, for example, writing a sentence might rightly be regarded as a huge achievement), and there is 'consolation' success. Pupils recognize that teachers will often give 'consolation' praise, which is not really sincerely meant praise, but like a pat on the head. Hatfield (2004) and I (Stern 2009a) both asked the following research question: 'Describe the three most recent and memorable times the school made you feel good about yourself.' It is a fascinating question to ask of pupils and also of adults remembering their schooldays. One pupil aged seven in Hatfield's research could not think of any times. He was in a good school, and had been much praised by his teachers for the three years he had been there, but had achieved at lower levels than his classmates. Encouraged to think of any times the school made him feel good about himself, he finally said, 'My first day at school'. 'Why was that?' the researcher asked. 'Because I thought I could learn', the pupil answered. For all the praise he had been given, he understood that it had been 'consolation' praise, not 'normal' praise.

Teachers and pupils need ways to develop their confidence and dignity without being given insincere praise to 'boost their self-esteem' when the teacher knows that they are being insincere. Smith (2002) writes of this kind of insincere boosting of self-esteem as a 'kindly apocalypse'. Pupils bring with them an expectation – a hope – that they will learn and flourish in school, and teachers and pupils can all use research to help understand barriers to successful learning and flourishing and, even better, ways in which success can be promoted. Whether children bring to school their social class (which may affect their language codes), their wish for dignity (which teachers may fail to supply), their wish to learn (which may generate only 'consolation' praise from teachers), their gender (which may make them 'invisible', Spender 1982), it matters what they bring, and it matters even more how teachers deal with what they bring. And to add an absolutely crucial item to that list, children bring their religious or non-religious understandings, practices, experiences, and perspectives to school, and how teachers (and fellow pupils) deal with those characteristics is important throughout school and especially in RE lessons. Returning to an issue mentioned in the introduction to this chapter, I will describe my own experience of teaching RE lessons about death – and how various pieces of research changed my approach.

The lesson I learned, which seems so obvious now but took years for me to grasp, was that children will bring to school their own understandings of death and their own experiences of bereavement. The educational psychologist John Holland has written about how staff in school are often 'lost for words' when it comes to pupils who are bereaved (Holland 2001, 2016). Teachers tell him they don't know what to say to a child whose parent has died. 'What do you want to say?' he asks. 'How sorry I am that their mum has died', they often answer. 'Well, why don't you say that, then?' Such simple advice (and much more complex advice, too) highlights the need to be able to talk with pupils about their own experiences, and not block it all out. Another author, Maureen Oswin (1991), writes of a child with significant learning difficulties who was told that her mother had died. 'Am I allowed to cry?' the child asks, heartbreakingly. Oswin used the question as the title of her book, and I sometimes wonder if 'Yes, you are allowed to cry' should be a motto for all schools, especially when they deal with sensitive issues. Teachers are not professional counsellors, of course, and there are good reasons why teachers will be encouraged to ask others to help when children are upset. But teachers do not need to pretend that their subject matter is entirely objective and brush under the carpet any personal experience, and any feelings, that their pupils might have of the subject. I taught the topic of religious and non-religious views of death for quite a few years. Christians believe this, Hindus believe that, Buddhists and Humanists have their distinct practices and beliefs, and so on. I can still remember the yellow-covered book that I used. In 1997, by which time I was working in a university, a questionnaire was sent out to hundreds of schools in the UK taking part in an RE Festival. Many thousands of responses were received. The paper copies were held for a while in my university, and I was entranced by the pupils' responses. Several hundreds of the responses were put online, and they are still available (at old.natre. org.uk/db/, and see Blaylock 2001a, 2001b; Weston 2003). One of the questions was this:

> Here are two comments about death. 'When we die, we lie in the grave, and I'm afraid that's the end of us.' 'I think dying is like being born. You leave the place you know, but you go to a wonderful place you don't know.' What are your thoughts about death, and life after death?

Here is a brief selection of responses from 11-year-old respondents, who would have been a couple of months into their new secondary (high) school. I transcribed the responses myself, from the original documents. (The online responses are all 'tidied up' to correct spelling and grammar infelicities.) Some of the respondents expressed relatively conventional views that might have been drawn from RE, and external religious and humanist, learning. For example, 'Death is not a nise [*sic*] feeling but when you go to heven in [*it*] will be like wonderful land', or 'I think there isn't really a heaven. I think we just get buried and that's it, nothing else'. However, the complexity, the depth of thought, and the personal engagement with the issues of many of the responses all suggest that pupils are able to tackle some of the biggest questions. One child says with great eloquence:

> I think you die because you have been on earth for a while and now God wants you up there with him. Up where the sky's always blue, where you can never leave the ones you love and treasure.

Many children, religiously self-identified as Christian or as 'none', write about coming back or reincarnation. One child, identifying herself as Christian, says, 'I think you could come back but as a spirit to help with good but I could feel something at my Grandmas house when my Grandad died and my dad can too.' Another respondent (religiously described as none) says thus:

> I believe that when we die our body rots away, but our spirit (excluding) our memory) goes into a new born baby. However if the person has some unfinished work or business to take care of their spirit will try and correct it.

A more complex view, from a child who does not indicate her religion:

> I beleive that when you die, you do have an afterlife because i find that when you do die you go to a place eg: heaven and live an afterlife, not into another person but a living creature or plant. I have always thought that when my hamster died she was the tree I had planted on her grave. So I think there is an afterlife.

It is fear that comes through, however, as dominating a number of responses.

> I believe in afterlife but sometimes I am afraid of death. I think when people die they live in another world I think the criminals are still acepted by god becasue god will forgive everyone if you want be forgiven.

One of the most poignant of all the responses simply is, 'I afraid of death but part of me want's [sic] to die'. It is difficult to see how the issues raised by these pupils could be discussed and built upon other than in RE. RE has a special place in the curriculum as a subject able to tackle death, in ways that do not deny the real feelings and fears of pupils. Pupils have a right to a curriculum that actively engages with those views, and RE is put forward as a vehicle for such engagement.

When I first used these examples, I said that the audience might wish to compare the children's views with the level of religious development of adults who trivialize death or killing. However, that missed the more obvious point. I was an RE teacher who had been teaching about religious views of death for several years, and I hadn't thought children had such complex, deep, and well-articulated views on what happened when we die. As the professional teacher of such matters, it was much more shocking that I had such little empathy for or understanding of the children I had been working with, than that a celebrity or political figure might have a lack of empathy for the dying or bereaved. At that point, I realized a simple survey could turn my life upside down, and it can also turn upside down the lives of other people – young and old.

Activity 3.2: A survey can turn your life upside down

People often get anxious about the work they have to do. Teachers and pupils alike have a lot of tasks and targets, and never seem to have enough time. However, in RE all the rush to detail can mean that teachers never find out what pupils really think. One survey (with some responses at *old.natre.org.uk/db/*) turned my own RE-related life upside down. As an activity with pupils, ask each pupil to find someone on the database of roughly their own age, but in other ways *as different as possible*. If the pupil is female, she should tick 'male', and choose a different religious position. Then, choose one of the questions and look at the written and video responses. Which respondent is the most different to how the pupil thinks? The pupil chooses that person and then writes three questions in the form of an email/tweet to the person. What does the pupil think the reply would be to these questions? (Pupils may want to work in a group on this task, to give themselves more ideas about how the conversation might go.)

Then ask each pupil to find someone who is *similar* – the same gender and religious position and, on a particular question, a similar response to the one you would have given. What three questions would you like to ask that person?

Pupils can present this research as a series of emails/tweets, including their questions and the responses of the respondent – their real response, from the database, and then their imagined responses to the pupil's questions. As some of the responses on the database are in the form of videos, pupils may want to make their own videos, too.

In this way, pupils will get to know what other people of the same age are thinking about important issues, and will be able to talk about what they know themselves.

The questions and answers on the database cover sensitive issues. Pupils should be told that they should only talk about things that they are happy discussing – with the teacher and with others in their class. Nobody should be made to 'confess' what their own religious position or beliefs are, if they don't want to do this.

As I say, the initial results of this survey changed how I understood RE and how I understood the pupils I had been teaching. By making this a class activity, you will be able to hear first-hand from your pupils, writing or talking about issues of great importance. If dealt with sensitively, it can transform your – and their – views of the subject and of themselves.

Without trying to understand pupils, not only will you be missing out but they will be missing out too. Responses to important questions like the ones quoted by Linda Rudge should always be of interest. An Ofsted inspector was reading the work of 11-year-old pupils who had been writing about themselves. One boy had written, 'I am John; I am 11 years old; I am nothing' (Rudge 1998, p. 155). 'I am nothing' is a response that can upset, and there are those who sincerely believe that teaching about atheism in RE is 'deceptive' (Felderhof, in Felderhof et al. 2007, p. 87). But the *problem* of invisibility is supported by some sociological research.

Some non-religious young people reported how atheism was not represented at all in the media, due to a shortage of sensational stories, the perceived lack of conflict caused by atheism in comparison to religion, and the invisibility of those with no specific faith. In a predominantly religious environment, such as the neighbourhoods in which this study was undertaken, having no faith could be viewed as a potentially stigmatising, spoiled or deficient identity, requiring appropriate coping mechanisms in response. *(Madge et al. 2014, p. 63)*

'I am nothing' or being invisible is as upsetting, I think, as 'Am I allowed to cry?' (Oswin 1991), quoted above, or.... Well, you try asking interesting questions of your pupils, and listen carefully to their answers, especially the answers of those who don't usually answer, those who are not the first to put their hands up, those who all too often get left out. RE can inform, engage, and empower pupils. Let it not be the subject that rejects children (who are 'nothing', for example) or that tells a pupil (and that pupil's family) that their own experience of a religion is 'wrong'.

It matters (differently) what teachers bring

It matters what pupils bring, and it matters, too, what teachers bring to the RE classroom. The relationship between a teacher's own beliefs and ways of life and the subject of RE is very complex. Issues arise of professionalism and how to deal with one's own beliefs in a contested classroom. It matters now, and it matters across a teaching career that may last for forty years or more. There is not a huge quantity of research on the lived experience of RE teachers. Judith Everington has spent many years studying the experience and life histories (or teaching histories) of RE teachers, and talked about this in the Westhill seminars. Earlier work with Pat Sikes looked at the use of life histories in general (Sikes and Everington 2001, followed up in Want et al. 2009), and at the contrast between the image and reality of being a new teacher of RE (Sikes and Everington 2004, with the compelling quotation in the title 'RE teachers do get drunk you know'). For many, becoming an RE teacher has seemed to 'just happen': most did not plan, for long or at all, becoming an RE teacher. (The 'happenstance' theory of how people develop their careers is a common issue in all areas, for which see Krumboltz 2009; Krumboltz and Levin 2010.) More recently, Everington has worked on more of the specifics of the classroom, including how much new RE teachers reveal of their own beliefs (Everington 2012, 2014). One teacher (quoted in the title of the 2012 article) says, 'We're all in this together, the kids and me' and that – for that teacher and many others – justified teachers in revealing their own beliefs and talking of their personal experiences in RE lessons. More recently, qualified RE teachers seem more willing to do this than those who qualified some time ago. This may be affected by an increasingly 'revealing' culture – a culture of telling all on social media. There certainly are advantages, in terms of pupils seeing teachers (with their religious or non-religious beliefs and practices) as 'real human beings', and as having had experiences of relevance to the pupils. There are also dangers of what is referred to as the 'tyranny of intimacy' and the dangers of giving pupils no protection of 'distance' from their teachers. Hence pupils may be 'denied privacy and lose the sense of security that should be provided by an 'objective' professional who is entirely focused on their learning' (Everington 2012, p. 350).

Teachers need to think, and need the time to do this. Vivienne Baumfield talked in the Westhill seminars about how teachers need permission, almost, to ask what is important, what matters, and why am I doing this? Baumfield thinks that it is through curriculum development that teachers are most often empowered to think, if given the opportunity (see also Baumfield 2016, 2017). This is important to RE teaching, where most come to the subject with some kind of personal 'investment', their own way of life. It matters what the teacher brings to the classroom, and it matters, sometimes in a different way, what the teacher *reveals* in the classroom. In a later study of Hindu, Muslim, and Sikh RE teachers in the UK, Judith Everington writes of the advantages of pupils having 'models' of religious adults who do not necessarily fit the stereotypes of Hindus, Muslims, or Sikhs. Yet here, and even more in a recent article on 'being professional' (Everington 2016), she notes the balances that must be struck, and the need, above all else, to train and support teachers in knowing how to balance the competing pressures of wanting to be a 'real person' in the classroom with the wanting to maintain suitable professional boundaries. And for every pupil enlivened by learning that their RE 'gets drunk', or is a Muslim woman who doesn't wear hijab, there will be another pupil who may think one or other (or both) is acting inappropriately.

There are approaches to teaching RE that say all personal religious characteristics of the teacher must be hidden. In France, no religious clothing or any other religious identifier may be worn in schools – by pupils and staff alike. As Bérengère Massignon and Séverine Mathieu describe an RE classroom in which a pupil assumes the teacher is Christian,

> The teacher insisted upon his need to remain neutral and said to them: *'Here I am neither Christian nor Muslim nor Jewish, I am your teacher'*, without even addressing their categorisation of him as a Christian. *(Massignon and Mathieu, in Avest et al. 2009, p. 102, also quoted in Chapter 2)*

The attempt to entirely set aside your religious or non-religious identity is tough and for many would be impossible to achieve whilst retaining your dignity. To give a personal example of my own (as a vegetarian), there have been some attempts to ban vegetarian options in school canteens in France, on the grounds that providing food to meet people's religious or ethical positions would break with the required 'neutrality' (Haurant 2011; Chrisafis 2015). Meanwhile, in Québec, there is a legal 'requirement that teachers adopt a professional stance of impartiality' and 'refrain from sharing their points of view, so as not to influence students as they develop their own positions' (Estivalèzes 2017, p. 55). How much of yourself are you prepared to leave at the school gate?

John I'Anson (2004) studied the transition from religious studies student to RE teacher. His research indicated that the need for the inclusion of teachers is as significant as that for pupils. UK-based RE teachers who have completed religious studies degrees may have to readjust their way of thinking about religions when they start teaching, as religious studies is a broadly modernist social scientific discipline, whilst RE in the UK has some more subjective and personal elements – described in a number of curriculum documents as adding 'learning from religion' to the more social scientific 'learning about religion' (Grimmitt 2000, p. 18; Chater and Erricker 2013, p. 2). An alternative approach would be to recast RE in the UK to suit the traditions of religious studies, and I'Anson has also been working on such a project (Jasper and I'Anson 2017). This work is 're-imagining Religious Education (RE) as this is practised in schools, colleges and universities throughout the UK and in a wide variety of international educational contexts' (Jasper and I'Anson 2017, back cover). Of course the nature of religious studies in higher education and its relationship to theology, and the relationship of both those disciplines to the school subject of RE, have been much argued over, notably by Denise Cush (Cush 1999). This is also part of a larger debate about the nature of school subjects, either as 'junior' versions of academic disciplines (Stenhouse 1975) or as having their own distinct value with quite different purposes to the disciplines with similar names studied in university (Beane 1995).

Teachers may bring to the RE classroom their own beliefs and practices, but whether these 'come through the door' and are made explicit to pupils can say a lot about how schools work. Lynn Revell has worked on this as an issue of 'performativity': the importance of teaching as 'performance' and what this means for religious and personal and professional identity (Bryan and Revell 2011). I am interested, myself, in how a teacher can both include and exclude pupils, through how they 'appear' in the classroom. Teachers *represent* the subjects they teach, for many pupils. As a student, you may feel the discipline you are studying is 'your' discipline, but as a teacher, you 'are' the discipline. (I wrote about it, for history teachers, as moving from 'your history' to 'you're history', Stern 1999, p. 23.) One approach – developed from the idea of teaching as performance, and views on performers and artists – is to practise 'negative capability'. This was the phrase used by the poet Keats to describe artists such as Shakespeare, who was 'capable of being in uncertainties, mysteries, doubts, without any irritable reaching after fact and reason' (Keats 1947, p. 72). It does not mean being vague or fuzzy, but performing or writing in such a way that others feel they can take what they want or need from you, without feeling that you have battered them into submission with a particular viewpoint. Gloria Durka writes eloquently of the 'teacher's calling' being 'mysterious and fascinating':

> The longer we do it, the more we become aware that we can never fully know our students or the subjects we teach. The more we think about them, the more clearly we see the limits of our understanding. This insight has been called the

'learned uncertainty of teachers'. … It is my hope that this modest book can affirm in some measure the role of teachers as ministers of personal and social transformation, and that it might help readers to celebrate the mystery and wonders of a teacher's calling. *(Durka 2002, p. 1)*

The ability of a teacher to live in uncertainty, as Keats and as Durka describe it, can be of value in RE classrooms, especially, where pupils can – understandably – want much more certainty than RE teachers could or should ever provide. (Chapter 10 explores more about the related issue of 'truth' in RE classrooms.)

Fedor Kozyrev tells of a pupil aged 15–16 in Russia who had been asked an apparently simple question in a questionnaire about what religion he belonged to, and who, in turn, asked his teacher: 'Marie-Anton, who are we, we are Orthodox or we are –?' (Kozyrev, in Stern 2016, p. 166). Is it up to teachers to tell pupils what religion they belong to, or is this a sign that there is much more RE to be done with those pupils?

Activity 3.3: Negative capability

The relationship between a teacher's own beliefs and ways of life and the subject of RE is very complex. Issues arise of professionalism and how to deal with one's own beliefs in a contested classroom.

Work with pupils to get them to script the best possible responses to these questions. Small groups of pupils could come up with a 'best thing to say', and perhaps a 'worst thing to say', and then you and the class could discuss *why* you and they believe the answers to be good (or not good).

1 Pupil says: Is it only Christians who go to heaven?

Teacher replies:

2 Pupil says: You keep saying, 'Muslims believe this' or 'Christians believe that'. What do *you* believe?

Teacher replies:

3 Pupil says: What's the point of RE if I'm not religious?

Teacher replies:

4 Pupil says: If evolution is true, does that mean Judaism, Christianity, and Islam are all wrong because they all say Adam was created as the first man?

Teacher replies:

5 Pupil says: I really like Buddhism: Can you tell me how to become a Buddhist?

Teacher replies:

6 Pupil says: If I do yoga, does that mean I'm a Hindu, and if I do mindfulness, does that mean I'm a Buddhist?

Teacher replies:

Conclusion

Everyone has a view on RE: pupils and teachers, others who work in schools, families of pupils, members of religious organizations, politicians, and others. Research within the school can help uncover some of these views. Ignoring them leads to a conspiracy of silence: RE continues with everyone talking to each other but nobody listening. That is not a good recipe for learning in any subject. In a subject as complex and personally challenging as RE, it is a guarantee that, even if helpful information is exchanged, there will be little real learning about or learning from religious and non-religious ways of life. Earlier in this chapter, I described my own very late realization that children had sophisticated and well-developed views on death, views that were quite different to the information I had been telling them in RE lessons. Joyce Mackley and colleagues wrote a fine guide for RE and personal and social education called *Looking Inwards – Looking Outwards: Exploring Life's Possibilities* (Mackley 1997). If considering our own mortality is the essence of looking inwards, then travelling around the world is, I guess, the essence of looking outwards. In the next chapter, therefore, there is something of a world tour. Since writing the first edition of this book, the biggest change in my own understanding of RE has been as a result of reading about and, even more, discussing with colleagues from other countries, the RE that is practised across the continents. I started with the – perhaps inevitable – feeling that RE in other places should be judged according to how closely it matched RE in my own country. Over the years, I have become no less confident in the value of UK RE, but I have become a great deal more confident in the value – often, the quite different value – of RE around the world.

Chapter 4
RE Around the World

RE lessons give you the peace of mind in a world, where peace and mind no longer go together.
(a 17-year-old)

Introduction

I think it will be clear already in this book that what seems obvious about RE in one country would be surprising in another. Whichever country you are working in, it is worth exploring RE in other countries around the world in order to understand RE in your own country. In many countries, RE is 'confessional', which can either mean it is taught according to the religion of the pupils (with a class only containing pupils of a single religious tradition) or it can mean the purpose of RE is to induct pupils into a particular religious tradition. My own experience in the UK was of confessional RE slowly disappearing from the 1970s and being regarded as inappropriate in community schools by the time I started teaching in the 1980s. It was only when I started travelling and working with colleagues in other countries, notably in the ten years since I wrote the first edition of this book, that I realized how popular confessional RE was around the world. In that earlier edition, I did refer to those who promoted confessional RE in the UK (e.g. Thompson 2004a, 2004b), but this was described as something of an 'underground' movement. It remains a minority approach in the UK, although it has become more common in a wider range of schools with church foundations. (Most UK church schools had practised non-confessional RE roughly from the 1980s to the 2000s, to the consternation of many of those working in church foundation schools in other countries.) Around the world, though, it is very common and institutionalized and accepted as the 'normal' way to do RE. So, if this book remains dominated by non-confessional approaches to RE, covering a range of religions and non-religious traditions, this is as much to do with what is most familiar to me as it is to do with what I find most educationally appropriate.

By taking a tour of RE around the world, I hope that readers will come to understand better what their own situation is and what alternatives are available. I remain a supporter of UK-style RE, but I no longer judge RE in other countries simply by how close it is to UK RE. And I have found – to my surprise – that RE is a lively, hotly debated, interesting and politically contentious subject in almost every country around the world, even those countries where I had previously thought no RE existed at all. Of course, a single chapter cannot possibly cover the variety of RE in every country. I am hoping to provide some interesting stimulus to further research – by you and your colleagues and pupils – which, I hope, will also lead to more international dialogue amongst pupils and teachers and other researchers.

Overviews and international policies

In the past, it was rather difficult getting clear pictures of RE in different countries around the world. This was partly because 'RE' has such a variety of meanings, making it hard to compare one country with another. It was also because it is easier for the 'big educational theories' to claim universality (even if they are not) than it is for individual curriculum subjects in schools – where most of the discussion is local and national, and there was less of an appetite for international discussion. Happily, things have got more fluid – if not universal – in recent years. One of the most influential figures in RE in UK schools, the Scottish religious studies scholar Ninian Smart (1927–2001), also worked in and influenced religious studies (mostly in higher education) in the United States, and wrote of religious and non-religious philosophical traditions across the world in his remarkable final book *World Philosophies* (Smart 1999). The Australian John Hull (1935–2015) was hugely important to UK RE, and also brought together RE researchers from more than thirty countries across six continents in ISREV, the International Seminar on Religious Education and Values (*www.isrev.org*), which he co-founded with the American character education specialist John Peatling. ISREV remains the biggest forum for research in RE around the world and has more than 250 of the leading researchers around the world, meeting every two years since 1978.

Bob Jackson built up the very important RE research community in the University of Warwick (*www2.warwick.ac.uk/fac/soc/ces/research/wreru*) and has worked tirelessly with international research projects across Europe and beyond. The US-based Religious Education Association (*religiouseducation.net/*) currently has Bert Roebben, from Germany, as president, and Mualla Selçuk, from Turkey, as president-elect. Different countries are becoming more familiar. Some handbooks have been produced, summarizing different RE traditions. Marian de Souza et al. (2006) produced a massive two-volume account of RE and spiritual and moral education. The book by James Arthur and Terence Lovat (2013) ranges across RE and values, while that of Derek Davis and Elena Miroshnikova (2013) is remarkably comprehensive, albeit focusing mostly on the legal position of RE. Covering RE across the hugely varied European landscape are many books developed from the

REDCo (Religion in Education: A Contribution to Dialogue or a Factor of Conflict in Transforming Societies of European Countries) and ENRECA (The European Network for Religious Education in Europe through Contextual Approaches) projects (such as Bob Jackson et al. 2007; Ina ter Avest et al. 2009). Elza Kuyk et al. (2007) is a systematic comparison of RE practice in thirty-one European countries, and Rothgangel et al. 2014 and 2016 are the first three of a six-volume study of the whole of European RE. Schreiner et al. (2007) investigates RE in primary schools across Europe, and there's more in Schreiner et al (2002). The European Forum for Teachers of RE, EFTRE (*www.eftre.net*), links teachers of RE and researchers across the continent, too, and their website provides guides to RE in member countries.

RE research and policy development have come together in a number of international agreements. Bob Jackson has been writing about RE across (and beyond) Europe for many years (e.g. Jackson 2006), and he has also supported the development of international policies. The best known of these are the *Toledo Guiding Principles* (ODIHR 2007), which are European principles on teaching about religions and beliefs in public (i.e. community) schools. Designed by a European organization, they are also promoted beyond Europe. It is worth quoting their 'key guiding principles':

1 Teaching about religions and beliefs must be provided in ways that are fair, accurate and based on sound scholarship. Students should learn about religions and beliefs in an environment respectful of human rights, fundamental freedoms and civic values.

2 Those who teach about religions and beliefs should have a commitment to religious freedom that contributes to a school environment and practices that foster protection of the rights of others in a spirit of mutual respect and understanding among members of the school community.

3 Teaching about religions and beliefs is a major responsibility of schools, but the manner in which this teaching takes place should not undermine or ignore the role of families and religious or belief organizations in transmitting values to successive generations.

4 Efforts should be made to establish advisory bodies at different levels that take an inclusive approach to involving different stakeholders in the preparation and implementation of curricula and in the training of teachers.

5 Where a compulsory programme involving teaching about religions and beliefs is not sufficiently objective, efforts should be made to revise it to make it more balanced and impartial, but where this is not possible, or cannot be accomplished immediately, recognizing opt-out rights may be a satisfactory solution for parents and pupils, provided that the opt-out arrangements are structured in a sensitive and non-discriminatory way.

6 Those who teach about religions and beliefs should be adequately educated to do so. Such teachers need to have the knowledge, attitude and skills to teach about religions and beliefs in a fair and balanced way. Teachers need not only subject-matter competence but pedagogical skills so that they can interact with students and help students interact with each other in sensitive and respectful ways.

7 Preparation of curricula, textbooks and educational materials for teaching about religions and beliefs should take into account religious and non-religious views in a way that is inclusive, fair, and respectful. Care should be taken to avoid inaccurate or prejudicial material, particularly when this reinforces negative stereotypes.

8 Curricula should be developed in accordance with recognized professional standards in order to ensure a balanced approach to study about religions and beliefs. Development and implementation of curricula should also include open and fair procedures that give all interested parties appropriate opportunities to offer comments and advice.

9 Quality curricula in the area of teaching about religions and beliefs can only contribute effectively to the educational aims of the Toledo Guiding Principles if teachers are professionally trained to use the curricula and receive ongoing training to further develop their knowledge and competences regarding this subject matter. Any basic teacher preparation should be framed and developed according to democratic and human rights principles and include insight into cultural and religious diversity in society.

10 Curricula focusing on teaching about religions and beliefs should give attention to key historical and contemporary developments pertaining to religion and belief, and reflect global and local issues. They should be sensitive to different local manifestations of religious and secular plurality found in schools and the communities they serve. Such sensitivities will help address the concerns of students, parents and other stakeholders in education. (ODIHR 2007, pp. 16–17)

There has been some debate about the organization that 'hosted' this project, as it is a security-focused organization (the Organisation for Security and Co-operation in Europe) (Gearon 2013; Jackson 2015). But the document itself – with all the careful wording characteristic of international policy documents developed by a large group of legal, educational, and religious bodies – is surprisingly readable and recognizable by RE teachers.

Activity 4.1: If I ruled the world

The *Toledo Guiding Principles* (ODIHR 2007) are available online (at *www.osce. org/odihr/29154*). Starting with the 'ten key principles', work with colleagues and pupils to do an audit of your own school, or the cluster of schools with which you work. Are each of the principles fully met, partially met, or not met at all? (The full document provides more explanation of each principle to help with the audit.)

After the audit, if there are any partially met or unmet principles, you may want to write a plan of how to move closer to meeting those principles.

Next, work with your colleagues and pupils to add an eleventh principle. What else would be good as a basic principle for RE?

One of the leading researchers on the interconnections between RE, religion, and politics, internationally, is Liam Gearon (e.g. 2002a, 2002b, 2003a, 2003b, 2004, 2005). His work – described in a Westhill seminar – explores religion's place in the world, its relationship to the United Nations and citizenship or human rights education, and the connections between RE and citizenship or human rights education. He starts from the idea that religion's role in public and political life has been underplayed. Talk of 'secularisation' has often meant that religion, in Western contexts, has been pushed into the 'private' sphere since the eighteenth-century Enlightenment. However, this appears to be changing as there is increasing evidence of the importance of religion in post–Cold War public and political life, often but not exclusively centring on issues of human rights, including freedom of religion or belief. The post–Cold War context is particularly important, with Bowker and Smart working on this since the 1960s, attacking the secularization thesis (as well described in Smart 1999). For example, in 1998, the US legislature passed the International Religious Freedom Act: a requirement for the US government to have a report on religious freedom every year (available on the internet at *www.state.gov/*). Religious freedom is therefore seen as a barometer of wider freedoms, although this should not be regarded as uncontroversial.

The United Nations system incorporated and defined freedom of religion or belief since the 1948 *UN Universal Declaration of Human Rights* (*www.un.org/en/universal-declaration-human-rights/*), but the early history of the UN tended, according to Gearon, to downplay religious and ideological diversies. The notion of 'universal' human rights itself may downplay diversity, as the universality of the declared rights itself seems to deny the specificity of religious context (it can be described as a 'humanist' text), even though it may be the religious contexts that provide, for many people, the reasons for having such rights. However, freedom of religion and belief, incorporating non-religious beliefs, was incorporated in the 1981 *UN Declaration on the Elimination of All Forms of Intolerance and Discrimination Based on Religion or Belief* (*www.un.org/documents/ga/res/36/a36r055.htm*). This has meant that, after a long neglect or low-level treatment of religion explicitly, the UN system from the late 1970s and with the 1981 Declaration began to recognize the international significance of religion for a stable world order. There is a UN Special Rapporteur on Religion and Belief, with that role having considerable relevance to education, including UNESCO, work (see *www.unesco.org/*). The 1992 *UN Declaration on the Rights of Persons Belonging to National or Ethnic, Religious and Linguistic Minorities* (*www.un.org/documents/ga/res/47/a47r135.htm*) is further evidence of a move to considering these issues as important, despite or perhaps related to the conflicts precisely over those issues in (and since) the 1990s.

Such large-scale comparative texts are fascinating, but it may be more immediately interesting to describe some of the research findings from individual countries. In the following sections, there is a bit of a world tour – some of the places I've found interesting RE research, albeit knowing there's plenty more still to be discovered.

East Asian, Southeast Asian, and Middle Eastern RE

One country where many people expect to find little RE is China. As Hirotaka Nanbu says, from the 1950s to the 1970s, 'it was thought that religion would disappear' (Nanbu 2008, p. 223), but it was eventually accepted that religion would continue – with a separation from the state, similar to that in the United States. High schools nevertheless teach about religion, especially in geography lessons, and there are said to be 100 million members of officially recognized religions of whom 14 million are Christian (with Confucianism not legally recognized as a religion) (Nanbu 2008, p. 226). Jinghao Zhou (in Davis and Miroshnikova 2013) notes the teaching of RE in China, and describes it as 'in revival', but 'it is difficult to offer a detailed report on religious education in China' (in Davis and Miroshnikova 2013, p. 76). Within China, there is much variation. Jing Li and Danièle Moore (2014) write of the Yunnan Province in southwest China, for example, where there is a considerable influence of Buddhism. There is a large number of private Buddhist Temple Education schools and a set of state-funded 'minority' schools and boarding schools that cater for many of the Buddhist children, alongside conventional state schools. Meanwhile in Hong Kong, there is a flourishing RE in most schools, and a large number of state-funded schools with religious foundations, including Buddhist and Christian. Wong Ping Ho, director of the Centre for Religious and Spirituality Education in the Hong Kong Institute of Education, is an expert in research and practice that crosses religious boundaries and promotes wide-ranging understanding of religion and spirituality in China (Wong 2006a, 2006b).

My own research on spirituality in UK and Hong Kong schools (Stern 2009a) confirmed for me the possibility of understanding spiritual issues, notwithstanding the significant language and cultural differences. My own belief is that there is such variation in understandings and culture *within* any community that it is not much more of a cognitive and imaginative 'leap' to understand those in a quite different community. Hong Kong is often described as the most 'European' part of China, but it is still part of China – a country that surely incorporates more peoples and languages and beliefs than any other country. Descriptions of Japanese society, in contrast, tend to focus more on its homogeneity. And yet it is a plural society, and research by Hideko Omori (2013), for example, looks at the influence of Christian-based schooling on women's progress in Japan. Finding an interesting relationship between Japanese religious practice and 'Western' Christian practice, Dennis Klass writes of Japanese ancestor worship and how it may illuminate bereavement practices in Europe and North America – the 'continuing bonds' with the dead (Klass et al. 1996, chapter 4).

Mohd Shuhaimi bin Haji Ishak and Osman Chuah Abdullah (2013) describe the tensions between Malaysia as a 'multi-racial, multi-cultural, and multi-religious pluralistic nation', with half the population either not (ethnically) Malay or not Muslim ('a meeting point of various religions including Islam, Christianity, Buddhism, Hinduism, Taoism, and others'), with a promotion through Islamic education of 'Malay hegemony' (Ishak and Abdullah 2013, p. 298). A parallel could be drawn with the UK, in which Christianity has a prominent place (both in RE and, separately, in the statutory 'collective worship' expected to be of 'a predominantly Christian character'), and this is connected to the government's wish for school to reflect the Christianity that is the 'predominant religion in Great Britain' (DfE 1994a). Perhaps the similarity between UK and Malaysian education is not surprising, given the history of the two countries. But as Ishak and Abdullah explain, the picture of Malaysian Islamic RE and its role in political as well as religious life is an interesting and subtle one. A different approach to religious pluralism is described by Syafaatun Almirzanah (2014), who writes eloquently of Indonesian society, and an RE that is broadly confessional (based on the principle of a 'belief in the one Supreme God', Almirzanah 2014, p. 234) and dialogic – in which '[r]eligious pluralism calls for active engagement with the religious other not merely to tolerate, but to understand' (Almirzanah 2014, p. 242). The comparison made by Mirjam Künkler and Hanna Lerner is between this situation in Indonesia and the contrasting one in Israel, where religion is more often a dividing point in schools, with state-funded religious schools increasingly moving away from a 'secular' education, and therefore moving away from other state-funded schools, and closer to private religious schools (Künkler and Lerner 2016).

The possible fragmentation between different schools in Israel ('secular public education, religious public education, ultra-Orthodox-independent education, Arab education and private education') is also seen by Ilana Paul-Binyamin and Shahar Gindi (2017) as a challenge to developing both individual autonomy and political integration. Others researching education in Israel stress the importance of teacher development, as in Shlomo Back's account of a humane approach to teacher development based on Charles Taylor's identity theory (Back 2012). Zehavit Gross (in Parker et al. 2015, chapter 4) focuses on one of the most sensitive topics taught in Israeli RE: that of the Holocaust. She says that the Holocaust 'should not be viewed as a unique historical issue that relates to a specific nation but rather as a moral and religious threat to liberal values and human rights that was committed by apparently "civilized people" who chose to cling to that evil' (Gross, in Parker et al. 2015, p. 79). RE is certainly as challenging in schools that are dominated by a single religion as it is in more plural schools. Research by Jarallah Abdulaziz Al-Buraidi on Saudi Arabian Islamic education (the country's approach to RE) provided evidence of surprising challenges. These included the relatively low status of RE compared to other subjects, RE teachers having a large number of relatively short once-a-week classes, the dearth of effective training of specialist teachers, the lower use of teaching aids, the need to develop more effective uses of assessment for learning, and the perception of RE as less 'relevant' and old-fashioned (Al-Buraidi 2006).

European RE

Adam Anczyk and Joanna Grzymała-Moszczyńska (2016) write of RE in Poland. It is a confessional subject that is funded by the state but controlled by the Catholic church. The subject is not compulsory, with parents able to opt their children out of the subject, and there is an option also to study ethics. Since 2012, the subject has had a somewhat lower status in schools, as it does not count towards pupils' transition to the next grades, and it counts as a 'complementary' rather than 'core' subject. The situation in Croatia is somewhat similar, with elective Catholic confessional RE described by Denis Barić and Josip Burušić (2015), although the subject does provide 'an opportunity for growth in [pupils'] personal, religious and cultural identities through dialogue, ecumenism and acceptance of different people, worldviews, religions, and confessional and cultural expressions' (Barić and Burušić 2015, p. 294). Moving East from Poland and Croatia, Russia is one of the most interesting countries in its approach to RE. Until the 1980s, Russia rejected most forms of religion and RE. Since then, it has not only moved to allow more public recognition of religion but the Orthodox church has also gained considerable political influence. And in 2010, RE became a required subject on the country's national curriculum. Within less than a generation, the political upheavals have been more than matched by religious and educational upheavals. One of the leading Russian researchers on RE, Fedor Kozyrev, had a career as a research biochemist, under the old regime, but came to active religious engagement in the 1990s and then, through reading John Hull's work, to RE in schools (Kozyrev, in Stern 2016 chapter 9). He had worked within the REDCo project on dialogues about religion in Russian schools (in Avest et al. 2009), focusing on dialogues of different voices in RE classrooms. Those dialogues have been changing, as the cultural and political climate changes. He describes an interesting incident:

> In one piece of research of REDCo, there was a question 'What religious group do you belong to?' and children raised their hands, not children, these were guys of fifteen or sixteen years old, and they asked the lecturer, 'Marie-Anton, who are we, we are Orthodox or we are – ?' They understand that everyone should put the 'right' answer: the person never thought about who is he personally. So of course there is a sort of change in their identification, caused by the introduction of religion into public sphere. But also there is less and less of those who are afraid of showing themselves Orthodox. *(Kozyrev, in Stern 2016, p. 166, quoted in part in Chapter 3)*

Alexandra Blinkova and Paul Vermeer provide a systematic study of RE in Russia since it became part of the national curriculum. They compare the Russian RE curriculum to those of Sweden, Denmark, and the UK. There is an 'objective' or social scientific approach to much of RE, rather like Swedish RE, but there is a stronger emphasis on RE having an important role in citizenship education, and (like in the UK) several religions have an input into the syllabus. 'Confessional' modules are provided by the Russian Orthodox church, and by Buddhist, Muslim, and Jewish communities. Pupils start with a common 'general lesson' entitled 'Russia is our Motherland' and finish with another general lesson called 'Love and respect for the Motherland' or 'Patriotism of multinational and multireligious Russian people' (Blinkova and Vermeer 2016, p. 7), and between these, parents can opt for one of

'Fundamentals of Orthodox Culture, Fundamentals of Judaic Culture, Fundamentals of Islamic Culture, Fundamentals of Buddhist Culture, Fundamentals of World Religious Cultures or Fundamentals of Secular Ethics' (Blinkova and Vermeer 2016, p. 7). Mararita Kostikova and Valentin Kozhuharov (in Kuyk et al. 2007), writing during the 'in between' period, when religious freedom had been instituted in Russia, but RE was not yet part of the national curriculum, provide a helpful account of how the subject was developing.

However, it is not just the political transformation in Russia that led to a transformation in RE, something similar happened in France. Although France had a much greater degree of religious freedom through the twentieth century, in terms of private practice, the public and political separation of church and state – the ideology of secularism or *laïcité* – has meant dealing with religion in schools has been a significant challenge. However, in the last twenty years, there have been several developments. Bérengère Massignon and Séverine Mathieu describe the changes in France in recent years (in Avest et al. 2009), and increasing course material dealing with religion has appeared, generally 'presented in a secular perspective within existing school subjects (History/Geography, French, Philosophy, etc.)', with 'no courses on religion only'; 'nor do religious authorities take part in teaching this material' (in Avest et al. 2009, p. 86). The French education ministry has portrayed the issue as one of 'religious illiteracy' and the need to teach 'religious facts', although the practice went further than this (as described in Chapters 2 and 3). A fascinating piece of research on RE in France by Carol Ferrara investigated the extent to which understanding religions and being tolerant with respect to religion were 'codependent'. In other words, is RE helpful in creating more tolerant people? The research was completed in two community schools (with little teaching about religion), and in an Islamic and a Catholic school (where RE was well established).

> While it is easy to jump to the conclusion that the more students learn, the better off they will be, this study has demonstrated that certain types of learning influence student tolerance and understanding differently, sometimes with undesirable and/or unintended results. For example, this can result in some students being *blindly* tolerant and others having understanding without tolerance. In order to better channel the efforts of religious education planners into effective policies and models, context needs to take priority in the planning process. *(Ferrara 2012, p. 528)*

Ferrara continues, saying that '[i]n some cases, it may not be more education about religion that is needed, but perhaps education in culture, moral education, critical analysis skills, team-building skills, understanding media bias, and so on' (Ferrara 2012, p. 529). There is a problem, still, of 'a lack of tolerance in private religious education and a lack of tolerance in public education', so RE planners should do more than 'simply pushing for more education about religion' (Ferrara 2012, p. 529). The French region of Alsace-Moselle has been an exception, with a history of RE stretching back to the nineteenth century, and a syllabus that includes work on religion and peace, religious persecution, and debates on transcendence, conviction, and tolerance (Kuyk et al. 2007, pp. 72–73). I have not seen comparisons between Alsace-Moselle and other regions in France, but contexts provide such distinct influences that it would be difficult to generalize from one to the other. (It is just as difficult to compare Northern Ireland, Scotland, England, and Wales with each other, or the different Canadian Provinces and Territories, or Australian States and Territories.)

I have found it difficult finding a wide range of research on RE in France, and this is not so surprising given their history of *laïcité*, but I have found a similar challenge in Italy, notwithstanding very well-established RE throughout the country. I would welcome enlightenment on this issue: I may well be looking in the wrong places, but Flavio Pajer (in Kuyk et al. 2007) explains that no state universities have theology faculties, and this may therefore limit the pool of staff wishing to research RE. In schools, the Catholic religion is taught as a confessional subject, with one or two hours a week offered to all children – with parents deciding whether or not their children take the lesson. In community schools, although the RE is confessional (and approved by the church), 'the educational outcomes ... are scholastic in nature, which means it is cultural, informative, critical, and not pastoral or catechetic ... [and t]he didactic approach is mainly hermeneutical-anthropological, and less historical-cultural' (in Kuyk et al. 2007, p. 117). There are some Catholic private schools (for about 5 per cent of the population), but other religious groups have very few private schools and none contribute to RE in community schools. Valeria Friso and Roberta Caldin have produced fascinating research on RE and disability in Italian schools. They refer to ways in which RE, in dealing with universal human experiences such as bereavement, can help with inclusion in schools. They conclude that '[t]he attempt has always been ... to promote the concept of individual differences and the sacredness of each individual in order to impel the inclusion of children with disabilities' (Friso and Caldin 2014, p. 223). Teachers therefore need the skills 'to dismantle, rebuild, reshape, and reinvent subject content in order to make it more understandable' (Friso and Caldin 2014, p. 224).

RE teachers around the world will no doubt recognize the need to do that for all pupils. Italy has in recent years become more religiously diverse. Although I have not found research on how schools are adapting to this in their RE lessons, Roberta Ricucci, of the University of Turin, has researched young Muslims in Italy (aged 18–24) and their use of social media. What seems to be happening is that many will have three Facebook pages, one for family and relations, a second for friends of the same age from all groups, and a third for young people who are Muslim (Ricucci 2015). Young people – perhaps unsurprisingly – reflect the country's separation of public and private, and the different roles of family, with respect to religion. The Republic of Ireland provides an interesting contrast to Italy. Unlike Italy, the country's constitution 'acknowledges God as the source of its authority' (Andrew McGrady in Kuyk et al. 2007, p. 108), and most schools have church foundations – mostly Catholic. The church also controls RE that is provided in all schools. McGrady suggests that '[y]oung people are drawn to issues of spirituality, personal development and global ethics (especially justice issues) but remain aloof from the doctrinal stance of the Church' (McGrady, in Kuyk et al. 2007, p. 112).

Germany has a very rich tradition both of RE and of research on RE. The investigations of Thorsten Knauth on dialogue in Hamburg were mentioned in Chapter 2, along with Wofram Weisse's work there and in South Africa. Peter Schreiner leads the Comenius-Institut in Münster, a centre for research and professional development in RE across Europe as well as in Germany. He writes of RE in Germany as reflecting both the secular nature of the state (guaranteeing both freedom *from* and freedom *of* religion) and its federal nature – with 16 *Länder* (states) each having distinct control over education. Roughly a third of the population is Protestant, a third Catholic, and a third members of other religions or none. RE in schools is mostly confessional – being taught to pupils of that same 'confession' (i.e. denomination), but it is broadly educational rather than indoctrinating pupils, and it may at times address different religions and inter-religious dialogue. In some states, Islamic or Orthodox education is provided for Muslim and Orthodox pupils, respectively, and all pupils may be 'opted out' of RE by their parents, and will usually follow a secular ethics, philosophy, or values education course instead. RE syllabuses are developed jointly by the state and churches. However, such is the variation between states that it is difficult to give a straightforward account that covers the whole country. Schreiner's account suggests that key issues include the further support for teachers of Islamic RE, the need for closer co-operation on RE between different religious groups, and more work on inter-religious dialogue (Schreiner, in Kuyk et al 2007). Dan-Paul Jozsa has researched precisely these issues within North Rhine-Westphalia (in Avest et al. 2009, p. 134). One of his concerns is that the study of Islam, unlike Protestant and Catholic RE, is not regarded as 'religious education' and so – unlike for the Christian denominations – is entirely under the control of the state, and teachers of Islam, for example, 'are not allowed to wear a headscarf in school' (Jozsa in Avest et al. 2009, p. 137).

Eva-Maria Kenngott researches the interesting 'Life Design-Ethics-Religion Studies' (LER) in the federal state of Brandenburg, which is, according to Kenngott, the only wholly non-confessional form of RE in Germany. LER developed out of the tradition in what had been socialist and secular East Germany, although other former East German states have not followed this pattern. However, whilst there is some pressure to develop less confessional RE in other parts of Germany, there appears to be some movement in the other direction, as 'the number of students choosing confessional RE is increasing ... [f]rom 2004 to 2015 ... from 9% to around 16.5%' (Kenngott 2017, p. 43) and as the proportion of LER-trained teachers falls. The value of *confessional* RE, in the German style, is described by Christoph Scheilke (2011) in terms of twelve good reasons for a confessional RE in plural schools. Within a confessional, Christian, German RE, and history, Reinhold Boschki researches how pupils can or might remember the Holocaust, in an interesting project that complements the work of Gross in Israel, described earlier in this chapter. He promotes a 'culture of remembrance' which 'is more than dealing with knowledge about history': it is 'an ethically-reflected, self-reflected, critical culture ..., and a moral culture … where the suffering of the past is remembered in order to never repeat the injustice, oppression, and destruction of former times' (Boschki, in Parker et al. 2015, p. 37). Manfred Pirner researches religious freedom in religious schools in Germany (Pirner, in Parker et al. 2012). Elisabeth Naurath's research on teaching about Judaism and the Holocaust in German primary schools (in Parker et al. 2015) notes the need to avoid associating Jews *only* with the suffering of the Holocaust (i.e. more of Judaism should be taught than just this topic). She also recommends that pupils should learn through research, and teachers should teach through research, especially on this difficult topic. That, of course, complements the theme of this whole book.

Continuing the travelogue, RE in the Netherlands is affected by what is known as the 'pillarization' of schools. Ina ter Avest and colleagues research the effects of schools being separated (in 'pillars') by denomination, with 60 per cent of primary schools Protestant or Roman Catholic, 30 per cent community, and 10 per cent private (Avest et al. 2008). It is interesting to note how this affects a society that has a long history of pluralism and an approach to religion summed up by a government minister as 'Iets-isme' ('whatever-ism') (Avest et al. 2008, p. 320). Kuyk notes how the pluralism and the openness of schools (so denominational schools will be open to those outside that denomination) used to be combined with a 'confessional' RE for many pupils. In the Netherlands, confessional RE means RE with the teacher and pupils belonging to the same denomination, as is also common in Germany. However, this is one option amongst many, with pupils (and their parents) often receiving more 'multicultural and even inter-religious teaching' with 'elements of philosophy and ethics' (Kuyk, in Kuyk et al. 2007, p. 136). The move away from confessional RE is rather slow, Kuyk says. My 'outsider' view of the Netherlands as a very secular and liberal country does not quite match my understanding of how RE works in schools there. As in so many countries, RE is a good 'test' of how schooling works and what the relationship is between schools, governments, and other – especially religious – organizations.

Moving North, to Norway, we find another country where RE's position in the curriculum has in recent years been challenged – including major legal challenges. Geir Skeie (1995, 2002, 2017) researches RE in Norway (and across Europe) and focuses on the tensions between pluralism in the curriculum and the religious or non-religious position of the teacher. RE is non-confessional in Norway, although this is a relatively recent development, and the subject is largely determined at national level, with religious organizations often involved, but without the final say, at local level (Leganger-Krogstad, in Kuyk et al. 2007). How the subject has worked in what was often regarded until recently as a monocultural country such as Norway is interesting – and as multi-religious RE has grown, the subject has become of interest to a number of researchers. Marie von der Lippe notes how non-confessional RE was intended to prevent conflicts rooted in religion, but the characteristic understanding of religious conflict was conflict *between* religions, not *within* a religion. Lippe herself therefore explores dialogue in Norwegian RE classrooms (using videos of lessons) and how both conflict and agreement can be part of healthy educational conversations (in Avest et al. 2009). Oddrun Bråten (in Parker et al. 2015) compares the development and practice of Norwegian RE with that in England, noting the differences in national 'styles' and approaches to key issues – such as the role of Christianity in national culture. A fascinating piece of detailed research on pupils' exercise books in RE, by Elisabet Haakedal (in Parker et al. 2015), addresses – amongst many other things – the political challenge of drawing and labelling maps related to the life of Jesus that also recognize contemporary Israel's borders.

While Norwegian and English RE are similar in many ways, Swedish RE is distinctive in a number of ways. There is more discussion of Swedish RE in Chapter 11. Here, I will mention the research by Karin Sporre, who has explored RE and ethics in both Sweden and South Africa. She set up a South-North dialogue on diversity and the future of education (Sporre 2012), and this dialogic approach to research, as well as to educational development in the two countries, is a model of effective collaboration across borders. (See also Berglund et al. 2016, on RE 'in a global-local world'.) Within Sweden, Pernilla Liedgren has explored how Jehovah's Witnesses experience how schools deal with religion. There are few legal ways in which pupils can be withdrawn from classes for religious reasons, so modules on sexuality or evolution, and social activities based on religious festivals, have been problematic for Jehovah's Witness families. Interviewing teachers and adult Jehovah's Witnesses about their school days, Liedgren notes that 'positive experiences concerning their religious identity occurred at school when teachers were clear, respectful and open with their opinions' (Liedgren 2016, p. 5). One interviewee 'described an occasion in which he was taking a test on the theory of evolution and wrote everything that the teacher wanted him to write but also added the Jehovah's Witnesses perspective', and the pupil 'appreciated that the teacher gave him more than the full points for the test' (Liedgren 2016, p. 5). Another 'described an occasion in which a biology teacher firmly but kindly declined further discussion on the theory of evolution as interpreted in a Jehovah's Witnesses-published book that this pupil had given to the teacher', and 'returned the book after a week and stated he had reviewed it but was not convinced'. The pupil said that 'he appreciated the teacher's forthrightness, which contrasted with the approach of other teachers who would say that they wished to read Jehovah's Witnesses booklets, books or magazines but would then discard them in a bin shortly after receiving them' (Liedgren 2016, p. 6). It is interesting to note that honest disagreement was welcomed more than fake interest. How a country like Sweden deals with challenging religious issues – whether in RE or science lessons – is complex and unexpected. There is no easy route to living and learning together.

Finnish RE has been broadly confessional, with Lutheran RE available for most pupils, at their parents' request, and RE in other religious traditions available if there are enough people requesting it (Luodeslampi, in Kuyk et al. 2007). However, more recently, multi-religious RE has been introduced, including work on the pupil's own religion, work on 'world religions', and 'a good life', with all three activities available to pupils who may still learn together with pupils of the same religion (*www.eftre.net*). Recent research by Martin Ubani (2015, 2016) investigates how those training to teach RE in Finland are dealing with the changing nature of – still broadly confessional – RE and their professional identity as teachers. Moving South,

Olga Schihalejev's research in Estonia suggests the biggest change for pupils in RE is the change from the old Soviet approach in which children were expected to be 'listening to the teacher's lecture and filling up a work-sheet with a clear and safe border between right and wrong answers' (Schihalejev, in Avest et al. 2009, p. 72). Increasingly, RE is becoming dialogic. However, as Pille Valk noted, it was an optional subject – albeit one that was non-confessional and 'contextual', dealing with the issues that are of relevance to the pupils themselves (Valk, in Kuyk et al. 2007) – until the 2010 national curriculum made multi-religious RE a subject within the Estonian national curriculum (*www.eftre.net* and *usundiopetus.weebly.com/eng.html*). Latvian RE has been researched by Lāsma Latsone, exploring confessional RE in parishes and 'intercultural education' in schools and teacher education (Latsone 2013a, 2013b; Latsone, in Stern 2016). However, confessional RE has been the dominant form since the early 1990s, with the subject supported by relevant denominations (Dzintra Iliško in Parker et al. 2012, Ilishko, in Kuyk et al. 2007). Hungary, also a former communist state, has similar confessional RE for those who opt for it, in 'secular' schools (Szabo, in Kuyk et al. 2007).

Marios Koukounaras Liagkis describes the recent development of compulsory RE in Greece, based on 'constructivist and critical approaches to RE' (Liagkis 2015, p. 153), following the work of Andrew Wright and Michael Grimmitt – as '[t]he new curriculum is explicitly infused with British RE approaches', even though 'there is a veiled layer of a monocultural RE' (Liagkis 2015, p. 157). (Until relatively recently, Greek had confessional and catechetical Orthodox RE, according to Tsakalidis, in Kuyk et al. 2007.) Another secular state with non-confessional RE that can – increasingly – seem to be somewhat monocultural is Turkey. Significant research on Turkish RE has been carried out, with Mualla Selçuk and John Valk suggesting a 'worldviews' model of RE as a further development of the subject (Selçuk and Valk 2012, and see also Selçuk and Doğan, in Kuyk et al. 2007). The subject, under the name 'religious culture and ethics', is a valuable comparator for those looking at secular non-confessional RE in Christian-majority, Muslim-majority, and Jewish-majority states. (India, as a Hindu-majority state, does not, as far as I know, have well-established RE in community schools.)

African RE

Moving from Europe to Africa, it is in South Africa that there has been the greatest flourishing of RE research. Cornelia Roux's extensive research on spirituality is reported in chapter 16 of Ota and Chater 2007, and focuses on the communitarian and non-dualist principle of *Ubuntu*, and Karin Sporre's work in Sweden and South Africa has been mentioned earlier in this chapter. Elaine Nogueira-Godsey provides a very useful overview of recent developments. 'Religion education' is the distinctive name for the subject, to distinguish it from the confessional 'religious education' in apartheid South Africa. RE became 'integrated into a subject named Life Orientation' as a non-confessional and multi-religious subject, and that subject was later renamed 'Life Skills' (Nogueira-Godsey 2016, p. 230). The subject addresses major religions in South Africa: Judaism, Christianity, Islam, Hinduism, Buddhism, Bahá'í Faith, and African Religion. There remain some issues of teachers who, although supportive of the curriculum, remain 'confessional' in their approach in the classroom:

> Through the interviews, it is explicit that those obstructing an effective implementation of the Policy on Religion Education are not necessarily against the curriculum's goals of religious diversity, but rather the obstructions are wrapped up with teachers' inability to recognise and move beyond a confessional pedagogical approach to religions in their own practice. *(Nogueira-Godsey 2016, p. 234)*

Petro du Preez researches the relationships between morality, human rights, and religious freedom as it affects RE (du Preez in Parker et al. 2012). René Ferguson also researches religious diversity in South Africa (Ferguson in Parker et al. 2012), focusing on how research uncovers the unexpected. It is the traditional African Religion, and tradition more broadly, that is the focus of Glynis Parker's research. Her conclusion, like that of Roux, centres on *Ubuntu*, the approach to community described by Bishop Desmond Tutu as being 'generous, hospitable, friendly, caring, compassionate' and as indicating that 'we belong in a bundle of life' as 'I am human because I belong' (quoted in Hoppers and Richards 2012, p. 58). Parker concludes that

> Tradition and culture are not static; they move and interact and get modified through time. Tradition can be seen as a collage, an assemblage of diverse elements grouped together and considered as a whole; it is composed of original and borrowed material. It is this ability of tradition that gives it its resilience to survive in the new South Africa. All of this can arguably be ascribed to adherence to the philosophy of *ubuntu*, which is the vehicle through which traditions can be carried forward and which keeps them alive in contemporary South Africa. *(Parker, in Parker et al. 2015, p. 339)*

The influence of tradition on contemporary RE is also described by Sarah Croché in the similarly secular Senegal. Teachers tend to 'teach for religion in public schools (in a devotional sense)' rather than 'teach about religion (in an academic sense)' in Senegal, notwithstanding the 'official curriculum' (Croché 2015, p. 37). My own experience of RE in the UK suggests that in the UK, too, there are teachers whose personal religious position seems to undermine the non-confessional nature of RE in their schools. Perhaps this is a universal – and inevitable – feature of the subject that some teachers (no doubt a minority, a tiny minority in most countries) will work in this way. Croché gives the example of a Senegalese teacher who teaches about evolution and also tells his pupils that the theory is clearly incorrect (Croché 2015, p. 45). Paul Thomas (2012) describes how the influence of African Traditional Religion is greater in Ghana because the multi-religious subject ('religious and moral education') comes in and out of fashion (or up and down in its priority) in Ghanaian schools. In contrast, Zimbabwean RE is avowedly 'bible-oriented and confessional', according to Lovemore Ndlovu. Ndlovu's research suggests that 'most Religion Education stakeholders prefer an authentic values-oriented multi-faith model that would contribute to the teaching of values such as citizenship, human rights, ubuntu/ unhu, nationhood, etc' and so suggests a 'values-oriented multi-faith approach' for Zimbabwe secondary schools (Ndlovu 2014, p. 174).

American and Australian RE

North American RE is as varied as European, Asian, African, and Middle Eastern RE. In both Canada and the United States, there are massive variations between states/provinces as well as national interests in RE. Oddly, Canada is a less religiously active country than the United States, but it is a country with a far more fully developed tradition of RE than the United States. Stephen Prothero compares undergraduate students in the United States and Europe, as he discussed the issue with an Austrian colleague: 'European students can name the twelve apostles and the Seven Deadly Sins, but they wouldn't be caught dead going to church or synagogue themselves', whilst 'American students are just the opposite', as 'here religious ignorance is bliss' (Prothero 2007, p. 1). Prothero might have found a similar contrast north of the border. In Canada, Mireille Estivalèzes researches RE in Québec, where an 'ethics and religious culture' programme was introduced to all schools in 2008. That programme of multi-religious RE included the 'requirement that teachers adopt a professional stance of impartiality' and 'refrain from sharing their points of view, so as not to influence students as they develop their own positions' (Estivalèzes 2017, p. 55). There were critics of the programme, including 'Catholic parents who were denied a request to have their sons exempted from the ... programme', because they felt the programme was 'putting forward a relativistic view of religious and moral knowledge' (Estivalèzes 2017, p. 59). In contrast, 'the Mouvement laïque québécois (a secular movement) ... considers that the ... programme is an apology for religion, mainly Catholicism, and that it manipulates the minds of young people, at the risk of indoctrinating them' (Estivalèzes 2017, p. 59). A third critique 'considers that the programme is a propaganda tool for Canadian multiculturalism and its objective is to weaken the national, political and religious identity of Québec by overvaluing diversity' (Estivalèzes 2017, p. 61). (See also Montreal Gazette 2008, 2010 for news reports of protests.) Who said RE was easy?

These issues are put in historical context by Lorna Bowman, who suggests that there is more work to be done to enable the many religions and worldviews 'which make up the Canadian mosaic' to catch up with the legally 'privileged position of Catholic education, not only in Ontario but also in Alberta and Saskatchewan' (Bowman, in Parker et al. 2012, p. 44). More recently, Bowman has researched the problems with the religious education of Canada's 'aboriginal children' (Bowman, in Parker et al. 2015). The importance of Catholic education in Canada, noted by Bowman, is explored more fully by Myrtle Power, who writes of RE in Canada's Catholic schools (Power, in Parker et al. 2015), and Catholic education not only in Canada but across the world is the topic of Mario D'Souza's research on religion in pluralist societies (starting with Canada) (D'Souza 2000; D'Souza, in Parker et al. 2012), and in his magisterial account of Catholic philosophies (and philosophers) of education (D'Souza 2016).

Rather like the Toledo Guiding Principles, described above, Diane Moore and colleagues in the American Academy of Religion have produced helpful guidance for teaching about religion in US schools (Moore 2010). But it was Prothero's research on religious literacy, stimulated by his concern about religious ignorance, that introduced this section on North America. His work promotes a relatively straightforward knowledge of religious 'facts', somewhat in the style of French teaching about religion. He is not naive in his views on education and realizes that there is much more to understanding religions than mere facts – but he insists that without key facts, the rest of learning is of little value: 'the challenging conversations I coveted were not possible without some common knowledge' (Prothero 2007, p. 5). Religious illiteracy is 'dangerous', he says, and his focus is specifically 'on spreading knowledge rather than inculcating virtues' (Prothero 2007, p. 21). Haynes (2012) provides a good example of the dangers of illiteracy, Nash and Bishop (2010) put the whole of religious literacy into the 'Post-9/11' context, and Hess (2017) puts RE into its political context. This approach appeals to those in the United States who are nervous of the constitutional separation of church and state, notwithstanding Prothero's (and many others') accounts of how the US constitution restricts public bodies from promoting a particular religion, but does nothing to limit teaching *about* or learning *from* religions (Feinberg 2014). The 'safe' character of this form of religious literacy (which is a long way from the theological religious literacy of Andrew Wright 1997) has made this approach popular in a number of other countries – including the UK.

A different approach to research, and to RE, in the United States is provided by Matthew Geiger. Geiger taught RE in an Episcopal (Anglican) high school whilst completing his doctoral research and publishing several articles. He promotes forms of relationality in RE classrooms: that is, he is interested in how RE teachers and pupils relate to each other in and through the subject itself. A 'notebooking' activity was developed, where teachers and pupils correspond on matters that are of importance. This could be portrayed as a type of formative assessment (and he credits the complementarity to my own work on assessment, published as Stern and Backhouse 2011) (Geiger 2016b), but extracts from the notebooks are evocative of a tremendously powerful personal influence of those teachers who took this approach to heart. Pupils 'used notebooks to write personal reflections on course content, which were read by the teacher and responded to in a sometimes more, sometimes less, relational manner' (Geiger 2016a, p. 18). The 'more' or 'less' in this phrase are important: in two of the three schools, the teacher responses were perceived as genuinely conversational; in the third school, they were not and the pupils said that they 'were faking it' (Geiger

2015, p. 177). Here is an example of what Geiger considers a genuinely relational correspondence in one of the notebooks:

> Maddie: When my father died, I shunned God altogether. Some have stories of coming closer to this God, but I only put distance between the already small connection I had. . . .
>
> Mr. Lisbon: I can only imagine.
>
> Maddie: Now, upon reflecting, I realize I still sort of acknowledge this God.
>
> Mr. Lisbon: Isn't it strange that not believing is still sort of a relationship?
>
> Maddie: I am angry. Angry at this one entity. I question the existence, but no matter how much I question, I am still frustrated. This might be my covenant. This, of course, is nothing light-hearted or joyous, but this God might let me blame him, even if he doesn't exist. (Geiger 2016a, p. 21)

Conversation of this kind is, for Geiger, at the heart of developing personhood, and he later described the pupils' and the teachers' positioning in terms of 'personae': how we act our parts and, in acting, discover (or develop) our 'real' selves (Geiger 2016c). Geiger's hope was that teachers doing research 'will further explore the nature and function of relational pedagogy in the nurturing of purposeful, socially informed democratic citizens' (Geiger 2016b, p. 10). There is a significant amount of US research about religion and education in general, such as that of Prothero, Warren Nord (1995), and David Purpel and William McLaurin (2004), and there is some tremendous work on broad spiritual (educational) themes such as that of Rachael Kessler (2000, 2002), Linda Lantieri (2001), Gloria Durka (2002), and Parker Palmer (1993, 2007). I find it harder, though, to find much of the kind of empirical, school-based, research of the kind that Geiger has completed – and that seems easier to find in other countries. Chris Sink, who researches young people's well-being and spirituality, notes how in US community schools, he refrains from explicitly surveying spirituality, because of the difficulty of gaining approval for such research, although such research (part of the same project, indeed) can be completed in Korea and in South Africa (Sink and Bultsma 2014; Sink, in Stern 2016, p. 155). Sink, like Geiger, found it viable to study religion directly by going into the small number of private schools with church foundations (Sink et al. 2007).

Latin American research in RE is limited (in the English language accessible to me), and the subject has mixed fortunes – as in North America. There is a small number of countries in which the teaching of religion is forbidden (such as Cuba), a much larger group of countries in which RE is forbidden in state-owned schools but allowed in private schools (such as Mexico, Uruguay, Argentina, Paraguay, and Ecuador), and another group where, legally, RE can be taught, but where it is rarely taught (such as Brazil and Venezuela; Juan G Navarro Floria, in Davis and Miroshnikova 2013, pp. 199–200). A small group of countries have substantial RE (with an 'opt out' for pupils or parents), which is mainly Catholic teaching

(Chile, Peru, and Bolivia), with some optional teaching of, for example, Evangelical Christianity in Colombia (Juan G Navarro Floria, in Davis and Miroshnikova 2013, p. 200). According to Floria, there is increasing debate on the place of religion in school, in part as a result of increasing religious diversity and a weakening influence of Catholicism, and this view is also supported by research in Brazil (by Sérgio Rogério Azevedo Junqueira) and on Chile (by Rodrigo Fuentealba Jara and Patricia Imbarack Dagach) in Buchanan and Gellel 2015 (chapters 23 and 24). And Maria Concepción Medina González found that in Mexico, although RE is not a subject in state schools, 'civic and ethical formation' lessons may indirectly touch on religion (in Davis and Miroshnikova 2013, chapter 30).

Australian RE research is much more widely available, especially – also – on Catholic RE. Australian community schools have a similar difficulty with religion that US schools have, but Australia also has a large number of publicly funded Catholic schools – attended by more than 20 per cent of the population. (Australia has much lower church attendance than the United States, and Catholic schools are not restricted to practising Catholic pupils.) Research in RE – at least, Catholic RE – has flourished for a long time. Michael Buchanan has researched the role of heads of RE in Catholic schools (Buchanan and Engebretson 2009) and moved on to broader issues of leadership in schools with a religious foundation (Buchanan 2013). Brendan Hyde explores the details of Catholic RE and spirituality (Hyde 2006, 2008a, 2008b) and the tensions between the purposes of RE and the purposes of Catholic education (Hyde 2013). Peta Goldburg, in the same sector, explores the role of RE as a foundation for freedom of religion and belief (Goldburg, in Parker et al. 2012). Some of the challenges are expressed by Marian de Souza, who researches spirituality. She notes that 'the secular character of Australian society creates a serious barrier to any recognition that spirituality may have a role in the educational process since, for many, spirituality and religion are seen as synonymous, or certainly, very closely intertwined' (de Souza, in Ota and Chater 2007, p. 165). de Souza attributes this to the Cartesian Enlightenment views brought with the European settlement of Australia. Andrew Singleton (2015) writes of children in Australia who say they have no religious affiliation, 8 per cent of whom say they believe in God, 12 per cent of whom pray, and 30 per cent of whom believe in the afterlife. His conclusion, that religiously unaffiliated Australians 'overwhelmingly' avoid 'religious practice and belief', may be less significant than his sensible call for further study of this group. Notwithstanding these challenges, in community schools there are – as in the United States and France – some opportunities for teaching about religion. Paul Babie and Ben Mylius provide a legal background, saying that '[r]egular provision shall be made for religious education at a government school' (in Davis and Miroshnikova 2013, p. 24). And Andrew Peterson writes about how, in all Australian schools, religion can be taught as part of the 'civics and citizenship' curriculum, where pupils are required to be 'taught that Australia is a secular nation and a multi-faith society, learn about the religions practised in contemporary Australia, and understand the Judeo-Christian traditions of Australian society' (Peterson 2017, p. 208).

Activity 4.2: What should we do?

Using the brief guides in this chapter, pick two countries (outside your own country) that have contrasting approaches to RE. Describe them to your RE class, ask the pupils to investigate further, and list the advantages and disadvantages of having RE in the style of that of each country. You (and they) could follow up the references in this chapter or use websites such as *www.eftre.net*, *religiouseducation.net/*, or newspaper sites such as *www.onlinenewspapers.com/*.

This long chapter does not need much of a conclusion. I have provided some research on countries on several continents and have avoided making too many judgements about the RE or about the countries. The more I research, the more I achieve what Gloria Durka refers to as the 'learned uncertainty of teachers' (Durka 2002, p. 1, quoted in Chapter 3). And as readers, you will want to come to your own conclusions. What is clear is that RE is hugely varied. The next chapter returns to the RE classroom and looks at the variety that might be present within a single school, within a single teacher's teaching career.

Chapter 5
Understanding Pedagogy in RE

*Teacher: Come on, you still have all those questions to finish. You can finish
colouring in that candle after you have done them.*
Pupil: But miss, you said to make it look nice!
(Trainee teacher, responding to the question 'What is typically said in RE?')

Introduction

The RE curriculum brings together teachers (whose work is pedagogy) and pupils
(whose work is learning). 'The curriculum' describes *what* may be taught and
learned, whilst 'pedagogy' describes *how* it might be taught and learned. The *what*
and the *how* are of course intimately linked. This chapter investigates some of those
links, starting in this introduction with the role of religion in RE (part of the *what*),
continuing with the nature of pedagogy in general (part of the *how*), and bringing
both together in models of RE pedagogy. Research has been completed on all of
these areas, especially on the nature of the RE curriculum, and research can stimulate
further development of the subject and of the teachers of the subject. However,
Grimmitt has noted that, of the various approaches to RE pedagogy represented in his
book, '[i]t is quite remarkable that to date there have been no extended, independent
evaluations of any of the pedagogies of RE represented in this book, other than as
pilot studies undertaken during the life of the projects themselves' (Grimmitt 2000, p.
22). Some of the research on RE pedagogy will therefore need to draw on research on
pedagogy in other subjects, and that is one of the purposes of this chapter. However,
there has been more work in recent years that explores RE pedagogy in general (such
as the *Does RE Work?* project, Conroy et al. 2013, building on *Making RE Work*,
Bell 1999; Zamorski 2000; Rudge 2001), and specific aspects of pedagogy (such as
Geiger's and Franck's work on assessment described in Chapters 4 and 11).

In one of the Westhill seminars, Vivienne Baumfield – a key member of the *Does
RE Work?* team – noted how difficult it was to pin pedagogy down. She described

it very broadly, following John Dewey, as concerned with the relationship between society's view of what education should be and the work of the classroom. Baumfield also noted how difficult it was to pin RE down, and she asked whether RE in church schools and non-church schools had enough in common for it to be considered a single subject. Participants in the project, exploring RE in England, Wales, Scotland, and Northern Ireland, agreed on the role of RE in challenging pupils' thinking and being subversive – whether from church or non-church contexts. There is a need to acknowledge controversy within and between different faiths and not avoid it by being anodyne. But consensus broke down, Baumfield said, when trying to articulate how the broadly stated intentions of RE could and should be enacted in the practice of the classroom – with teachers from non-church schools separating education from nurture, whilst those from church schools finding them more tenably combined.

Research on RE

In order to research how RE is taught, you need to explore the specific role of RE in its context. But it is hardly controversial to quote Wintersgill, who says that 'what RE offers uniquely is *the study of religion*' (Wintersgill 1995), or to quote Teece, who says,

> I judge good RE to be happening when students are enabled to develop
> their own beliefs, values and critical faculties by learning about and from the
> interaction between the study of living religions and our common, shared human
> experience of the world. *(Teece 2004)*

This approach, related to that of the Westhill Project (published, for example, in Read et al. 1988), is often described as the three-circle model of RE, addressing traditional belief systems (beliefs and spirituality), shared human experience (issues and ultimate questions), and individual patterns of belief (beliefs and values). Yet it is still not clear what 'traditional belief system' or 'religion' mean in the model. For Teece, a member of the Westhill Project team, one of the problems is that religions are often understood naturalistically, non-religiously, sociologically, phenomenologically, anthropologically, or historically: religions are not always understood 'religiously'. Teece's concern – expressed in a Westhill seminar – is to have a religious understanding of religion that is more spiritual than phenomenology, broader than theology, and that better aids pupil learning from religion (Teece 2010). According to Teece, relating his views to those of Hick (1989), religions share a view of human nature as essentially unsatisfactory or incomplete, along with the possibility of human transformation: they share these views, but interpret them in many different ways – all of which can be explored in RE. This can lead to us viewing the phenomena of religions in a transformed way. William Cantwell Smith says that it is not 'religion' but 'religiousness' that should be understood through RE:

Religion is ... inherently human, and integrally so ... if abstracted from ... the men and women whose humanity it informs it wilts, even if it is abstracted for the purposes of intellectual scrutiny ... It is not a thing but a quality: of personal life (both individual and social). ... [Smith is here considering an example of a Hindu man:] If we would comprehend ... we must look not at their religion but at the universe so far as possible through their eyes. It is what the Hindu is able to see, by being a Hindu that is significant. Until we can see it too, we have not come to grips with the religious quality of his life. And we can be sure that when he looks around him he does not see 'Hinduism'. Like the rest of us, he sees his wife's death, his child's minor and major aspirations, his money lender's mercilessness, the calm of a starlight evening, his own mortality. He sees things through coloured glasses, if one will, of a 'Hindu' brand. *(Smith 1978, p. 138)*

As Fowler (1981) says, students of religion should not be asking, 'What do you believe?' but instead should be asking, 'How do you see the world?' Teece's own approach is well expressed in *A Third Perspective* (Baumfield et al. 1994). There, the work on the human condition, for 11–14-year-olds, fits with the way people are, focused around guilt and reconciliation, why we are not perfect, what is the problem, what should people be like, facing up to the truth about ourselves, and an ideal human being in an ideal world. In such ways, Teece says, we need to help our pupils gain a greater understanding of what religion is all about, as so many people fail to understand this issue.

Activity 5.1: What does religiousness mean?

What makes something 'religious' is worth investigating by all RE teachers. All teachers can have their own views of religiousness, but it is understanding the views of pupils as well as colleagues that can help clarify and, it is hoped, improve the subject.

The question should be asked in a way that is appropriate for those of any religion and of no religion. All can be asked both of these questions:

- If you say someone is 'religious', what do you mean?
- If you say someone is 'not religious', what do you mean?

Pupils could produce their own answers, and then work in pairs and fours, to come to an agreement about what they think 'religiousness' means. It is important that there is not a simple 'right answer' to the question: the question can be answered in many useful and meaningful ways. Once the pupils have generated some answers to the questions, they can be asked the following question:

- What has been done in RE lessons that helps us to understand being 'religious'?
- What has been done in RE lessons that helps us to understand being 'not religious'?

These four questions are helpful in analysing pupil views on religiousness and pupil views on how RE lessons tackle religiousness. They are therefore central to understanding how the subject works in a school.

Research on pedagogy

The previous section looked at religion, ending with work on the subject of RE itself. Here, the issue of pedagogy – the *how* of teaching – is tackled. Understanding pedagogy is centred on understanding learning theory, and there are two traditions of learning theory worth describing here: behaviourism and constructivism. These initial descriptions are adapted from Stern 2009b, and can be followed up in standard textbooks such as Wood 1988, or Daniels and Edwards 2004.

Behaviourists tend to look at how people respond to 'stimuli' (so they may be called 'stimulus-response' theorists), which in practice generally means 'rewards and punishments'. If the theory underlying teaching is based on giving pupils incentives to do the 'right' thing, and sanctions to prevent them from doing the 'wrong' thing, then the teaching is working on behaviourist principles. The rewards may be praise or marks or stars or credits or exam results or sweets or bicycles; the sanctions may be criticism or detentions or missed break-times/recess or fines. Of course, every teacher will use rewards and punishments. It becomes more 'behaviourist' if the teacher believes this is the *only* way to get pupils to act in a certain way. Famous behaviourists include Pavlov, Skinner, and Eysenck, with Pavlov known for demonstrating that dogs can be trained to salivate on the ringing of a bell if the bell has been rung every time the dog is fed. Their theories are not so 'fashionable' amongst contemporary psychologists, or amongst RE researchers. But within schools, the practical application of behaviourist theories can dominate teachers' lives. In addition to star charts and merits, a concern with physical conditions (e.g. having carpeted rooms in order to reduce noise) might – if it dominates teaching – be based on these same theories. It is an unfair stereotype of behaviourism to say that teaching is like training dogs, but it is a memorable analogy. Equally unfair, and equally memorable, is the description by Rumi, the thirteenth-century Sufi Muslim poet who wrote *Two Types of Intelligence* (also quoted in Chapter 1, from Rumi 1995, p. 178), of 'acquired' intelligence that flows into a schoolchild from books and teachers, weighing them down as 'retaining all that knowledge is a heavy load'. What behaviourist approaches tend to have in common is the idea of adding extrinsic rewards or punishments to what is happening in the learning itself and having more rewards than punishments.

For RE, behaviourism might mean getting pupils to learn RE by rewarding the completion of work, marking and returning work quickly (so that the feedback 'stimulus' is associated with the original work), rewarding good quality work, being careful to avoid associating RE work with punishment – especially unfair punishment. A behaviourist approach could also lead to setting up RE classrooms with good conditions for studying (tables, lighting, displays, resources), to help stimulate positive feelings about the subject. Many see behaviourism as tied into debates on 'standards of achievement', as a concern with standards leads many to introduce incentives and punishments related to the achievement of such standards.

Constructivists, in contrast, tend to look at each pupil's current understanding or 'worldview' (whatever subject is being studied), and see teaching and learning as building on, or reconstructing, that worldview. It is easy to see how controversial this might be, in terms of religious worldviews, if pupils or their families think that the role of RE is to 'reconstruct' pupils' worldviews. As the educationist Bruner once said, '[p]edagogy is never innocent' (Bruner 1996, p. 63). To constructivists, pupils are seen as active rather than passive learners: they are not 'empty vessels' into which teachers pour knowledge or 'behaving machines' that teachers can re-programme with appropriate stimuli. Vygotsky used the term 'scaffolding' to describe constructivist approaches. Helping children understand what it is that they know and can do, and giving them the tools with which to develop or change their understanding, is typical of those supporting this theory. Classical, or more individualist, constructivists include Piaget, who sees the process of learning primarily as an individual pupil and teacher working together: pupils are sometimes like 'lone scientists'. Social constructivists include Vygotsky and Bruner, who see children as learning 'in conversation' with peers and teachers, and may look at systems (classes, families, schools, and communities) rather than just at individuals. The process of learning involves groups of pupils working collaboratively with a teacher to build up their understanding. (Vygotsky and Bruner, then, can be 'blamed' for group work.) It is an unfair stereotype of constructivists to say that teaching is all about waiting around while pupils discover everything for themselves, but it is a memorable analogy. Equally unfair and equally memorable is Rumi's description of the learning that comes from within, from the heart or soul, and that flows outwards and 'gushes continually from the house of the heart' (Rumi 1995, p. 178). What constructivist approaches tend to have in common is the idea of looking at the intrinsic features of learning, to support learning 'from the inside', either individually (often using 'cognitive' strategies) or collectively (using social strategies).

For RE, constructivism means getting pupils to learn RE by encouraging pupils and teachers to talk about the topics and tasks, encouraging purposeful and interesting and creative activities, that provide intrinsic motivation. Pupils can work long hours on tasks that really interest them, making incredible discoveries, whilst extrinsic rewards and punishments may have little effect and will never make routine and repetitive work interesting. Indeed, constructivists will often say that extrinsic rewards and punishments will distract, not encourage, pupils: if you are working on a project because you will get a merit mark or avoid a detention, you will not be wanting to learn the subject, and will be unlikely to develop a lifelong interest in the subject, but will merely be learning how to get a reward. Teachers expressing an interest in RE, and demonstrating how important it is as a subject, should help, too. The more that RE can build relationships and conversations within and particularly beyond the school, the more the social constructivists will say this is how people learn best. Many see constructivism as more loosely tied into debates on 'standards of achievement', and yet in the last ten years, debates on how to raise standards in UK schools have been dominated by various versions of 'assessment for learning' (well described in Black and Wiliam 1998a, 1998b; Assessment Reform Group 1999; Weeden et al. 2002), which is clearly based on constructivist theories of learning. (And see Blaylock 2000b, on RE.)

Most of the traditions of RE pedagogy described in Grimmitt (2000) are broadly in the constructivist tradition, although it is only Grimmitt himself (within that book) who writes extensively about constructivism. A constructivist approach also matches UK government descriptions of the importance of RE, as national guidance focuses on intrinsic values of the subject. The National Framework document asserts that RE 'encourages pupils to learn from different religions, beliefs, values and traditions while exploring their own beliefs and questions of meaning', and 'encourages pupils to develop their sense of identity and belonging' – enabling them 'to flourish individually within their communities and as citizens in a pluralistic society and global community' (QCA 2004). Nevertheless, as has already been said, teachers' lives in schools are often dominated by behaviourist, not constructivist, approaches. In that context, some research on how pupils and teachers themselves see their learning is worth carrying out, in order to understand which traditions are most influential in the classroom.

The following activity is based on the work of Daniels (2001), which is itself an investigation of the social constructivist approaches to schooling of Vygotsky. The terms used in the analysis of the activity are 'classification' and 'framing', themselves taken by Daniels from the sociologist Bernstein. Stronger and weaker classification and framing refer to the divisions between subjects ('classification') and the degree to which pedagogy is teacher-centred rather than pupil-centred ('framing'). Stronger classification and framing are more likely in schools using more behaviourist approaches, and match Rumi's view of 'acquired' learning. Weaker classification and framing are more likely in schools using more constructivist approaches, and match Rumi's view of learning 'from the inside'. The differences are illustrated by Daniels from art lessons in two of the schools. In the school with stronger classification and framing,

> the teacher read a story called 'Where the Wild Things Live' [*sic*]. ... The teacher had prepared a number of different pieces of sugar paper and proceeded to assign children to these pieces of paper. Each piece of sugar paper had an outline of a 'Wild Thing' on it and most of them had sections/areas of the paper marked off. Each section contained a code number and thus could be translated by a key at the bottom of the piece of paper. ... The department head said of art lessons, 'We are interested in the results of art, of good productions rather than "experiencing" the materials'. *(Daniels 2001, pp. 162–163)*

In the school with weaker classification and framing,

> the children were given different grades of paper, powder paint and a piece of foam rubber or sponge. The teacher then told the children to wet the paper and flick paint at it with the sponge. The children were encouraged to use different kinds of paper with different degrees of dampness. They were told to experiment with ways of applying the powder paint. *(Daniels 2001, p. 163)*

In this way, Daniels contrasts classrooms where 'you paint what you see' and those where 'you paint what the teacher sees' (Daniels 2001, p. 170).

Activity 5.2: What is typically said?

Derived from the work of Daniels (2001), here is an activity that asks what might typically be said in a classroom, in a number of subjects. Examples of the tasks are given here for RE and for English, but it would be helpful also being completed for a number of subjects or for a single subject across year groups and, as appropriate, ability groups or gender groups.

In analysing responses, teachers should bear in mind the indications of 'classification' and 'framing'. Indications of stronger or weaker classification will be in how different the descriptions are of different subjects or how 'bounded' those subjects seem. Indications of stronger or weaker framing will be whether pupils are 'painting what the teacher sees' or 'painting what they see'. According to Daniels, weaker classification and framing are likely to be more inclusive, that is, more suited to classrooms where pupils have a wide range of educational needs.

What is typically said in RE

We are in an RE lesson in a school. What do you think the teacher is saying, and what do you think the pupil is saying, in this picture?

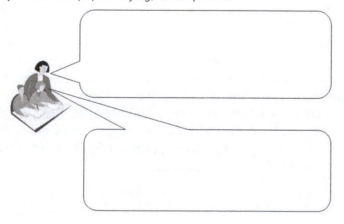

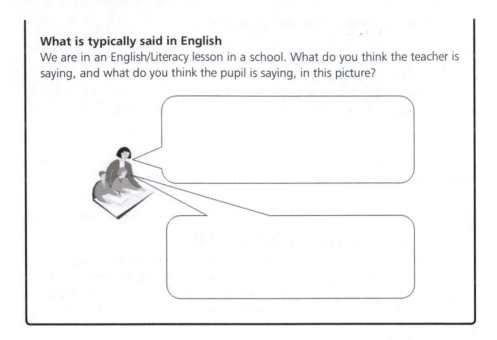

What is typically said in English
We are in an English/Literacy lesson in a school. What do you think the teacher is saying, and what do you think the pupil is saying, in this picture?

Discussion of the outcomes of this activity – completed by teachers, as well as by pupils – suggests that there is a concern with the difference between the 'self-image' of RE and how the subject works in classrooms. Pupils often see RE in terms of 'right and wrong factual answers', and/or a confessionalist promotion of religious belief.

The varieties of RE pedagogy

Blaylock (2004a) describes six schools of thought in RE, with phenomenology providing a platform, a 'given', for RE, even if it is not the whole pedagogical toolkit for RE. What is interesting is that, for Blaylock, phenomenology and the other pedagogies described here can be cumulative, and can work in any order. A 'humaniser' start can be complemented by a 'postmodern' piece of work, and, crucially, *vice versa*. It is worth noting that Blaylock is not describing all the possible pedagogies of RE, and that confessional RE is not included in his modelling, despite its popularity across many countries (described in Chapter 4). First is Blaylock's diagram covering six schools of thought (adapted from Blaylock 2004a, with each also represented in Grimmitt 2000). These approaches could be described as competitors or as complementary, with complementarity illustrated in the following narrative from Blaylock.

	Focus	Impact	Questions raised
Phenomenology E.g. Smart (1969).	Learning in RE is focused upon assembling, broadening, and deepening understanding that takes each religion's phenomena on its own terms. Examining the 7 Smartian dimensions of religion brings balance to the study.	From the 1970s until now, this set of approaches has defined a baseline for English and Welsh RE: children should learn lots of information about the religions. Its best practice takes comprehensive account of whole religions.	Is it supportable to argue that 'dry factuality' goes with phenomenology? Can a phenomenological pedagogy which takes theologies and philosophies on their own terms be envisaged? Practised?
RE as human development E.g. Grimmitt (1987).	Pedagogy is guided by the need for RE to enable human development. The links between psychology and other social science disciplines, and philosophy and questions of meaning, establish a creative tension. The place of religion as a distinctive human discourse, in flux and flexible, is defended even in relatively secular cultures like those of the UK.	The term 'learning from religion' originates in this articulation of RE's purposes and has been highly influential as an 'attainment target'. The focus on finding and making meaning through RE has become axiomatic for many RE teachers.	Is this set of approaches tied to an existentialist philosophy (the idea of meaning making)? How can the tensions between religionists and educationists be balanced? If RE is a part of the curricular 'meaning making', then should religionists control what is taught at all? Or is it enough to 'treasure the questions'?
Spiritual development E.g. Hay with Nye (2006), Hammond et al. (1990).	Concepts of spiritual dimensions of life lie behind the intention to enable learners to access their own spirituality. The psychological defence of the spiritual dimension is linked to the examination of spiritualities from various different religions.	Hammond et al. (1990): widely influential on some teachers, but the momentum is slower now. The emphasis on spirituality and psychology leads to opposition from phenomenology, and little government interest.	Are these approaches to RE dualist? Individualist? Is there a danger for RE in being 'more spiritual but less religious'? Does the spiritual focus here draw RE too far from religions and their communities as found in the UK?

	Focus	Impact	Questions raised
Religious literacy – conceptual approaches E.g. Cooling (1994a, 1994b), Wright (1993).	Since religion is about truth, the critical evaluation of claims and schemes for establishing the truth about religious propositions are the key skills for young people in their RE. These skills are especially necessary in a philosophical climate of relativism and post-modernity.	Through teacher training and academic writing, these approaches, allied to 'critical realist' philosophical discourse about religion in a postmodern society, are popular with many teachers. It is a bit less clear that there are resources to support classroom work in this style.	By focusing on the conceptual, and the 'truth-claiming' elements of religion, what is marginalized? Does a conceptual approach carry the danger of making too little space for cultural and social aspects of religion? Do these approaches set phenomenology and community cohesion too lightly aside?
Interpretive pedagogy E.g. Jackson (1997).	In religious terms, the focus is on internal diversity as well as religious plurality, and on a serious engagement with the layering of religion, culture, and philosophy. In terms of learners, the key skill is interpretation.	By linking resources, methodological publications and research the 'Warwick school' has made a substantial impact on teaching and learning. Versions of interpretive pedagogy are practised, increasingly widely, from 5 to 16.	Is it possible for teachers to grasp this set of methods with sufficient clarity to be effective? Do the subtleties of reflexivity suit the learning needs of all 5–16-year-olds? What is the place of 'neutrality' in the stances of the teacher and the learner now?
Deconstruction and the 'world view' E.g. Erricker and Erricker (2000).	If the task of education is constructing the 'self', then pedagogies for religious (and spiritual and moral) education should facilitate this task with regard to the 'philosophical' or 'spiritual' self. To enable this, some 'inappropriate' prior practice must be swept away.	The UK National Framework (QCA 2004) and the lobbying interests of the British Humanist Association (*www.humanism.co.uk*) have created a climate in which 'world views' are part of the RE of the future. As yet, little curricular resource supports this, but the impact is likely to grow.	What effect would deconstruction in RE have for children whose family culture is evangelical Christian, traditional Islamic, or humanist? What effects would follow if the deconstructionist tools were turned upon consumerism or soft agnosticism? Is this their commonest use?

Six ways around Easter: A pedagogical fantasy

At the start of term, the new RE teacher Miss X noticed in her syllabus that she was to teach the 11-year-olds about the Festival and stories of Easter, the beliefs associated with the celebration, and the impact of these beliefs in the Christian community. She had just been trained by some phenomenologists (as in Smart 1983), and so planned two lessons on the phenomenon of Easter. Using artefacts – a variety of crosses, some icons, some 'He is Risen' badges, hot crossed buns, and a video of the Easter celebrations in an Orthodox and an Evangelical setting – she taught them about the festival, its terminology, and its diversity.

After two lessons, Miss X read Michael Grimmitt's book on RE and human development (Grimmitt 1987) and realized she had been neglecting pupils' learning from religion. She planned some fresh activities: pupils were asked some provocative questions. What if you were in charge of the Easter celebrations for the two churches nearest school? What music would you choose for Good Friday and Easter day? What does the idea of 'life out of death' or 'resurrection' or 'life after death' mean to you? Can you explain an occasion when hope seemed hopeless, but you held on anyway? More good work emerged as pupils related the festival to their own experiences.

After these two lessons, she went on a course with Trevor Cooling and learned the methods of 'concept cracking' (as in Cooling 1994b). Inspired by the new pedagogy of the conceptual analysis of truth claims, she planned two lessons of Biblical study in which the claims of the resurrection were presented to the class. They responded to the challenge – some who thought it would be impossible discussed their view with others who thought it a miracle. Some Christian children in the class stayed at the end to say how affirming they had found the exploration of their own faith.

During half term, she checked her notes from college and remembered all about the deconstruction of religion for postmodern young people (as in Erricker and Erricker 2000). The next two lessons were used to dissect how the Easter festival is sometimes used to keep people in their place – a heavenly reward for a life of drudgery. One child asked, 'So, Miss, is religion just a way of keeping people in their place?' She knew she was getting somewhere when a group of boys announced they didn't believe in Easter, and wouldn't be bothering to wait till Sunday before eating the chocolate.

There was another course on interpretive approaches to RE (as in Jackson 1997), and Miss X was edified. She decided to plan a couple more lessons, the first on the diversity of Easter as Christian children describe it (she used accounts from 13-year-old Catholics, Methodists, and Quakers, from Bristol, Birmingham, and Nigeria). Then she asked pupils to write interpreter's notes on the *Hallelujah chorus*, making sense of its origins, use today, and impact within and beyond the Christian community.

As the term wore on, Miss X was visited by the local adviser, who was signed up to a spiritual and experiential approach to RE (as in Hammond et al. 1990). She realized what was missing in the terms' lessons and used a guided fantasy based upon the appearance of Jesus to two disciples travelling to Emmaus. Pupils finished the term creating works of art inspired by the work on a choice of themes: 'Back from the Dead' or 'My Hope for the Future'.

Activity 5.3: Evidence for perspectives

Having looked through these descriptions of six perspectives, following up with further investigation of each of them (e.g. from Grimmitt 2000), investigate evidence, from the RE in your school, for each of the six perspectives being followed. The evidence should be in the form of 'learning tasks', and not simply principles and policies.

It might be that one perspective dominates RE in your school, there may be elements of all six, or there may be little evidence for any of these. Nevertheless, the investigation allows an RE department to see how it might develop further in the future.

Evidence for a phenomenological approach

Evidence for an approach based on RE as human development

Evidence for a spiritual development approach

Evidence for a religious literacy approach

Evidence for an interpretive approach

Evidence for a worldview approach

Perhaps by swapping evidence from a number of schools, RE teachers may discover the extent to which the various approaches to RE pedagogy dominate RE. Asking pupils for their views (as suggested throughout this book, and supported by Rudduck et al. 1996 and Flutter and Rudduck 2004) will be important, too, as will understanding the cultures and perspectives of university theology and religious studies departments which generate RE teachers (I'Anson 2004). It may be that the culture and pedagogy of each school, rather than the training and beliefs of the RE department, will dominate, especially if many of those teaching RE have not trained in the subject (as described by Gates 1989, 1991, 1994). Clearly, a school dominated by a more behaviourist approach to learning is unlikely to find it easy dealing with constructivist approaches to RE or any other subject. Yet the variation between departments within UK secondary schools is wide ('the range of variation by department *within* schools is probably three to four times greater than the average variation *between* schools', Reynolds in Stoll and Myers 1998, p. 167), suggesting that there may be room for departments as 'islands of constructivism'. I'Anson's (2004) research on trainee teachers negotiating a route between post-structuralist religious studies (at Stirling University) and modernist school RE gives further hope for intelligent negotiation rather than giving in to the context and saying, 'There is nothing we can do'.

Conclusion

This chapter has touched on a small part of research on the RE curriculum – itself probably the most-researched aspect of RE – and on some broader issues in pedagogy that could be applied to RE. It is clear that teachers wishing to develop themselves will want to be researching their own pedagogy using some of the techniques described here. By researching RE pedagogy, teachers can thereby come to understand the impact and value of their work. They may also come to feel a part of the whole process: not merely 'speaking textbooks', but members of the community of learners learning and developing together with colleagues and pupils. This links back to Chapter 3, on the real lives of teachers and pupils, and it is also a good link to the following chapter on inclusion – in this case, the inclusion of teachers, not just pupils. RE is and always will be a demanding subject, not because its status is in doubt (even if it is), but because it deals with real religions, religions that have been at or near the heart of most of the world's controversies and conflicts.

Chapter 6
Inclusion, Diversity, and RE

People have to learn *to be adults.*
(An 8-year-old with learning difficulties, saying what they had learned
from the Zen story of the sound of one-hand clapping)

Introduction

Everyone thinks inclusion is a good idea and that exclusion is a bad idea. This chapter investigates a variety of issues in inclusion for RE and relates those to research on inclusion, with education research identified by O'Hanlon (2003) as a method of inclusion in itself. By bringing pupils together in dialogue (as in Chapter 2), RE can bring pupils together in all kinds of ways. It is important to start with what inclusion itself means, however, as a simple 'bringing together' is only the start of the story. Some have even suggested that an uncritical promotion of inclusion, without evidence for its value, is reminiscent of some methods of promoting religion: hence the reference (in Hornby 2001) to the 'church of inclusion'.

Inclusion is a key concept whose history is tied in with the histories of other key concepts such as 'poverty' and 'special educational needs' and 'equal opportunities'. In the first place, consider poverty, a concept that has in some ways been superseded by the concepts of inclusion and exclusion. While poverty might be described as a simple 'lack' (of money or resources), social deprivation or social exclusion involves an inability to take part in activities or aspects of life that others take for granted. An example to illustrate this might be the consequences of what are called 'natural disasters' such as floods and famines. Sen (1981) notes how in most famines, there is not a lack of food in a country: there is, rather, a group of people who are excluded from access to food. The opening words of his influential book are worth quoting:

> Starvation is the characteristic of some people not *having* enough food to eat. It is not the characteristic of there *being* not enough food to eat. While the latter can be a cause of the former, it is but one of many *possible* causes. (Sen 1981, p. 1)

Poverty might suggest having less of something, whilst exclusion suggests not having something. This was why, in the late 1970s – especially with the publication of *Poverty in the United Kingdom* (Townsend 1979, and see also the more internationalist Townsend and Gordon 2002) – definitions of poverty began to be centred on measuring how many activities people took part in, rather than simply what income or wealth people had. There are tremendous advantages in this change. Being unable to have hot meals, or holidays, or a home, or seasonal clothing, are 'absolute' deprivations, albeit not as serious, perhaps, as starvation – the measure of poverty used in the late nineteenth and early twentieth centuries. Not only this, but the inability to take part in activities might be the result of, say, racism, sexism, physical or mental illness, disability, or, as Sen says, a lack of entitlement, not just a lack of money. By the mid-1980s, few people in the mainstream political parties in the UK talked of poverty, and by the mid-1990s, UK politicians were talking instead about 'social exclusion' and creating a 'Social Exclusion Unit'. Inclusion and exclusion are also used by other European politicians, with the trend well represented in Council of Europe 1996, which suggests that poor children should be given pocket money by the state 'in order to integrate them into the consumer society' (Council of Europe 1996, p. 75, with more culturally sensitive views of inclusion in the European context given in Schreiner et al. 2002; Jackson 2004), and the United Nations describing 'overall poverty' as, amongst other things,

> limited or lack of access to education and other basic services; ... unsafe environments and social discrimination and exclusion. It is also characterised by lack of participation in decision-making and in civil, social and cultural life ... [for example] the utter destitution of people who fall outside family support systems, social institutions and safety nets. *(Quoted in Townsend and Gordon 2002, p. 59)*

When it came to education, the term 'inclusion' has taken over many of the uses of the term 'special educational needs'. The move to a concern with this kind of educational inclusion first developed in the UK in the 1970s, when all young people were to be educated (including those with severe learning difficulties, formerly catered for only by the health service), and educated up to the age of 16. By the 1980s, further moves were being made, in the UK and well beyond, to cater for most or all pupils in mainstream schools, rather than having a large number of special schools. By the 1990s, landmark legislation such as the UK's SEN Code of Practice (DfE 1994b) and the UN's *Salamanca Statement* (UNESCO 1994), an assumption came to be built into the system that 'inclusion' was a good in itself. This, notwithstanding the warnings of people such as Garry Hornby, who worries that the policy change 'has resulted in what can, at times, appear to be a tidal wave of inclusive intent preached with overpowering zeal by the church of inclusion' (Hornby 2001, quoting O'Brien). Hornby stresses that we should look at the outcomes of inclusion, and see what they are, and not simply opt for inclusion into the mainstream at all costs:

> inclusion in an unsuitable curriculum directly contributes to the disaffection of many pupils which leads them to be disruptive and eventually results in the

exclusion of some of them. The priority for children with SEN must, therefore, be that they have access to curricula which are appropriate for them, not that they are fitted in to a curriculum designed for the mainstream population which may not meet their needs. *(Hornby 2001)*

It is particularly interesting for RE specialists to read of this use of the metaphor of the 'church of inclusion'. Notwithstanding Hornby's warnings, that particular church has many members, and the third strand of contemporary inclusion, related to equal opportunities, developed in part from the UK inspection framework of 2000 (and the related training materials), which said that 'an educationally inclusive school is one in which the teaching and learning, achievements, attitudes and well-being of every young person matter', which 'involves taking account of pupils' varied life experiences and needs' (Ofsted 2000a). The remarkably inclusive Ofsted list of those groups of people who might for one reason or another be excluded is as follows:

girls and boys, minority ethnic and faith groups [it is not entirely clear whether 'minority' qualified only 'ethnic' or also 'faith groups'], Travellers, asylum seekers and refugees, pupils who need support to learn English as an additional language (EAL), pupils with special educational needs, gifted and talented pupils, children 'looked after' by the local authority, other children, such as sick children, young carers, those children from families under stress, pregnant school girls and teenage mothers, and any pupils who are at risk of disaffection and exclusion. *(Ofsted 2000a)*

Such guidance, by bringing together 'educational' issues such as special educational needs and 'social' issues such as seeking asylum and gender and ethnicity, inevitably brings together the issues of inclusion, equal opportunities, and social justice.

This modern concern with inclusion as a concept encompassing poverty and special educational needs, makes it an immensely significant concept, then, and RE can contribute to inclusion, in its content (the curriculum) and in its pedagogy (the relationships between teacher and pupils). Important research on how RE can in itself model inclusiveness has been completed by Hull (as in Hull 1998, 2003, 2005), and by Ipgrave (on dialogue in RE, for example, in Ipgrave 2001). Both of these authors are concerned with the 'deep' issues of the nature of humanity, and both can be related to theological theories. My own work on inclusion (e.g. Stern 2007a, chapters 2, 5, and 8) is set in the context of the philosophies of Macmurray (on the nature of community, as in Macmurray 1996) and Buber (on dialogue, as in Buber 1958). Searching for those underpinnings is a tremendously important aspect of research, often encouraged by the discipline of research degrees (such as masters or doctoral degrees) or by the discipline of systematic religious reflection, but of course a search for theoretical underpinnings can happen anywhere. The following activities can be used to analyse both the curriculum and the pedagogy of RE in a particular school or classroom. Each of the activities aims to draw out how inclusive the RE is, based on inclusive, dialogic, models of RE described throughout this book.

Activity 6.1: How inclusive is the RE curriculum?

This activity does not list the content of the RE curriculum, but looks at how that content is joined together or 'mapped'. Each pairs of statements is joined by a line. For RE in one classroom or one school, work out how far it is along the line, from one extreme to the other. It may help to copy the statements onto cards and separate them with a rather longer line, to make the position on the line, and the justification of that position, clearer.

1 Loose learning	1 Mapped learning
No connection is made between systems, cultures, religions, and worldviews.	In describing any system, get the pupils to say what it is *not*. This is particularly important in RE, as RE is beset by descriptions of religious systems that make them all sound the same (e.g. 'be nice to people').

2 Every classroom its own world	2 Connected learning
No connection is made between different kinds of worldviews, for example, cultures, religions, philosophies, political systems.	RE must never teach about religions in isolation from other systems: it must address citizenship, for example, whether it likes it or not. A simple activity like describing the activities and consequences of a putative 'religion police' is helpful here. (This is expanded in Activity 3.1.)

3 Island or siege learning	3 Learning in a community of communities
No connection is made between worldviews, pupils, and pupils' communities.	RE pupils and teachers should, for example, frequently set homework that captures the views and ways of life of people outside school. Easy examples include counting up and analysing the breaking of the Five Precepts or the Ten Commandments in a soap opera, or accompanying a member of the family to a shop and agreeing what would be the most appropriate gift (from the available goods) for Jesus as a baby (as in Stern 2009b).

Activity 6.2: How inclusive is RE pedagogy?

This activity does not list the pedagogies of RE (as described in Chapter 5 and in Grimmitt 2000), but looks at how the relationships between teachers and pupils can be broadly described. Each pair of statements is joined by a line. For RE in one classroom or one school, work out how far it is along the line, from one extreme to the other. It may help to copy the statements onto cards and separate them with a rather longer line, to make the position on the line, and the justification of that position, clearer.

1 Exam factory The school tries to gain the best possible exam results.	**1 Learning community** RE should be in the school because it helps people to learn to live in community. Good exam results are a bonus. RE teachers and pupils must be able and prepared to justify RE in these terms.
2 Learning for the academy The school subjects are taught for the benefit of those subject disciplines, usually as embodied in universities and described as 'academic subjects' such as religious studies and theology.	**2 Learning to be human** RE should be in the school because it helps people to learn to live in community. The good of academic religious studies or theology is a bonus.
3 Hedonistic learning The school tries to make everyone happy.	**3 Learning for flourishing** RE addresses pupils' lives (and the lives of communities in and beyond the school) in their own terms, perhaps including hedonist communities but only as special topics.

RE and the range of pupil needs

How can RE meet a wide range of needs? Pupils with special educational needs (as described in Wearmouth 2001) and those with other special needs (such as the gifted and talented, or those with English as an additional language) have always completed RE. RE has notable advantages in meeting a wide range of needs, as it can

exploit the richness of religious and other traditions and the ways in which all those traditions have, in turn, had to meet the needs of the whole range of adherents. Yet there is some evidence that RE does not have a distinguished record in meeting such needs. Fortunately, in recent years there has been a significant growth in research and professional development concerned with RE meeting the range of needs. Erica Brown has written widely on the 'regular' teaching of RE to pupils with special needs (as in Brown 1996), and has also researched and written on important issues for RE such as special needs and bereavement. Anne Krisman (e.g. Krisman 2001), John Hull (e.g. Hull 2004), and Lesley Beadle (2006) have written on a range of RE and special needs issues. Liz O'Brien (2002) has researched pupils on the autism spectrum and those with severe and complex learning difficulties, and Janet Orchard (2001) has researched challenging pupils aged 11–14.

It is helpful to describe a case study of research involving pupils with special educational needs. This case study was carried out by me and Marie Stern, at that time head of a London special school. It involved taking a group of pupils aged 9–11 from a special school to a Hindu *mandir* (the Shri Swaminarayan Mandir and Hindu Mission, London, www.swaminarayan.org/) and, after the trip, asking the pupils three questions (also outlined in Activity 7.3). Prior to the visit, the pupils had worked on some Hindu beliefs and stories (from Rose 1995), making use of some *murtis*, images on cloth, and a *puja* tray. However, most of the work was planned for after the visit. All the pupils had what are described as significant learning difficulties and were working at levels below those of the UK National Curriculum, but the purpose of this case study is not to highlight the needs of the pupils, but to describe how RE can help meet the needs of pupils including those having considerable difficulties with learning. The three questions were in this case as follows: What did I learn about Hinduism? What do Hindus want us to learn from a *mandir*? What did I learn from Hinduism to help with meeting my targets? The first activity, aiming to explore the first question, was an 'adjectives' activity. This involved attaching adjectives to pictures of the *mandir*, a school, and a hospital, and saying why they had chosen them. The adjectives were 'angry', 'frightened', 'cold', 'peaceful', 'relaxed', 'busy', 'safe', 'happy', 'sad', 'beautiful', and 'interesting'. This is how the pupils justified putting particular adjectives by particular pictures.

Then the pupils were asked more about what they learned about Hinduism from the visit and what they thought Hindus wanted them to learn from the *mandir*.

They believe in gods and I saw beautiful statues of Sita and Rama like a Princess and a Prince. They put money in a bowl.
I learned about where Hindus pray and that they like to do yoga. I liked the ornaments and you had to put your hands on the light.
I saw the temple.
I learned how to do the hand movements [copied, perfectly], and how to do *Aum*. They put red spots on their head.
I learned about the music and how they use the *Aum* sound. (Why do they do this?) To help them pray.

Adjectives	Mandir	School	Hospital
Angry	I was afraid they would be angry if we teased them about their precious things.	Cussing. Nasty people.	Upset and crying. Angry when the baby died. (This pupil's newborn sibling died on the day of the visit. The same pupil is the second of the contributors to hospitals being 'cold'.)
Frightened	Before we got there, I thought they might be mean. (Why?) Because they had so many rules. I was scared because I'm a Christian and I thought that when I was there I wouldn't know if I'm a Christian or a Hindu.	Cussing. Bullying. Kicking. Punching.	Going to die. Loads of needles. Heart attack. Meningitis.
Cold	It was warm.	School can be cold, warm, or hot.	Hospitals can warm you up from the cold. My mum was cold when the baby died.
Peaceful	When we went 'Aum'. No shouting. When we walked and saw stuff. When there was praying.	When your friends are there. When you are playing.	If you get good news.
Relaxed	When the music made my headache go. When we took our shoes off. Nice music. The people were excellent to us.	When we did yoga.	When you rest and calm down.
Busy	There were lots of people looking around. Some people were working and giving us advice.	Teachers do lots of work.	It is very busy, with lots of patients and doctors. Helping babies to come out.

Adjectives	Mandir	School	Hospital
Safe	It's peaceful there because there is no talking and no silliness. There was no bad people. There's no fighting. It's all nice and peaceful. It's relaxing.	You can see the teacher so she will look after you. Teachers protect you. Teachers are good to you. You do nice things.	If you're really sick, they can protect you. Nurses help you.
Happy	It's peaceful because there is no talking and no silliness. The statues made you happy. I liked the flowers and books in the shop.	You are happy when you learn. It's better than staying at home. You can play with your friends.	You are happy when someone's alive.
Sad	–	You might hurt yourself. If you hurt yourself.	If someone's dying or hurt or has a heart attack.
Beautiful	The building was beautiful. The statues were beautiful.	It has all the things we need.	–
Interesting	You can go and listen and see what they do. It makes you go to sleep when you are looking at the ceiling. (The ceiling at this *mandir* is very ornately carved.) The elephant God (i.e. *Ganesha*) was interesting.	You do lots of work.	–

Before I went there I didn't know they had so many pictures and you could see
   so many things.
I learned that they do yoga there to help them pray to the gods.
Now I know why they put a red mark on their head and I know that they ring the
   bell when they want to pray.
The Hindus made the temple with carving then the man blessed the gods. The
   monks wear orange and lay on the floor.

The teachers involved in this case study assessed these responses (using guidance in
QCA 2004), and said that the responses were working at levels considerably higher than
the level of work the pupils achieved in the rest of their schoolwork. This suggested
that the engaging, experiential, learning, based on traditional Hindu teaching, enabled
the meeting of many of the pupils' needs. The pupils themselves were asked about how
the visit might have helped them meet their own targets. This is what some said:

The music helped me to be quiet. (A pupil with targets including avoiding
   inappropriate shouting.)
It was good – it made me good. (A pupil with targets including attempting to
   take responsibility for his own actions.)
I learned some new words. (A pupil with targets including learning new words.)
Not to be rude. (A pupil with targets including avoiding rudeness.)
It was quiet; it helped me to be quiet. (A pupil with targets including calming.)

There are many conclusions that could be drawn from this work, not only for teaching
pupils with special educational needs but for pupils with a wide range of needs,
including those deemed 'gifted and talented'. Here are three conclusions, drawn
from a range of research on RE:

- When teaching RE, trying to meet a wide range of pupil needs, it is valuable
  to focus on the key concepts. RE can easily become a set of descriptions of
  religious 'phenomena' such as clothing or celebrations, with the descriptions
  made more simple or complex for pupils with different needs. Yet it is the
  concepts – concepts in the case study such as 'calm', 'respect', the *Aum*,
  'safe' – that carry more of the essence of the religious traditions to be
  studied. Unlike some literacy strategies, RE does not simply add a word to a
  vocabulary list and then move on. Rather, it introduces concepts like change,
  peace, kindness, or happiness, early in a pupil's education, and then helps
  deepen that concept year after year. Progression in RE, then, is a matter of
  deepening concepts, not simply increasing vocabulary.

- Religions themselves have a long history of attempting to meet a very wide
  range of learning needs of members. RE can follow suit. Think about the 'multi-
  sensory' methods of establishing and promoting religions – making use of text,
  art, music, smell, dance, and so much more. Simply using religious music,
  as described in detail in Stern (2004), can allow pupils access to authentic

elements of religious and other traditions, and can do so in a way that allows a profound response from all pupils.

- Pupils' own needs, including special educational needs, may provide insight into religions. For example, although aspects of autism can be understood as barriers to learning, the need for and comfort in ritual is often better understood by those on the autism spectrum than by others. Similarly, those with behavioural difficulties are more likely to understand, say, the Buddhist story of Angulimala (the fierce robber who learned how to change, as described at *www.angulimala. org.uk or Chödzin and Kohn 1997*). One might as easily consider the insights provided by a pupil's speech difficulties into the life of Moses (who appeared to consider himself unworthy to be a prophet, due to his stutter) or pupils' literacy difficulties with the 'unlettered' Prophet Muhammad (pbuh).

One way of systematically researching pupils with a wide range of needs – a way of finding out that allows a range of pupils to respond meaningfully – is to use a 'Salmon Line' (as described in Salmon 1994). This is exemplified for RE in Judith Lowndes' work (e.g. Lowndes 2001, also in Stern 2001), and it is worth considering how the Salmon Line could be used further to understand how pupils develop. This work comes from a psychological tradition called 'personal construct psychology' (an example of constructivism), which is particularly identified with Kelly (Kelly 1955; Ravenette 1999) and described by Grimmitt as related to learning *from* (in contrast to learning *about*) religion (Grimmitt 2000, p. 18).

Activity 6.3: Salmon line

Pupils should consider one aspect of their learning in RE, for example, their written explanations or their ability to take part in discussions or their 'learning about' religion or their 'learning from' religion (as described in QCA 2004).

For the first stage of the activity, pupils should, on their own, make two marks on a 'Salmon Line', a straight line with contrasting words at either end of the line:

Mark **Present** or **P** on the line where you think your (written work) in RE is at the moment.

Mark **Future** or **F** on the line where you would like your (written work) in RE to be in one year from now.

Excellent _____ Poor

There is no precise 'scale' on this line – it simply involves making two marks, for the present and the future.

For the second and most important stage of the activity, pupils should discuss with each other and with the teacher how they can get from the 'present' to where they would like to be in the 'future'. This discussion can take place between pairs of pupils, in groups of four or five pupils, or between each pupil and the teacher (who could go around the class discussing this, whilst the pupils got on with another piece of work). If discussion is difficult, pupils could write, on their own, about how they might get from one point to the other. The discussion should include what might be needed – including what pupils might need to do, but also what help might be needed, and what other things would need to change.

RE and the inclusion or exclusion of religions or ways of life

When considering inclusion, it is not just those pupils with special educational needs who need to be included. Broader groups need to be included. This is a general issue of the ethos of school and the nature of subjects, relationships with parents, and the overcoming of racism and sexism and various forms of bullying. The history of English and Welsh RE has in recent decades been dominated by the incorporation of many religious and non-religious traditions and the rejection of 'confessionalism' or the promotion of religious belief. (Some alternative views in the UK are described in Chapter 11.) The UK tradition is distinctive, even within Europe, and there is a need for research to investigate the impact of this policy, in terms of inclusion, especially as there is some tentative evidence that RE may be a lesson where – ironically – pupils who are religious may feel most ostracized or excluded (as in White 2001). Jackson has worked on inclusion and exclusion in RE across Europe (working, for example, on RE as a way of overcoming intolerance in plural societies, Jackson 2004), Joy Schmack and Brendan Schmack (e.g. in White 2000, 2001, and exemplified in Lovelace 2001) have worked on how pupils of religion can be included, Ipgrave has investigated pupils' own religious backgrounds and how they can be used in primary RE (in Ipgrave 2004), and Dodd (e.g. Dodd et al. 2002) has looked at issues of Islam and intercultural education. Good examples of inclusive practice across religious and non-religious traditions are embedded in the work of many local RE syllabus committees in the UK (as described in Hull 1998; Rudge 2001). The active approach exemplified in Lovelace 2001, in which pupils and adults talked about their beliefs and ways of life, can also be used in research, as described in Activity 2.3.

All this research investigates how the RE policies of inclusion are implemented and how at times RE may unintentionally exclude some pupils. However, there are some ways in which RE policies may intentionally rather than unintentionally exclude. For example, in the UK and a number of other countries, parents or carers of pupils may withdraw them from RE, or from parts of RE, schools with religious foundations may reject applications from pupils on religious grounds, and the subject as a whole may exclude some traditions from syllabuses. RE teachers can research the inclusiveness of their subject, with their own pupils, by completing the following activity.

Activity 6.4: When do you feel most included?

Provide pupils in RE with a definition of inclusion, appropriate to their age and understanding. The definition might be taken from your school or a regional or national policy on inclusion such as this one:

An educationally inclusive school is one in which the teaching and learning, achievements, attitudes and well-being of every young person matter. . . .

This does not mean treating all pupils in the same way. Rather it involves taking account of pupils' varied life experiences and needs. *(Ofsted 2000a)*

Then ask pupils to describe when they feel more included in RE lessons. The question should be asked of individual pupils, as an open question, initially, to allow for answers of many different kinds. Pupils should then work in groups of two, three, or four, to agree on a list of situations in which they feel more included in RE.

When this question has been asked, pupils have given a wide variety of types of answer. Some have written about the topics of lessons (topics that seem more 'relevant' or simply more enjoyable), and others have written about the style of teaching and learning (discussions or project work or group work). One surprising response was that of a pupil who felt most included when allowed to work on his own. Perhaps allowing for individual interests to be met, rather than always working collaboratively, can itself help include pupils.

It seems particularly strange that some religious traditions might themselves feel excluded from the RE curriculum. Of course, no syllabus could cover absolutely every tradition, yet some traditions are not only unlikely to be included in syllabuses but may be actively rejected as inappropriate. Examples include paganism and other traditions referred to as 'new age' religions (as described at *paganfed.org/*) and other new religious movements (NRMs) such as Christian Science, Scientology, and Jehovah's Witnesses (*www.christianscience.com/* and *www.scientology.org/* and *www. jw.org/*, with information on many groups at *www.religioustolerance.org*). James Holt has researched and published on the Church of Jesus Christ of Latter-day Saints (CJCLDS) and on Jehovah's Witnesses (JW) (i.e. Holt 2002, 2004), and has completed research on NRMs more generally, especially Christian NRMs. In a Westhill seminar, Holt explored definitions of NRMs. Eileen Barker (e.g. Barker 1982, 1984, 1989, 2013) writes of the members of NRMs being first-generation converts, atypical of society, with a founder or leader who wields charismatic authority. George Chryssides (e.g. Chryssides 1999, 2003; Chryssides and Wilkins 2006) writes of NRMs being recent, outside the mainstream, and attracting converts from the indigenous culture. Holt himself writes of an NRM as having been founded within the past 200 years, and placing itself or being placed by the majority of its 'parent' faith, outside of the mainstream – because of either tradition or doctrine. The idea of a 'parent faith' is determined by the group itself. For example, the Nation of Islam identifies with Islam and the CJCLDS considers itself Christian, whether or not the 'parents' acknowledge their 'offspring'. Bahá'í no longer identifies with any 'parent', so although it is new, it should not, according to Holt, be considered an NRM.

Pupils' own views are important. *Speaking for Ourselves* (Lovelace 2001) includes a Jehovah's Witness and a Rastafarian, which is helpful. RE could continue without NRMs, but it would miss a lot of diversity, a lot of discussion points, and the backgrounds of a lot of pupils. For Holt, the best approach would be phenomenological, that is, the clear systematic study of individual NRM traditions, so that the curriculum is richer, and pupils from NRMs feel free and confident enough to share their beliefs as appropriate in lessons. Exam boards might also recognize the possibility of a number of NRMs being used in answers to examination questions on ethics. In the study of religions, there will always be issues of proportionality: it would be impossible to give substantial time to all religious traditions, even within the most generous timetable. More important than a simple statistical proportionality is an appreciation of the reasons for the inclusion or exclusion of a particular tradition. If for example there are pupils in the school following a tradition, this seems to be a good reason for inclusion. (That is the principle used in the syllabus of Birmingham City Council 2007.) In contrast, if a tradition is included only if it is 'safe' and 'respectable', this seems to be a weaker justification for inclusion. In Chapter 4, there are accounts of RE in other countries, where different religious and non-religious traditions are included or excluded – with Confucianism not regarded, legally, as a religion in China and non-Orthodox Christianity not included in Russian RE (although secular ethics *is* included). Who is 'in' or 'out' is therefore an interesting and contested issue for RE.

Conclusion

When it comes to inclusion, RE has the immense advantage of access to thousands of years of multi-sensory, affective, teaching that uses various forms of language, symbols, music, art, and dance. On the other hand, RE also encompasses traditions of rejection and exclusion – not only in religious traditions but in its own history as a subject. The former advantages can be used to outweigh the latter disadvantages, to help schools as well as RE become more inclusive. One strategy that would help pupils and teachers alike, in RE, would be for teachers to be able to say, 'I don't know', if that is accompanied by 'so I/we will try to find out'. This might lead on to what is called 'reciprocal teaching' (Oczkus 2003), making the classroom environment acceptable for asking questions. Reciprocal teaching involves a dialogue between teachers and students for the purpose of jointly constructing meaning from text with five strategies for structuring the dialogue: predicting, clarifying, visualizing, question generating, and summarizing.

Having made use of research in RE to investigate, illuminate, and inspire further inclusion of pupils, it is important to retain a sense of teachers, too, being included. The lives of teachers are complex and challenging. The research described in Chapter 3, by Judith Everington and John I'Anson (Sikes and Everington 2001; I'Anson 2004), indicates that the need for the inclusion of teachers is as significant as that for pupils, and there is sufficient indication of teacher stress for it to be worth pointing out such a need. Many would recognize the comment from Macmurray that '[t]he tendency to sacrifice the adults to the children [in school] is as disastrous as it is widespread' (Macmurray 1946c, p. 6). Many other people can and should be included in classrooms, and this might sensibly start with those who write and engage with sacred texts – the topic of the following chapter.

Chapter 7
Working With Sacred Texts

*My Grandmother read to me when I was young, a piece from the Bible
and taught me those things.*
(A 13-year-old responding to the question 'Religions sometimes teach their
followers about freedom, truth, justice, love and forgiveness. Who has taught you
about these things?')

Introduction

Teachers of RE have always been exploring sacred texts, and the best use of sacred texts in RE should be enlightening, imaginative, literate, provocative, and sensitive to context. However, this is inevitably not always the case, and the ways in which texts are studied in RE differ from the ways they are studied in history or English lessons. Research on the use of sacred texts in RE can help teachers understand what is happening and what is possible. Research on the use of sacred texts can also connect contemporary RE to its past, as the detailed study of sacred texts is one of the few activities that teachers from centuries past might recognize in today's classrooms.

Texts themselves – in contrast to oral communication – are attempts to communicate at a distance. Space and time are not barriers to textual communication, even if the texts themselves and their significance may seem to change as they are re-read over the years and as they are passed around the world. It is therefore important to investigate context, as well as text. Amongst the research on sacred text in RE is a small-scale study by the UK RE advisers' organisation (*www.areiac.org.uk/*). That study is a good starting point, as it simply compared the typical use of texts in history and RE:

History	RE
Tasks tend to require pupils to • read multiple source materials • make decisions and choices about the material they are reading	Tasks tend to require pupils to • rarely use multiple texts • simply recycle their reading

History	RE
• work with original texts • handle challenging text material • process reading so that their writing output is significantly different from the material they have read	• use second-hand rather than original texts • engage with over-processed simplified language • paraphrase reading doing little with the original; too much emphasis on low-level comprehension and recall

It is surprising that there is such a gap between the approaches to the use of texts in these subjects, given the way the subjects both depend on old and original texts, and given that many teachers teach both subjects. It is hoped the situation will improve. The availability of texts may help, as multiple, original, sacred texts are becoming much more easily and cheaply available, especially in electronic formats. On the internet, general sites include *www.religioustolerance.org* and *www.sacred-texts.com* and sites with access to key texts include *www.buddhanet.net/* and *www.biblegateway. com/* and *www.krishna.com/* and *qurango.com/* and *www.jewishvirtuallibrary.org/* and *www.Sikhs.org/granth.htm*. However, the availability of sacred texts does not necessarily mean they will be used most effectively in RE classrooms. What about the 'challenge' of the material and the ways of reading texts? Five overarching issues can be identified when dealing with sacred texts in RE:

- The format in which we present sacred texts, for example, in snippets on dog-eared worksheets, or in the form of the full text, or somewhere in between. It is worth noting the importance of oral traditions in most religions: the *telling* of stories, not just the *reading* of stories.

- The quantity of sacred text that can be put in front of a pupil, whether in snippets or longer extracts or full texts. If English lessons comfortably handle complete novels and plays, RE lessons should be able to handle complete sacred texts, even when only a short piece is studied in detail.

- The degree and format of translation, paraphrasing, and retelling, taking account of different traditions in different faith communities. There can be a tension between authenticity and accessibility, although this can be tackled directly in the lessons, as it is, for example, in many history lessons and English lessons. ('Tension' over translations has – historically – included executions and wars: no one should underestimate the power of the beliefs about a sacred text.)

- The assumptions we bring to sacred texts, and how we convey the assumptions a believer may bring to the text, and what happens when someone comes to the text who is not a believer. Assumptions include ideas on the truth: within religious traditions, for example, a single text may be treated as more literally true or more figuratively true. Again, teachers should tackle this head on, exploring possible assumptions.

- Issues of pedagogy, including appropriate ways of dealing with texts from the perspective of the RE teacher and from the perspective of the member of the faith community. Pupils should feel comfortable handling sacred texts and using all their skills and creativity to come to understand the texts. The 'framing' of texts is well developed in history textbooks such as those of the *Schools History Project* (at *www.schoolshistoryproject.co.uk/*), in which extracts from historical sources are explained in terms of how the texts were written, whether and how they are translated, what they would have been used for, and how they fit in amongst other related texts.

All these issues have been raised with respect to the Bible, by the Biblos project based in Exeter, and explored by Terence Copley in a Westhill seminar.

Exploring Bibles

One of the biggest RE projects of recent years has been the Biblos project, exploring the uses of the Bible in RE, and this is therefore a good place to start, in understanding research on sacred text. It is a superb example of the search for empirical evidence, to contribute to debates on the proper uses of the text. It also draws on that research to support the training and professional development of teachers and, notably, bases what it says on evidence provided by pupils and teachers as well as a clear understanding of theology. The respect thereby shown to the sacred text itself, in its religious context, and to pupils as well as to teachers is a model for research in RE. The project was led by Copley (Copley 1998a, Copley et al. 2001, 2004), with classroom materials coming from the project (Copley and Walshe 2002). For Copley, the Bible as a sacred text has a particular 'problem' in England, because it is regarded as a 'heritage text' as well as a 'sacred text'. Heritage is a big problem in this country, he says, as people are more likely, for example, to visit cathedrals as tourists than as pilgrims. Biblos tackles some stereotypes of the Bible in English RE: that the Bible has disappeared from RE, the Bible is only relevant to Christians, that teachers are reluctant to use biblical material, and that biblical material should be secularized.

An example of the loss of the Bible, even from nominal 'Bible stories', is the Joseph narrative as tackled with 7–11-year-olds. Joseph becoming an oppressor is not included in the narratives used in schools, and the central role of God in the Bible is suppressed, just as the central role of Allah in the Qur'an is at times suppressed. For example, in the musical *Joseph and the Amazing Technicolour Dreamcoat*, 'any dream will do'. God appears not at all: Joseph is a 'nice guy, who succeeds against the odds'. This, says Copley, is anti-RE. A proper consideration of biblical texts is vital as they are relevant to three religions, Judaism, Christianity, and Islam; they have a place in the history of Western civilization and are a proper subject for debate. The relevant cultural and historical contexts must be supplied, and for this, academic scholarship is important: the apparent 'divorce' of theology from RE, since the 1960s, may not have helped.

The criteria for the Biblos project's choice of stories, or narrative themes, were that they had to be relevant, a bridge between secular and religious, easily comprehensible, easy to remember, theological not secular, not exclusive, and progressive. The team, after abandoning hope (as a theme) and giving up taking 'God' seriously (as a topic), settled on 'destiny', 'encounter', and 'vulnerability' as the three themes. These themes are also themes of importance to children: what they want to grow up as, encounters with friends and enemies and teachers, and vulnerability in all those things. The Biblos project went on to study what young people know and think about the Bible and what has shaped these attitudes and perceptions. The work was replicated in New Zealand to see how 'British' are the responses.

Most of the 1,066 respondents in the UK (aged 10–17) could identify passages from the Bible, but when asked about meaning, 36.3 per cent found secular ethical meanings, compared to 22.9 per cent theological, 9.1 per cent literal, and 5.8 per cent irrelevant. Examples of the 'secular' meanings given to Bible passages were David and Goliath as hope for the underdog, the birth of Jesus meaning Christmas presents, and feeding the 5,000 meaning not taking things for granted and sharing things. There were many responses to questions on why the Bible is important, especially from respondents who themselves were members of religious groups other than Christianity. The 'heritage' importance of the Bible was certainly recognized. 'The Bible should be respected' (74.1 per cent) and it 'can show people how to live' (63.1 per cent), but to Copley's surprise 58.8 per cent disagreed or strongly disagreed with 'I look to the Bible for personal guidance'. Most positive were Christian church-attending females aged 10–11, with hobbies such as reading fiction/novels and watching soap operas, rather than film, music programmes on television, and computer games. What matters most to children? Family, education, and religion, for those more positively inclined towards the Bible; activities and hobbies, for those less positively inclined towards the Bible.

The project's overall conclusion is that, by presenting Bible narrative in its cultural context and by encouraging pupils to provide their own theological interpretations, we can open the Bible for children. It is the research of teachers to support the presentation of the appropriate context, and the research of pupils, as interpreters of the text, that can change passive lessons in comprehension into lively and scholarly RE. There are different ways of researching and teaching the Bible, such as those of Cupitt (1991), Erricker (Erricker and Erricker 2000), and Hull (1998), all of whom are described by Copley as looking for meaning in the *reader*, at times more than in the *text*. The Biblos project is clearly 'partial' in this way, in looking first for meaning in the text itself, and yet the contrast between those looking at the text and those looking at the reader may be something of a false dichotomy, as the Biblos project, in common with the other approaches, looks at *engagement* between text and reader: nobody looks to the text or the reader alone. (One of the interesting findings of Biblos was that many Christian children, whether in church or non-church schools, are apparently encountering more religion – engaging more – in school than they do at home.)

Activity 7.1: What to do with the Bible?

There are at least three conclusions from the Biblos research:

- Good RE teaching must not ignore the theological and God-centred dimensions of Bible narratives.
- Good RE teaching must recognize that the Bible is of particular (and different) importance to Christians, Jews, and Muslims.
- Good RE teaching must facilitate pupil engagement with the Bible and seek to raise their valuations of it, as the RE teacher is often the most important gatekeeper to, and cartographer of, the Bible for children.

RE teachers can investigate how each of these can be achieved. The process should involve three stages:

- A teacher or group of teachers should review the RE curriculum plan and highlight examples of the use of the Bible narratives.
- For each use, the teacher can assess whether theological issues are to be raised; how important the narrative might be to Christians, Jews, and Muslims; and how the lessons will help pupils to value the text.
- Where any of the answers are negative, the teacher could work out how to improve the plan so that, at least for some of the uses of Bible narratives, there are opportunities for theological engagement, consideration of the importance to religious believers, and pupils valuing the text.

Exploring the Qur'an

The Qur'an has been widely used in the teaching of Islam, both as an artefact, in lessons about how sacred objects may be treated, and as a text. However, relatively little research has been completed on its use in classrooms, although some initial surveys are being completed. From the Muslim Council of Britain, for example, Fatma Amer has considered approaches to using the Qur'an as a sacred text in the classroom. She starts with the question, What kind of sensitivities should teachers observe when using the Qur'an in teaching RE? On a school visit, Amer noticed one teacher who wanted to display a copy of the Qur'an apparently trembling, worrying about what the pupils, many of whom were Muslim, would say about her handling of the Qur'an. Such fear seems out of place: genuine respect is the appropriate attitude to this sacred text, as with all sacred texts. The Arabic text of the Qur'an is considered by Muslims to be the directly revealed Word of God, whilst a translated Qur'an is by definition part human interpretation of the meanings and is therefore no longer considered divine. However, both should be treated with respect.

Muslim pupils may memorize the Qur'an: Bill Gent has researched this issue for a number of years (e.g. Gent 2011). But teachers should avoid using pupils who memorize the Qur'an as a novelty. Rather, teachers could develop a knowledge of how and when this example may appropriately be incorporated into a lesson: it should be a voluntary activity. Comparisons may also be made with pupils who learn play scripts, or musical pieces, and the value and significance of such memorization. The time and background of the arrival of the first substantial Muslim community in the UK has influenced approaches to the Qur'an, as that group had a particular religious approach, reflecting particular cultural traditions rather than universal religious traditions. Whilst remaining sensitive to the specific cultural traditions, according to Amer, becoming completely tied to a set of 'taboos' deriving from a single tradition can restrict the possibility of studying the Qur'an in classrooms.

The Qur'an can be used in many ways, as a study text, as inspiration for daily life, as a catalyst for academically sound historical enquiry, as a linguistic framework, as a framework for modern ethical dilemmas, or as a way of facilitating acquisition of vocabulary for pupils with English as an additional language. Such uses can tie in with, but are not entirely addressed by, literacy strategies: these strategies tend to focus on literacy alone, and not on exploring the deeper meaning or the underlying messages. As with Copley's work on the Christian Bible, work on the Qur'an relates to Judaism, Christianity, and Islam.

Three issues are commonly raised by RE teachers on the use of the Qur'an:

- What are the best ways in which school RE can use the sacred texts of Islam? Amer suggests the use of narrative to inspire: the use of enjoyable games such as hopscotch to learn the stages of Hajj or snakes and ladders for steps to paradise (and see also Moksha Chitram in Chapter 13), the use of role-playing to assist in the exploration of the sense of awe and wonder in relation to the divine, and the use of poetry and creative writing (e.g. on birds, animals, insects, or water, in the Qur'an) for pupils of all ages.

- What potential for good learning in RE in general is there in the development of good uses of the Qur'an in RE? Exploring the transfer of concepts using the vehicle of translation, enhancing opportunities for social and emotional literacy, highlighting commonalities between three Abrahamic faiths whilst treating differences with integrity (as it is important to do both, especially with an increased prominence of interfaith issues), and the diversity and enrichment of religious literacy.

- How can teachers be helped to do more and better work with Qur'anic text in RE at the various different age groups? This is an issue of teacher training, increasing teachers' personal familiarity with the sacred text, and having good quality inexpensive in-service training. Amer talked about some of the resources that can be used, including the patterns of texts themselves as calligraphy, patterning used in texts, materials produced by the IQRA Trust (with information at *www.iqratrust.org*), story books that manage to avoid portraying prophets, and songs (including translations of meanings of Qur'an verses). With the involvement of the Muslim community in producing more resources, there is an increasing choice of resources. Publications of the

Islamic Foundation (*www.islamic-foundation.org.uk*) have been very helpful. Further ideas could be found from within Islam, such as from local mosques, the Muslim Heritage website (*www.muslimheritage.com/*), and Salaam (*www. salaam.co.uk*), in order to give some basis to valuable celebration traditions.

Those discussing the use of the Qur'an in RE often report a fear of making mistakes when using the Qur'an in any way. It is as though the Qur'an should, literally and metaphorically, be put 'out of reach' of the pupils. Yet it is surely better to engage with the text, even with the possibility of inadvertently making mistakes (and apologizing if mistakes are made), than to avoid all engagement.

Activity 7.2: What to do with the Qur'an?

- Good RE teaching must not ignore the theological and God-centred dimensions of Quranic narratives.
- Good RE teaching must recognize that the Qur'an is of particular importance to Muslims.
- Good RE teaching must facilitate pupil engagement with the Qur'an and seek to raise their valuations of it, as the RE teacher is often the most important gatekeeper to, and cartographer of, the Qur'an for non-Muslim children.

RE teachers can investigate how each of these can be achieved. The process should involve three stages:

- A teacher or group of teachers should review the RE curriculum plan and highlight examples of the use of the Qur'an narratives.
- For each use, the teacher can assess whether theological issues are to be raised, how important the narrative might be to Muslims, and how the lessons will help pupils to value the text.
- Where any of the answers are negative, the teacher could work out how to improve the plan so that, at least for some of the uses of Quranic narratives, there are opportunities for theological engagement, consideration of the importance to religious believers, and pupils valuing the text.

Exploring the Bhagavad Gita

A good example of research on using the Bhagavad Gita in RE is that of Naina Parmar (2001), who has been researching the use of translations of the Bhagavad Gita to raise questions fundamental to human experience. She worked with children aged 7, many of whom had experienced inappropriate teaching of Hinduism – for example, using cartoons that made the pupils uncomfortable. Parmar's own experience of Christian education, as a pupil, was not a challenge to her Hinduism, but enriched it, so, when Parmar took up her Bhagavad Gita, she used her interpretive skills as an historian as well as her life as a Hindu. The Bhagavad Gita is set on the eve of battle, with the battle metaphorically at the heart of every person. The problem is of right choice, happiness, and suffering, including the three *gunas* or qualities of light, fire, and darkness. Carrington and Troyna (1988) say that children should face controversial issues, and this is important in working with the Bhagavad Gita. Although the work is clearly important, the difficulty appears to be in getting teachers interested. Sometimes, new RE teachers see the subject as being about multiculturalism alone, without having a concern for the substantial sacred texts and other religious items.

An interesting issue is that of oral in contrast to literary traditions. Beckerlegge (2001b) investigates how religions represent themselves in their traditions, for example, in speech, texts, images, or ritual enactments, and how these are affected by cultural, historical, and technological contexts. The oral tradition, from which the Bhagavad Gita and other Hindu Vedic sacred texts derive, involved an immediate personal relationship between the speaker and audience. Written traditions, and later technologies such as film and the internet, changed that relationship and therefore affected access to and relationships with the sacred. Once photography was developed, according to Beckerlegge, photographs of such religious teachers as Ramakrishna were by some regarded as *murtis*, and more recently, there have been representations of deities and sacred narratives in films and on television, notably the 1987–1988 televised *Ramayana*. The qualities of the oral tradition must not be lost in all these changes.

Curriculum policy documents for English will not only address the development of reading and writing skills but will also usually include a focus upon speaking and listening. For example, pupils may be expected to demonstrate an ability:

> To speak with confidence in a range of contexts, adapting their speech for a range of purposes and audiences … [aged seven to 11, and to] speak fluently and appropriately in different contexts, adapting their talk for a range of purposes and audiences, including the more formal [aged 11 to 16]. *(DfEE and QCA 1999)*

This requirement, along with the importance of oral traditions in religion, gives considerable impetus to the use of storytelling in RE, and to assess pupil skills in storytelling, and listening to stories. Assessment of pupils rarely refers to oral work, except to complain of 'too much talking'. Activity 7.3 is therefore one example that ties together a vital sacred text with its oral origins, helping pupils develop their own oral skills as well as their understanding of religion.

Activity 7.3: What to do with the Bhagavad Gita?

The Bhagavad Gita is one of the texts most used by Hindus for guidance on making difficult personal decisions. Choose a topic of immediate importance to the pupils in your class, that is also addressed by the text, and create a storytelling (*telling,* not *reading*, if possible) of that text, and a lesson to follow it up. An example might be the apparent recommendation of violence in the story (generally noticed, with some glee, by more 'lively' pupils), noting the peace-loving Gandhi's response when asked about this. Questioner: 'At the end of the Gita Krishna recommends violence'; Gandhi: 'I do not think so. I am also fighting. I should not be fighting effectively if I were fighting violently' (quoted in Beckerlegge 2001a, p. 307).

Evaluate the lesson, on the basis of pupil answers to the following questions. The third question, about meeting targets, can only be asked where there is a clear 'target-setting' culture in the school.

- What did you learn about Hindu traditions or dharma from this lesson?
- What did you think Hindus would want you to learn from (this part of) the Bhagavad Gita?
- What did you learn from this Hindu story that will help you to meet your targets in RE or as a pupil?

Conclusion

Sacred texts communicate with us and are used to communicate between us. The relationship between text and reader, or between writer and reader, is much studied in literary theory (Rosenblatt 1994, 1995). In RE, sacred texts may have the religion extracted from them (as described by Copley with respect to the Bible), may be treated as unusable objects (as described by Amer with respect to the Qur'an), or may have their life-giving storytelling properties ignored (as described by Parmar with respect to the Bhagavad Gita). It is a measure of the importance of research that all three of these authors, along with others working in the field, can exemplify good practice with respect to sacred texts. The texts help communication across time and across distance: it is a kind of dialogue over space and time that can educate and inspire. Dialogue by text, across space and time, is now possible using computers, but the simpler technology of printing has already expanded the frontiers of dialogue, transcending space and time. And transcendence – in the form of spirituality – is the subject of the following chapter.

Chapter 8
Spirituality

All the things that are fundamental, all the things that, to the human spirit,
are most profoundly significant, can only be experienced, not expressed.
The rest is always and everywhere silence.
After silence that which comes nearest to expressing the inexpressible is music.
(Aldous Huxley)

Introduction

There is an ongoing debate between those who say that religion is just one aspect of spirituality and those who say that spirituality is just one dimension of religion. Whichever position you have, spirituality can hardly be avoided in RE. And however difficult it is researching religion, it is even more difficult researching spirituality. Nevertheless, in some schools, 'spiritual development' or 'spiritual education' is a significant aspect of education or even a separate subject. I jumped into these turbulent waters a number of years ago. Working in the UK, where all schools are legally required to promote the spiritual development of their pupils, I was interested in whether this was legitimate and whether it was possible. Some current legal requirements relating to religion I was happy with, including – unsurprisingly – the presence of RE on the curriculum. Some I was unhappy with, such as the requirement for a daily act of collective worship of a predominantly Christian character (described by Denise Cush as 'an abuse of human rights', Cush 1994). Spirituality, I wasn't so sure about, as a requirement for all pupils – not just those in schools with church foundations – and as an activity with no 'opt out' offered to pupils or their families. After a great deal of research, culminating in *The Spirit of the School* (Stern 2009a), I had just about worked out what I thought spirituality was and how it could appropriately be required of schools. (I also worked on the similar requirements for UK nurses to meet patients' 'spiritual needs', Stern and James 2006.) That gave me the confidence to continue working on spirituality but, as with RE, I have found that in different countries, spirituality was typically framed quite differently. Spending some time at a US university, giving seminars and public lectures, I noticed that the people I met generally had an expectation of presentations on 'spirituality' to be accounts of Christianity. In Hong Kong (where much of my research took place), there was a much more philosophical and worldly understanding of spirituality than was typical in the UK – where there is something of a 'magical moments' tradition in some guides to spiritual development.

This chapter therefore provides an account of some of the different traditions of spirituality, based on research that has been published – research in a variety of countries, from a variety of perspectives. My own research and my own views are in there, but the chapter is written to help stimulate further exploration, further research, on spirituality in RE classrooms. Although research papers and books on spirituality are all too often dominated by issues of definition, this chapter will also look at empirical research on spirituality in school contexts and how – whether – spiritual development can be explicitly taught.

What do people mean by spirituality?

There are so many definitions and understandings of spirituality; one of the most useful research tasks is to explore what people understand it to mean. This doesn't settle the definitional arguments (as the truth is not determined by a vote), but it helps illuminate other discussions of the topic. And it is worth starting with those who seem to say that defining spirituality is impossible. Aldous Huxley wrote this about the inexpressible:

> From pure sensation to the intuition of beauty, from pleasure and pain to love and the mystical ecstasy and death – all the things that are fundamental, all the things that, to the human spirit, are most profoundly significant, can only be experienced, not expressed. The rest is always and everywhere silence.
> After silence that which comes nearest to expressing the inexpressible is music. *(Huxley 1950, p. 19)*

A number of people do indeed use music to help with spiritual development, including Robert Nash and Penny Bishop (2010), David Hay (Hay with Nye 2006; Hay 2007a), Joyce Bellous (in Ota and Chater 2007), and Eleanor Nesbitt (2004). Others use silence, as I do myself (chapter 10 of Stern 2014b), and as do Helen Lees (2012), Rachael Kessler (2000), Linda Lantieri (2001), and Jerome Berryman (1999). And plenty of people who appreciate the value of education in spirituality also note the difficulty of pinning it down in a definition. Amongst these is Jack Priestley, who is very influential in this field. He investigated how 'spiritual development' became included in the 'preamble' to the 1944 Education Act in the UK. He asked the author, Canon Hall, why the word 'spiritual' was used rather than 'religious'.

He laughed but did not hesitate. 'Because it was much broader', he said and went on, 'if we had used the word "religious" they would all have started arguing about it'. *(Priestley 1997, p. 29)*

Priestley celebrates this ambiguity – this avoidance of narrow religious 'capturing' of spirituality – and does so with a valuable comparison.

[T]he spirit . . . is dynamic. The spirit denotes life. The traditional images of the spirit are those of wind, fire, running water and many others. They cannot be arrested without ceasing to be what they are. To freeze the spirit is to kill the organism. . . . This is why we surrender the whole argument the moment we fall into the trap of agreeing to define. To define is to put sharp edges round a blurred idea, to arrest motion. It is akin to asking a child on a stormy day to go out into the playground and to collect a jar of wind and to bring it back into the classroom for analysis. There can only be one outcome, namely the assertion 'there is nothing in it'. The wind, the fire, the rushing stream must be felt, they must be assessed by their consequences. One never steps into the same river twice, as the Buddhist saying goes. If education is a process and process is defined by dynamism then we have to acknowledge that static measurements are inevitably limited, with clear implications for inspection, it has to be said. *(Priestley 1997, p. 29)*

Priestley's description (not definition) of spirituality contains echoes of Aristotle's writing from more than two millennia ago. I sometimes think that Aristotle's *On the Soul* could be published under a pseudonym today in an article on spirituality, and readers would think the author was still alive. It is as good a description of soul or spirituality as I have read. In characteristic Aristotelian style, he gives helpful presentations on a whole range of contemporary beliefs and uses these to come to as broad and inclusive a description as he can achieve. (I copied this technique, in *The Spirit of the School*.) He describes some theories of the soul and notes that '[a]ll, then, it may be said, characterize the soul by three marks, Movement, Sensation, Incorporeality' (Aristotle 1984, p. 646), with 'incorporality' meaning the soul is not made of earth (one of the four recognized elements), though it might be made of water, as Hippo says, or air, as Diogenes says, or fire, as Democritus says. Today, a number of people refer to the spiritual as 'non-material', but Aristotle's use of 'incorporal' is quite different, as water (and air, and fire) are clearly also material, even if they are more 'moving'. And even earth is a possible constituent of the soul: 'earth has found no supporter unless we count as such those who have declared soul to be, or to be compounded of, *all* the elements' (Aristotle 1984, p. 646). 'Certain thinkers', he continues, 'say that soul is intermingled in the whole universe, and it is perhaps for that reason that Thales came to the opinion that all things are full of gods' (Aristotle 1984, p. 655). Is the soul part of the body or separable? Aristotle is – like Priestley – happy to leave things ambiguous.

[T]he soul is inseparable from its body, or at any rate ... certain parts of it are (if it has parts) ... Yet some may be separable because they are not the actualities of any body at all. Further, we have no light on the problem whether the soul may not be the actuality of its body in the sense in which the sailor is the actuality of the ship. *(Aristotle 1984, p. 657)*

So, Priestley and Aristotle, two of the leading writers on spirituality, leave us with *ambiguous* descriptions of spirituality. Some people think of ambiguity as being vague; I prefer to think of ambiguity as being rich in many meanings, as poetry and art is at its best. But both authors think spirit or soul is important and worth promoting. Others are less positive. John White is reported as saying, 'I would advocate an absolute embargo on the use of the terms "spirituality" or "spiritual development" in all official documents on education, all conferences on education, all in-service courses for teachers ... [as t]he words simply get in the way of thinking' (quoted in McLaughlin 2008, p. 245). Marilyn Mason writes of spiritual development as 'just the trendy, politically correct, egalitarian successor of the "character development" that was so much part of our public school system until quite recently', or, 'as Terence Copley called it "universal and inoffensive, the aromatherapy of the curriculum"' (Mason 2000, p. 5). (An education colleague of mine who was trained in aromatherapy celebrated Copley's statement as a positive endorsement of spiritual development, albeit realizing that he hadn't meant it that way.)

Copley's concern with spirituality is not really an attack on spirituality itself, but on its use in the curriculum. His worry is that an increasingly secular UK education system may replace religion with an uncritical form of spirituality, as many people 'are prisoners of modernity and post-modernity, yet still cling to spiritualities, some of them pre-modern, even though these are derided or ignored by many intellectuals' (Copley 2005, p. 150). There are, however, plenty of positive accounts of spirituality. Brenda Watson, for example, rejects – as Copley does – the idea of spirituality as an 'easy' alternative to religion: 'to advocate a secular spirituality on the grounds that it is open-ended by comparison with religion will not do' (Watson 2004, p. 58). She continues, '[t]o speak in terms of [spirituality] being either religious or secularist is inappropriate because this suggests some kind of possessiveness or competition, which I see as the very antithesis of the inclusiveness of spirituality' (Watson 2004, p. 58). In this way, Watson is echoing Priestley's description of spirituality as alive and dynamic, and able to be 'killed' by being put in a box. Her own description of spirituality is one that – without 'boxing' the concept – is in a tradition of spirituality as a 'separate substance' or 'separate dimension' of life. There is a large set of people in philosophy and in religion who are 'dualists', who believe there are two distinct types of substance or two dimensions. (Some believe there are *three* types of substance: I don't know of a word for that – trioist? – but hope that 'dualist' sufficiently covers the sense of separation.)

Spirituality may perhaps be best appreciated by putting it alongside experiences different from it. I suggest that there are three radically different kinds of human behaviour and attitudes:

A. one of these expresses habitual human nature – the plane in which we operate if we make no effort to avoid it;

B. one is the spiritual dimension – a quite different way of being which has to be actively chosen and is therefore capable of being deeply fulfilling;

C. one is the reverse of both – what might be called the 'demonic', whether that word is understood symbolically or not. (Watson 2004, p. 59)

Watson expands these descriptions, giving examples of each:

A. To be interested in what is of use or value or pleasure to me (ordinary plane)

B. To see things really and seriously from someone else's point of view – what is of use, or value, or gives pleasure to them (spiritual plane)

C. To be obsessively self-centred without any interest in what is important to others, or even to use knowledge we have to harm them and advance our own cause (demonic plane). (Watson 2004, p. 60)

For Watson, these different 'planes' or 'dimensions' are distinct, although they are not completely separate 'materials'. There is a continuum from the most dualist approaches to the least dualist. Thomas Moore, like Watson, talks of the 'soul' as 'essentially different, though by no means disconnected, from the mind and body', with 'its own qualities … [e.g.] eternal, unique, contemplative, poetic, erotic, aesthetic, and transcendent' (Moore, in Miller et al 2005, p. 10). Spirituality 'usually refers to a dimension of human life and understanding that goes beyond the physical or material', according to John Keast, and is 'often associated with an awareness of the transcendent, self-awareness, or the power of human spirit' (Keast 2007, p. 204). Guides to spiritual development have been produced by the UK's school inspection service, Ofsted, and these have sometimes been at the 'dualist' end of the spectrum. 'Spiritual development relates to that aspect of inner life through which pupils acquire insights into their personal existence which are of enduring worth' which 'is characterised by reflection, the attribution of meaning to experience, valuing a non-material dimension to life and intimations of an enduring reality' (Ofsted 1993). And more recently, '[s]piritual development is the development of the non-material element of a human being which animates and sustains us and, depending on our point of view, either ends or continues in some form when we die' (Ofsted 2004, p. 12). An even more recent guide from Ofsted is less dualist, and also perhaps less profound: spiritual development is shown by pupils' 'ability to be reflective about their own beliefs, religious or otherwise, that inform their perspective on life and their interest in and respect for different people's faiths, feelings and values', their 'sense of enjoyment and fascination in learning about themselves, others and the world around them', their 'use of imagination and creativity in their learning', and their 'willingness to reflect on their experiences' (Ofsted 2016, p. 35).

Kenneth Pargament and Annette Mahoney provide a more dualist account, as psychologists, saying that spirituality is a 'search for the sacred', with 'sacred' meaning 'holy' and 'set apart' from the ordinary (Pargament and Mahoney, in Snyder and Lopez 2005, p. 647). Rudolph Steiner has even more divisions, with 'four members of man's nature: the Physical Body, the Etheric or Life-Body, the Astral or Sentient Body, and the Body of the Ego', along with '[t]he Sentient Soul, the Intellectual Soul, and the Spiritual Soul, and beyond these the still higher members of man's nature – Spirit-Self, Life-Self, Spirit-Man' (Steiner 1965, p. 19). For children, he describes a simpler dualist approach to spirituality, with a description of how to get to the 'element of the spiritual': 'we can fly into the element of the spiritual, and we have two wings to fly there', he says; '[t]he wing on the left is called "hard work," and the other wing on the right is called "paying attention"' (Steiner 1996, p. 30).

At the other end of the spectrum – the less dualist end of the spectrum – are traditions of spirituality that can broadly be described as 'relational'. A 'relational' researcher (Klass 1999, pp. 98–99) quotes the ancient Buddhist philosopher Nāgārjuna:

The dualism of 'to be' and 'not to be',
The dualism of pure and not-pure:
Such dualism having abandoned,
The wise stand not even in the middle

Aristotle is one of the less dualist philosophers, especially when compared to his older contemporary Plato. Of modern writers, David Hay is a leading advocate of relational spirituality. Hay studied and taught science before moving into research on religion and spirituality. In these studies, based on research with children, he talked of 'relational consciousness', which he said was 'a biologically inbuilt aspect of our psychology' (Hay 2007b, p. 14, see also Hay 2006). This form of consciousness has 'the effect of ... shortening the psychological distance between the individual and their environment, so that damage to it, which had perhaps been hitherto a matter of indifference, now is of direct and personal importance' (Hay 2007b, p. 16). Relational spirituality is, for him, connected also to Martin Buber's 'distinction between relationships which have an "I-Thou" quality, where there is intersubjective recognition of the dignity and value of the other person, and those that are based on "I-It", where there is no such recognition and the other person is as it were, fair game, and legitimately open to manipulation for one's own gratification' (Hay 2007b, p. 17).

Hay's best known work was *The Spirit of the Child* (Hay with Nye 2006), and here, working with Rebecca Nye, he gave examples of how children talked about their 'awareness-sensing', 'mystery-sensing', and 'value-sensing' – all described as examples of spiritual experiences. Quotations from children help make the book popular, with occasionally grumpy 6-year-old Freddie, for example, talking about the film he has seen. 'The earth's so good [that God made], but sometimes somebody feels really sad, and like on Snow White, you know, Grumpy like, he feels very sad and grumpful ... but when he gets into know[ing] about life, he thinks more better about it, about Snow White and things like that', and 'I think Grumpy and Snow White learned about how clever and good life can be' as '[a]t the start he doesn't know nothing about life, so he don't like life and the planet of god and really later on he finds out all about it' (Hay with Nye 2006, p. 112, ellipsis and brackets in original). Nye goes on to say that '[i]t appears that when Freddie considered his religious views about creation, his personal conception of spiritual values was triggered', and '[t]hrough this storying about relationships we glimpse both his emerging and transformative self-consciousness, as well as some hints of his "God-consciousness" suggested in his comment about Grumpy's realization that he is a citizen of the "planet of God"' (Hay with Nye 2006, p. 112, see also Nye 2009).

David Scott says simply that '[t]he spirit(ual) is about relations and relationships' (Scott, in Ota and Chater 2007, p. 93). Various UK-based curriculum and inspection bodies have at times given relational descriptions of spirituality, too. RE 'provides opportunities to promote *spiritual development* through ... considering how religions and other world views perceive the value of human beings, and their relationships with one another, with the natural world, and with God' and 'valuing relationships and developing a sense of belonging' (QCA 2004, p. 14). 'There are many aspects of spiritual development', says one discussion document, including 'Relationships – Recognising and valuing the worth of each individual; developing a sense of community; the ability to build up relationships with others ... [and] steps to spiritual development might include: recognising the existence of others as independent from oneself' (SCAA 1995, pp. 3–4). The Ofsted inspection service noted that spiritual development was good in schools which 'provide opportunities across the curriculum for pupils to consider, for example ... the importance of relationships and the worth of each individual' (Ofsted 2000b, p. 32). Cathy Ota and Mark Chater end their book noting '[t]he central importance of relationality ... as the locus of spiritual education', which 'means that the visibility of relationality can be used as a measurement of the effectiveness of systems' (Ota and Chater 2007, p. 190). I took this task on myself, in *The Spirit of the School*, where I researched the relationships within and beyond schools, in order to explore and also help describe and promote spirituality in schools. After talking with 144 pupils, teachers, and head teachers in thirteen schools in the UK and Hong Kong, China, I developed a definition of the spirit of the school (in a shorter and a longer version):

> The spirited school is an inclusive community with magnanimous leadership that enables friendship through dialogue in order to create and evaluate valuable or beautiful meanings, valuable or beautiful things, and good people.
>
>   The spirited school is an inclusive (bringing in from past times and local and distant places) community (people treating each other as ends in the themselves) with magnanimous leadership (aiming for the good of the led) that enables (but does not insist on) friendship (by overcoming fear and loneliness and allowing for solitude) through dialogue (not monologue) in order to create and evaluate valuable or beautiful meanings, valuable or beautiful things (including the environment), and good (real) people. *(Stern 2009a, pp. 160–161)*

The intentions and relationships within the school (inclusion, community, leadership, friendship, and dialogue) also stretch beyond the school. When asked how to make the school more of a community, 'Desmond, aged ten ... wanted to draw people in to the school ...: "Just put famous pictures on the walls" and "get some ... people from the world to come and visit us sometimes"' (Stern 2009a, p. 96). The word 'spirit' comes from the word for 'breath', and Buber describes spirituality in terms of relationships, with a breathy metaphor:

> SPIRIT IN its human manifestation is a response of man to his *Thou*. ... in actuality speech does not abide in man, but man takes his stand in speech and talks from there; so with every word and every spirit. Spirit is not in the *I*, but between *I* and *Thou*. It is not like the blood that circulates in you, but like the air in which you breathe. Man lives in the spirit, if he is able to respond to his *Thou*. He is able to, if he enters into relation with his whole being. Only in virtue of his power to enter into relation is he able to live in the spirit. *(Buber 1958, pp. 57–58)*

So far, I have described some of the difficulties and ambiguities in defining or describing spirituality, and a range of descriptions of spirituality along a continuum from the more 'dualist' to the more 'relational'. It is important to note that these difficulties and that continuum are not restricted to one religion. There are more 'dualist' and more 'relational' approaches to Christian spirituality, to Hindu or Buddhist spirituality, to Muslim spirituality (well described at *www.islam101.com/sociology/spiritualPath.htm*), to Jewish spirituality, and to secular philosophical spirituality. I will end this section with a description from Douglas Hofstadter, a professor of cognitive science, writer on consciousness (and many science and computing topics), author of what has been called the 'nerd's bible' (*Gödel, Escher, Bach*, Hofstadter 1980), and 'sceptic'. In a more recent book about personhood, *I Am A Strange Loop*, he describes his mother looking at a photograph of her recently deceased husband (his father), and she says, 'What meaning does that photograph have? None at all. It's just a flat piece of paper with dark spots on it here and there. It's useless' (Hofstadter 2007, p. 9). He responds,

> In the living room we have a book of the Chopin études for piano. All of its pages are just pieces of paper with dark marks on them, just as two-dimensional and flat and foldable as the photograph of Dad – and yet, think of the powerful effect that they have had on people all over the world ... Thanks to those black marks ... untold thousands of people have collectively spent millions of hours moving their fingers over the keyboards of pianos in complicated patterns ... Those pianists in turn have conveyed to many millions of listeners, including you and me, the profound emotions that churned in Frédéric Chopin's heart, thus affording all of us some partial access to Chopin's interiority – to the experience of living in the head, or rather the soul, of Frédéric Chopin. The marks on those sheets of paper are no less than soul-shards – scattered remnants of the shattered soul of Frédéric Chopin. Each of those strange geometries of notes has a unique power to bring back to life, inside our brains, some tiny fragment of the internal passions and tensions – and we thereby know, at least in part, what it was like to be that

human being, and many people feel intense love for him. … Like the score to a Chopin étude, that photograph is a soul-shard of someone departed, and it is something we should cherish as long as we live. *(Hofstadter 2007, pp. 9–10)*

It is the phrase 'soul-shard' that echoes with me, and it is put by Hofstadter into an account of relational personhood. I don't know what Hofstadter's position is on religion, but his description of the soul, in this book, is interesting to the religious and non-religious alike.

Activity 8.1: Top ten views of spirituality

Here are ten views of spirituality (from the first half of this chapter), and you should work with colleagues or pupils to put them into a 'diamond nine' shape – with your favourite (or most relevant) at the top, working down the diamond to the ninth favourite, with a separate box for the 'discarded' statement:

a. The spiritual can only be experienced, not expressed.
b. Spiritual development should be required of *all* schools.
c. The spirit is dynamic; it denotes life.
d. The soul or spirit is characterized by movement, sensation, and incorporality.
e. Spirituality is the aromatherapy of the curriculum.
f. To be spiritual is to see things really and seriously from someone else's point of view, what is of use or value or gives pleasure to them.
g. The soul or spirit is essentially different from the mind and body, and is eternal, unique, contemplative, poetic, erotic, aesthetic, and transcendent.
h. Spirituality is the search for the sacred.
i. Spirituality is experienced through relational consciousness.
j. A person lives in the spirit who can respond to the *Thou*.

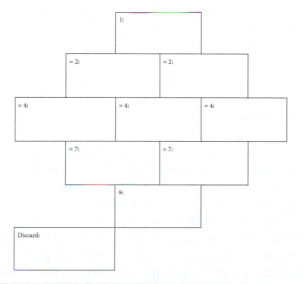

How can spirituality be taught?

Promoting spiritual development in school will look different, depending on what is meant by spirituality. And whatever description is followed, there will still be a variety of ways of teaching spirituality. Within RE, the specific traditions of spirituality can be taught. Hasidic Jewish mysticism and 'fervour', often experienced through music, can be compared with Sufi Muslim mysticism also at times musically expressed – as in the 'Whirling Dervish' practice. Hindu yogic exercises may be compared to Christian ascetic and monastic traditions. Recently, 'mindfulness' has become popular as a practice dissociated from its long tradition as a Buddhist spiritual discipline, just as yoga has been given a life apart from its Hindu roots, and meditation from its roots in so many religions. These are good topics for RE lessons, and controversies over whether yoga or mindfulness or meditation are 'religious' practices can be explored in newspapers – especially in contexts where religion is restricted, such as the US or French limits on religion in public life (including schools). Erricker and Erricker 2001 is a guide to using meditation in schools 'for calmer classrooms', within which are distinct guides to Christian, Buddhist, and 'educational' meditation and its use in Circle Time. As an RE teacher, whether you think meditation (or yoga or mindfulness) a religious or a secular practice, there will be pupils and families, and members of religious and non-religious groups, who will see the practice in a different way. This is therefore, at the very least, a good opportunity for exploring religious controversy with pupils in RE lessons.

There is research, though, on lessons and other activities intended to develop spirituality and on other activities that might, serendipitously, help promote spiritual development. A number of the activities in the 'experiential' approach to RE (Hammond et al. 1990) were adapted from, and in turn have influenced, spiritual practices. This is not surprising, as it was an attempt to help pupils to experience the world as religious people might experience it, and the more open-ended spiritual practices within religions were more likely to be possible within schools than the formal practices that would take place in religious services. The book is a helpful guide to 'teaching spirituality', and one researcher who used the experiential approach to explore and teach spirituality was Yee-Ling Ng. She developed a series of ten lessons for primary schools (for pupils aged 7–9) and then analysed how the children responded. These lessons included activities such as the following – with other authors of the activities described by Ng, where she had not developed them herself: 'Bodily awareness, silence and reflection', 'Russian doll as a metaphor of self (Hay and Nye 2006)', 'Beading activity and silence activity (Hyde 2008a)', 'Silence activity whilst outside', 'Use of photographs to elicit pupils' thoughts and experiences (Hay and Nye 2006; Hyde 2008a)', 'Explicating what is magical, mysterious or beautiful to the pupil through differing expressions', '"Mysteries questions": pupils writing down questions about which they ponder (Kessler 2000)', 'Use of important things as chosen by pupils as a channel to discuss meaning (Kessler 2000)', 'Questions: "I wonder what you think really, really matters …", "I wonder what you might wish for …" (Hay and Nye 2006)' (Ng 2012, p. 171). Each lesson started with a period of silence, after which the pupils drew or wrote what they were thinking about. Analysing the pupil responses, Ng said they fell into four categories: the 'world of self', the 'world with others (people)', the 'imaginary world', and the 'world of other' (Ng 2012, p. 172), and these categories also suggested a 'relational' spirituality that had guided the development of the lessons. What did the pupils learn? 'Pupils' journals and drawings provided a glimpse of what was meaningful to them, highlighting the personalised nature of this journey' (Ng 2012, p. 174).

> For example, Aerin (7–8 years) believed that the programme taught her 'to teller [tell] people minifel [meaningful] and speshel [special] things to one another'. Comparably, Holly (7–8 years) highlighted that during the lessons pupils were given an opportunity to reflect upon 'what is your harts [heart's] dirsiyr [desire]?' Wilson (7–8 years) also stated that these lessons allowed pupils to think about 'what makes you feel happy and why?' Furthermore, Camden (7–8 years) also believed he has learnt, 'want [what] is important to you?' Whilst Aidan (8–9 years) suggested, 'what is meaningful to you? Where is your special place?' … Class 6's teacher … stated that this programme may help develop a 'rounder child, it's them thinking deeper and thinking about themselves and thinking about the things that matter to them; it is really important'. *(Ng 2012, p. 174)*

Some people criticize the more meditative and 'quiet' lessons in spirituality as being self-indulgent or not engaged with the external world. Interestingly, although Ng found a great deal of self-reflection, the pupils often used this to gain an insight into the 'outside' world:

> Angie (8–9 years) stated that her favourite lesson was the 'silent time because it was intresting [interesting] to fin[d] out about what was going on around me'. She explained that 'I've learnt that if you just stop for a minute you can find out so much about what's around you'. Furthermore, Callum (7–8 years) also revealed that after the lessons he feels … 'as smart as my grandpa' … [because] 'now I know I don't have to open my eyes to see something'. Hence, pupils may have connected with self through partaking in moments of silence and reflection, which may have led to an awareness of not only themselves, but also the environment they inhabit. *(Ng 2012, p. 177)*

The approach to lessons in spiritual (and moral) development by John West-Burnham and Vanessa Huws Jones is intended to 'explore the most elemental human instinct to engage with that which is non-material, timeless and transcends the everyday boundaries of human experience and existence' (West-Burnham and Huws Jones 2007, p. 17). A number of experiences are described, and they provide an 'entitlement' list of twenty experiences every child should have done by the age of 16, including 'roll down a grassy bank', 'hands and feet painting', 'learn magic tricks', 'cuddle a lamb', 'sing in a choir', and 'see the stars at night' (West-Burnham and Huws Jones 2007, p. 104).

An experiential approach to developing spirituality is also recommended by a secular humanist group.

> Across the curriculum, it is possible to offer experiences which promote reflection, self-awareness and personal development, feelings of awe and wonder, a sense of unity with other human beings. First-hand and direct experience is probably best, but video, for example, can bring other people's experiences or the wonders of art and nature into the classroom powerfully and effectively. So can an enthusiastic teacher. *(BHA 2002)*

A church-based organization provides a guide that links spirituality more explicitly to religion, but which includes some similar experiential work. Spiritual development may be promoted in RE by, for example, 'becoming familiar with what "spiritual" means in the religions they study eg use of silence and meditation', 'developing their own beliefs and values', 'appreciating the beauty and order of natural and human made world', 'responding to their world with awe and wonder', 'asking ultimate questions – responding to the challenging experiences of life, death, suffering, goodness, evil and be challenged by the different answers offered by Christianity', and 'being aware of things other than the material and physical' (Chichester Diocesan Board of Education 2006, p. 21). A guide to RE suggests that spiritual development can be developed in the subject through 'discussing and reflecting on key questions of meaning and truth such as the origins of the universe, life after death, good and evil, beliefs about God and values such as justice, honesty and truth', 'valuing relationships and developing a sense of belonging', and 'developing their own views and ideas on religious and spiritual issues' (QCA 2004, p. 14). This is a noticeably less 'experiential' approach to spiritual development.

Understanding religious and non-religious ways of life through experience is in contrast to those who see religions as entirely 'cognitive', a set of beliefs about the world and the sacred, a set of 'worldviews'. Of course religions include beliefs, and these beliefs may fit together into a comprehensive philosophical system. I have many friends and colleagues around the world who spend their careers working on these systems, and I spend much of my own time doing the same. But understanding religion or religions is, for me, *also* about understanding how people live. And when I meet people with limited cognitive skills, children with profound learning difficulties, or adults with advanced forms of dementia, I still think that their particular ways of living are significant and of value – and captured within the framework of religious and non-religious approaches. John Gillibrand produced a moving account of his life in the church (as an ordained minister) with a non-verbal autistic son, Adam (Gillibrand 2010). It is a piece of theological, philosophical, and political research, and not simply biographical. At times, the father can only be silent:

> My reliance is upon silence. I find that in times of silence I am living most in solidarity with Adam, in his largely non-verbal world. That is where I want to be, where I long to be. ... Silence does justice to the simultaneous peace and pain

of the truly appalling. In silence, we stand at the boundary of the sacred and the secular. *(Gillibrand 2010, p. 66)*

Gillibrand refers to the 'absolute priority of care and kindness, indeed of love, over all things, and over all other values' (Gillibrand 2010, p. 51). Olivia Bustion interprets Gillibrand's work in a different way, as an example of academic theologians who have 'projected their own fantasies onto their nonspeaking autistic children, turning them into symbols of divine ineffability' (Bustion 2017, p. 2). I am not convinced that Gillibrand is merely 'projecting', although there is always that risk of that in anyone's account of another person, especially a person who can't 'answer back'. In my view, at the very least, Adam Gillibrand has helped his father describe what it means to be at the border of personhood. He may also have helped his father and the rest of us to explore the limits of and opportunities for dialogue. So experiential learning in RE and as a form of spiritual development can – even for (*especially* for) philosophers like me – help us better grasp religious and non-religious ways of life.

To use a word of Anne Pirrie (in Stern 2016, pp. 71–72), it is the *livingness* of schools that experiential work can both capture and exemplify. Rachael Kessler writes of 'the soul of education' in a way that – unusually – was seen as acceptable for community schools in the United States (Kessler 2000, published by the leading American professional learning body for teachers). Hers is a clearly relational view of spirituality, and she provides professional guidance for developing schools, with a seven-point guide. There are seven 'gateways' to the soul in education: 'the yearning for deep connection ... the longing for silence and solitude ... the search for meaning and purpose ... the hunger for joy and delight ... the creative drive ... the urge for transcendence ... [and] the need for initiation' (Kessler 2000, p. 17). She expands each of these seven, and I will mention her description of transcendence:

The urge for transcendence describes the desire of young people to go beyond their perceived limits. It includes not only the mystical realm, but experiences of the extraordinary in the arts, athletics, or human relations. By naming and honoring this universal human need, educators can help students constructively channel this powerful urge. *(Kessler 2000, p. 17)*

Throughout her book, Kessler provides examples of how to create each of these 'gateways' and further explanation of what they mean. In the same tradition is a teachers' guide written by Linda Lantieri. For her, in a 'school of spirit',

[t]he uniqueness and inherent value of every individual would be honored, and education would be seen as a lifelong process ... [s]chool leaders would shift from a centralized concept of power to approaches that help individuals and groups to self-organize ... [w]e would enlarge our ability to put to use our gifts of intuition, imagination, and creativity ... [t]here would be places and time for silence and stillness, to help us face the chaos and complexity of school life yet stay in touch with inner truth and the web of interconnectedness ... [and w]e would pay as

much attention to whether a student knows his or her unique purpose in life as we do to his or her SAT scores. *(Lantieri 2001, pp. 8–9)*

In promoting spiritual development, then, there is a balance of activity and contemplation, music and silence, thinking through big issues and focusing on the here and now. As the Hindu scriptures describe it,

For the sage who would climb [the heights of] spiritual exercise (*yoga*),
Works are said to be the means;
But for that same sage who has reached that peak
They say quiescence is the means. *(Zaehner 1992, p. 344, original parentheses)*

The research activity I recommend with this section comes out of my own work on spirituality. Describing spirituality (in the quotation earlier in this chapter), I then worked out six questions that would bring out each element of the description. These questions are who do you bring in, how do you treat people as ends in themselves, in what ways are you magnanimous, how do you enable friendship to thrive, are you in dialogue, and how do you take part in creating meanings, things, and people? The first four questions are focused on community, with the fifth and sixth being about dialogue and learning, respectively. Each can be applied to any aspect of schooling, and I have applied them, for example, to the use of computers and to the process of assessment. It is the latter that I present in the activity (taken from Stern and Backhouse 2011). Researching written assessment feedback – the ticks and comments that teachers put on pupils work – is very rarely done, yet it illuminates what is one of the most personal, individual, interactions between a teacher and a pupil.

Activity 8.2: The spirit of assessment

Find a sample of pupils' work in RE that has been marked by you. (If colleagues agree, it is good to use samples of work from several teachers, and it is also useful to compare marking in RE to marking in another subject.) Try to find examples that are both positive and negative responses to each of the six questions. For example, a positive example of teacher comments to the question 'Who do you bring in?' might be 'It would be good to know what someone from a different religion thought about this.' A negative example might be 'Why couldn't you write as well as your sister?'

There are fuller examples, and further explanations of the six questions, in Stern and Backhouse (2011), in my chapter in Franck (2017), and in Stern (2009a). In the article and chapter, the activity (suitably adapted) was also completed by pupils.

Writing these down can provide a good analysis of the quality of the dialogue teachers are having with pupils. For those – like me – who see relationality as central to spirituality, analysing written assessment feedback can help us understand how spirituality can be developed through assessment feedback – an aspect of schooling that is all too often regarded as 'soulless'.

Question	Positive examples		Negative examples	What could have been improved?
1 Who do you bring in in assessing pupils' RE work?				
2 How do you treat people as ends in themselves in assessing pupils' RE work?				
3 In what ways are you magnanimous in assessing pupils' RE work?				
4 How do you enable friendship to thrive in assessing pupils' RE work?				
5 Are you in dialogue in assessing pupils' RE work?	Real dialogue	Technical dialogue (information)	Monologue disguised as dialogue	
6 How do you take part in creating meanings, things, and people in assessing pupils' RE work?				

Conclusion

Spirituality is difficult to define or describe, difficult to research, and difficult to develop in schools. It is no less important for all those difficulties, and if RE avoids teaching about, and supporting, spirituality, it is unlikely to appear anywhere else on the curriculum. In the UK – where spiritual development is required of all schools – all subjects and other activities can and should contribute to spiritual development. But ignoring the histories of spiritual practices in religious traditions, or ignoring spirituality when teaching about religion, is inexcusable. And in recent years, at least, there has been a flourishing of research on spirituality. Two journals, the *International Journal of Children's Spirituality* and the *Journal for the Study of*

Spirituality, have a great deal of material from education and, in the second case, also from other professional contexts such as health and social work. And some people find spirituality a much simpler idea. Here are the words of the thirteenth-century Muslim poet Rumi (from Rumi 1995, p. 136):

> If anyone wants to know what 'spirit' is,
> or what 'God's fragrance' means,
> lean your head toward him or her.
> Keep your face there close.
> *Like this.*

Chapter 9
Ethnographic Research in Communities

They see us in a very funny way!
(Interview response of a young British Muslim)

Introduction

RE research is embedded in the everyday work of schools, and so ethnographic research in RE is interesting. Ethnography has at its heart the need to understand not only the people being studied, on their own terms, but also the researchers completing the study, and the relationships between researchers and researched. This chapter builds on the excellent ethnographic work in religious studies, over many years, and how it has been applied in school-based RE. And it also builds on the tradition of ethnographic research described by Jean Lave. Lave is well known for describing how people typically learn in a kind of 'apprenticeship' way as 'legitimate peripheral participation', in contrast to how schools usually work with formal 'instruction' (as in Lave and Wenger 1991). Her ethnographic research began with apprentice tailors in Liberia in West Africa. Amongst the many influences of that early research was Lave's reconsideration of the nature of research. People think of an apprentice as 'someone who doesn't know, learning from someone who does' (Lave 2011, p. 156, quoting Goody).

> From a relational perspective, I would now say, quite to the contrary, that we are all apprentices, engaged in learning to do what we are already doing. The differences between these two definitions are significant. To begin with, the distinction between one who knows and one who doesn't invokes the binary comparative theory and its epistemological politics. More interestingly, to *learn* to do what you are already doing is a contradiction in term; it implies that there is always more than one relation of knowing and doing in play – knowing and not knowing, doing and undoing, understanding theoretically but not empirically

and vice versa, starting from both ends of processes of production and coming together in the middle in (relational, concrete) ways that transform conceptions of the ends. It surely implies that apprenticeship is a process of *changing* practice. … Such relations also characterize research practice. … [W]hat we have been doing is … becoming apprentices to our own future practice. *(Lave 2011, p. 156)*

This sees researchers as always *apprentice* researchers, learning from the practice of research and changing the practice through engagement with it. And the same can be true of teachers: always *apprentice* teachers, however long we've been doing it, always learning and changing the practice through engagement. Lave's approach makes sense of the idea that all teachers are learners, just as pupils are learners, and all teachers and pupils can also therefore be seen as *researchers*. Such an approach to ethnographic research therefore underpins the philosophy of 'researchers in the classroom' (the subtitle of the book you are reading).

What connects just about all of the RE research in this book is how embedded research is in the everyday work of schools, and how sensitive research must be to the relationships and the ways of life that make up the whole school community. It is fitting, then, to have a chapter on ethnographic research in RE, as ethnography has at its heart the need to understand not only the people being studied, on their own terms, but also the researchers completing the study, and the relationships between researchers and the researched, as said above. It is not simply that we can have an 'ethnographic approach to life', attempting to understand people and communicate this understanding sensitively to others. It is that the ethnographic researcher is not, and should not attempt to be, a separate, impersonal, and neutral observer of life, looking at 'interesting objects of study'. Buber (1958) describes two forms of communication. A person can treat the other as an object, as 'it', or can treat the other as a subject, as 'thou'. Buber's contrast between 'I-it' and 'I-thou' relationships is used to understand people and to understand social and political structures. His is a good basis for the work of this book, as it also applies to teachers, pupils, and researchers, most especially ethnographic researchers.

Ethnography, pluralism, and RE

Since the early days of anthropology, ethnographers have dealt with the complex issues of understanding people who live in very different ways from that of the researcher. Ethnographers can therefore provide particular help in researching and understanding religion and RE. Many in RE see ethnographic approaches as the most appropriate approach to learning in RE, with Bob Jackson as a leading advocate of this method (e.g. in Jackson 1990). But there is a clue to its RE relevance in the etymology of the very word 'ethnography'. 'Ethnography' is derived from 'people-writing' or 'people-drawing', with 'people' perhaps meaning race or nation. So ethnography is related to ethnology (e.g. investigating tea ceremonies), and to anthropology, which in the past often involved investigating isolated and pre-literate communities, though it later developed into social anthropology often in urban settings. 'Ethnography' refers to immersive fieldwork in a real or a virtual community, and to the report of the fieldwork, which may be in print or a documentary or a film. It is an empirical study consisting largely of more-or-less participant observation, and semi-structured or unstructured interviewing allowing the interviewee some 'agency'.

This issue of agency is an important ethical and political issue. One of the leading ethnographic researchers working in RE is Eleanor Nesbitt, who in one of the Westhill seminars described researching young Hindu homes (reported in Jackson and Nesbitt 1993), and the potential problems of power, of having the power to interpret and use material gained from people. Increasingly, therefore, the subjects of research are being treated as active participants, with some editorial input. Such 'deep listening', and empowering people, can be an attitude to life as well as to research. We can have an 'ethnographic' approach to life, although we can also choose to reject that, as people and as researchers. The aims of ethnography are to understand human behaviour at ever-increasing depth, from the point of view of those studied, and to communicate this deepening understanding sensitively to others. When ethnographic research is completed for RE, as it is by Nesbitt and others at the Warwick Religions & Education Research Unit (*www2.warwick.ac.uk/ fac/soc/ces/research/wreru/*), there are therefore many benefits to RE teaching and learning, and to research in RE.

It is also, in contrast, important to be aware of some of the dangers of small-scale ethnographic studies. The dangers include the possibility of being superficial (simply looking for 'easy to see' characteristics), 'essentialising' an aspect of religion (making something that is incidental into something that is central to the religious life), homogenizing a 'religion' (assuming all those of a religion are like the people studied), or creating artificial boundaries between religions (by making differences between individuals into universal differences). A simple example given by Nesbitt was her self-questioning when studying Hindu children, asking why she was picking out the child's use of a *puja* corner to describe her life at home, whilst ignoring the child spending time watching soap operas on the television. A classroom example of my own is of a group of children watching a video of a Muslim wedding in Bangladesh, the wedding of family members of one of the classes. When the class was asked to say what they had learned from watching the video, the most striking 'lesson' was described by one pupil (not from Bangladesh), who said with real surprise in his voice, 'I'd no idea they had mopeds in Bangladesh!' Some of the advantages and challenges of the ethnographic study of religion are analysed and exemplified in the work of various writers, including Nesbitt (especially Nesbitt 2004, and other related work in Jackson and Nesbitt 1993; Nesbitt and Kaur 1998; Nesbitt 2001, 2003, 2005), Searle-Chatterjee (1997, 2000), Ballard (1994), Baumann (1996, 1999), and Geaves (Geaves 1998, and see also Geaves et al. 2004).

Ron Geaves himself presented in one of the Westhill seminars, and talked to the challenge of 'borderlessness' in religious traditions, making lived religions quite different to 'textbook' versions of religions, and making ethnographic research all the more important. His is an approach that is engaged: there is encounter in research, along with reciprocity and dialogue, and these qualities are of social as well as academic value.

Ethnography, pluralism, and RE all interconnect. Geir Skeie (1995) talks about pluralism as a commitment to an affirmative response to diversity or plurality. Plurality is a significant aspect of post- or late modernity, while pluralism is our response to this, according to Skeie. And there is an acknowledgement of religious and cultural plurality, which has driven much recent RE. Intercultural education, as exemplified in Nesbitt's book (Nesbitt 2004), is a phrase used more in French than in English, with 'intercultural' helpfully bypassing some of the conflict between multicultural and anti-racist movements. This can therefore connect the study of religion (as in Sutcliffe 2004) and RE. We should ask ourselves whether we, in universities or schools, can be more like ethnographers in how we work and teach and interact in schools. This is relevant to the whole school ethos, not just to RE. It may boil down to something pretty close to 'respect'.

Activity 9.1: Respect map

Pupils as researchers can construct a 'respect map' of their own school.

If work in RE has included how people identify themselves as, for example, an atheist, a Buddhist, a Christian, a Hindu, a Jew, a Humanist, a Muslim, a New Age follower, or a Sikh, pupils (in pairs or small groups) could become researchers concerned with one of those 'labels'. The questions and topics described by Nesbitt ('guidelines for teachers', Nesbitt 2004, pp. 154–166) may be helpful as preparation for pupils and teachers alike, as would her subtle analysis of identity (Nesbitt 2004, chapter 10).

Each group should be given a map of the school, with the rooms appropriately labelled with what subjects or activities they host. The pupils should interview other pupils and staff, asking about where in the school 'atheists' (or whichever group is being studied) would be most respected, and why. For example, pupils might say that 'atheists' are most respected in science laboratories, and in the staff room, or that Jews are most respected in RE rooms and in English rooms.

The analysis of the respect maps of members of all the groups can provide a subtle picture of the social organization of the school, how different subjects and activities of the school are regarded by pupils, and how much pupils understand about these issues.

Other 'respect maps' can be completed for boys and girls, or for members of different social groups. The value, for RE, of starting with those self-identified with religious categories is that it can provide a basis for much further RE, clearly connected to the lives of the pupils as lived in their own school.

Ethnography, Muslim diversity, and RE

Using ethnography can not only help teachers and pupils to understand the people being studied, it can also help researchers to see how they in turn are understood by those studied. This is particularly well illustrated by the research Sarah Smalley discussed in a Westhill seminar (Grove and Smalley 2003; Smalley 2005), on teaching about and learning from Muslims, in part in order to understand Islamophobia in the classroom. Smalley completed ethnographic work with two Muslim communities in the English town of Peterborough, and it is worth describing some of the processes of that research, as an example of some of the opportunities for ethnographic research with clear implications for RE.

Peterborough had two distinct Muslim communities, representing a huge diversity in terms of ethnicity, language, reasons for being in Britain, religion, and of course individual, personal, differences. There were interviews with twenty-four parents and further research with their children, with the sample coming from each of the two groups. One group was from Pakistani background families who were mostly labour migrants, Sunni Muslims, from a rural background and with varied educational backgrounds. These interviewees mostly had an expectation of marrying and doing business with other British people from Pakistani backgrounds. The second group were from African Asian background families, originally refugees, Shi'a Muslims (Khoja Shi'a Ithna'asheri), with urban backgrounds. They mostly had an expectation of marrying and doing business with a wide range of people from Britain, East Africa, India, Canada, the United States, and Dubai. Smalley looked across two generations: How did parents bring up children and how did this compare with how they were brought up? It is helpful to describe some examples of research findings, along with their implications for RE. As one respondent said, 'They see us in a very funny way!'.

One piece of research involved participant observation at a mosque during *Muharram* (related to the death of Hussein, the grandson of the Prophet), stressing suffering and martyrdom and moral issues for the contemporary world such as remorse and mercy. Preaching on one occasion was by a woman on the theme of Islam as 'all or nothing', on the death of Hussein, with breast-beating and, later, cheerful socializing. Later preaching also involved the congregation being drawn 'to a pitch of frenzied weeping', which 'ended as quickly as it had begun'.

For teaching RE content authentically, this work would bring to life characteristics of Sunni and Shi'a Islam. It could also help teachers to convey something of the power and purpose of ritual, thus providing a more accessible view of what might otherwise seem inexplicable. It could provide RE with a view of the practice and experience of women and girls (which is not always easily available), and connections with the expressions of remorse in other traditions (such as Good Friday processions in Southern Europe). In terms of the process of RE, this work would provide a way of recording and communicating religion, and an insight into how this experience fits into a bigger picture and tensions between different experiences within a tradition.

A second theme of Smalley's research involved interviewing Muslim women about the *hijab*. Texts on research methods (such as Cohen et al. 2011) point out many of the difficulties of completing interviews, including problems with leading questions and with confidentiality. Researchers are divided over the advantages of being 'insiders' and 'outsiders' (with a superb set of articles on the topic in McCutcheon 1999). Smalley helped create a 'connection' with the interviewees by talking as a parent, herself. Responses to talking about *hijab* varied widely, itself an important lesson for anyone wishing to teach 'the right answer' (or scared of presenting 'the wrong answer') on such issues. One respondent said, 'I just feel more comfortable in it now – I feel more confident'; others talked about the importance of inward goodness not (just) outward appearances, others about only doing things when they are understood (for the right reasons). However, such paraphrasing of the accounts takes away from their power and interest. The full accounts, and, even more, being involved in the interviews themselves, provide a much better sense of the individual life stories behind each decision.

Learning from home environments is a third theme of Smalley's research. This involved visits to homes in order to complete interviews, but the visits themselves provided further insights. For example, the pictures on the walls and the position of books around rooms all contributed to children's informal learning about Islam. The interviews took place, often, with children in other rooms or sitting with the mother, food being offered, and questions about schooling such as difficulties over homework. These 'ambient' characteristics, which could have been seen as distractions from the purpose of the interview, in fact helped retain a focus on people rather than on edicts and doctrines, and helped stress how people negotiate everyday life.

For RE, then, it is important to understand the variety of experience that children from different backgrounds bring to a diverse school. Overall, the qualitative fieldwork, according to Smalley, 'gives polyphonic depth and richness – we hear many voices'. Ethnographic research can add *authenticity* to RE, and can add personal – but not institutional – *authority* to RE. Smalley points out that this is no simple matter, as authenticity may not be 'positive' in the way many RE teachers would expect. In Smalley 2005, the question is asked: 'How can we be positive but realistic?', which is an extension of the same problem. It takes the argument back to the issues raised in Chapter 3, and elsewhere in this book, on controversy in RE: RE must be a gritty subject, and must not be a bland diet of 'niceness'. For Smalley, the answer to the question is in multiple views (i.e. seeing examples from the whole range of all traditions) and in active involvement (i.e. through ethnographic research and through dialogue within RE classrooms).

The following activity helps guide a piece of what might be called 'reverse ethnography'. As 'ethnography' has already been described as deriving etymologically from 'people-writing' or 'people-drawing', here is an attempt at the reverse: an attempt to 'draw with people'.

Activity 9.2: Reverse ethnography: Drawing with people

Most pupils and adults are familiar with 'photo-stories', where a kind of strip cartoon is not drawn but made up using a series of posed photographs. They have been popular in newspapers and magazines and have been often used to illustrate social and moral problems or dilemmas.

Pupils can create their own photostories. Such an activity has been made considerably easier in recent years, with the emergence of electronic photography and cameras on phones and the ease of editing pictures and text with the simplest of word processors.

Working in groups of four to six pupils, the pupils should be given a particular issue or dilemma related to their RE lesson topic and be asked to create a twelve-photo photostory to illustrate that issue. They will need to pose for, as well as photograph, the twelve scenes: hence, 'drawing with people'. They will also need to write the captions to each of the twelve scenes.

An example of a topic, related to Smalley's research, could be a discussion in a Muslim family about *hijab*.

Pupils creating photostories are often motivated by the task itself, as well as the topic. Further motivation might be added by an expectation that the photostories would be used to teach the topic to other pupils in the school.

Conclusion

Ethnographic research is by its nature small-scale research, developing complex accounts of the everyday lives of people rather than generalized accounts of society as a whole. It is the sharing of ethnographic accounts, the communication between ethnographic researchers, that can build up our understanding beyond that of the initial subjects of the study. The following activity should help spread the word about ethnographic research and allow teachers and pupils to share their experiences. Schools should consider the ethics of what material is appropriate to put on intranet or internet sites, and the consideration of online ethics is itself a valuable contribution to understanding RE and to understanding research.

Activity 9.3: Blogging for RE

If a class or an RE department wants to demonstrate the value of its research, they may be able to develop a class blog. Standard sites include Facebook and Twitter, and for more conventional blogs, there are programmes such as WordPress.

A class could create a blog for RE, accessible to other classes in that school. The ethics of presenting research in this way should be discussed with the class and with those having a responsibility for the school's Web policy (with general research ethics available from Cohen et al. 2011).

The blog may helpfully start with reports on ethnographic research as described in this chapter, and might also move on to include reports on other work based on the various activities described in earlier chapters of this book, reports on visits to religious and other communities, and reports on visits from such communities – perhaps including answers to questions posed by pupils. It might also include work by local students of religion, members of local organizations, and accounts of religious and other celebrations.

Chapter 10
Thinking About Philosophy, Truth, and RE

The child who 'saw' besought the gift to be taken from him and his vision to be restricted to a narrower span.
(Martin Buber)

Introduction

Religion and philosophy have similar arguments as religion and spirituality. Some see academic philosophy as just one tradition of beliefs/practices amongst many others (including religious traditions); others see philosophy and religion as wholly separate ways of looking at the world. Some schools teach RE and not philosophy, some philosophy but not RE. Some see philosophy as implemented across the curriculum (like spiritual development), whilst religion is a distinct subject. And one of the contentious concepts in both philosophy and RE is that of 'truth'. If aiming for the truth is seen as 'normal' elsewhere in the school, why shouldn't it be central to RE? But is there a 'truth' to be found, or is it all relative? It would be foolhardy to promise a comprehensive guide to all these issues in a single book, never mind a single chapter. But I hope to provide a guide to some of the important or high-profile aspects of the topic, how researchers have tackled the topic, and how research by teachers and pupils can help us understand even more.

I would like to start, though, with an odd experience. A group of RE specialists have recently been working on 'big ideas in RE', and I was a member of the group. (As I write, the results of the discussions are being finalized, to be published as Wintersgill 2017.) The initiative follows similar work in science, geography, history, and a number of other subjects. What are the big ideas that are fundamental to the subject that should be the basis for choosing the curriculum content to teach in school? Chairing the meetings was Michael Reiss, a distinguished science educator who was involved in the development of the 'big ideas in science' (Harlen 2010, 2015). At one point, the group was considering issues of truth in RE, and how difficult it was to deal with the presence of conflicting truth statements in RE (there is or there isn't a god, Jesus is or isn't the son of God, when we die we are or are not reincarnated). Most RE teachers have been asked by a pupil, 'Yes, but is it *true*?' Most RE teachers dodge that question with a response like 'Many people *believe* it is true.' There is a tension in RE between conflicting truths (there is a great deal of fundamental disagreement between – and within – religious traditions), and the wish to say, 'Let's not worry about truth for now, and try to understand what different people believe' (the epoché, or suspension of disbelief, of phenomenological research). A more extreme version of that tension is between those who believe there is one truth that should be promoted in RE (and all other views must be described as incorrect) and those who believe there is no such thing as absolute truth ('this is not a matter of true or false') and that all positions are equally valid. Truth, in other words, divides RE teachers. When the 'big ideas in RE' group raised this issue, what did Reiss say? He drew our attention to the 'big ideas in science' and explained that, in the science documents, there was no mention at all of 'truth'. I was surprised.

Here is a description of what science does:

> A scientific theory or model representing relationships between variables or components of a system must fit the observations available at the time and lead to predictions that can be tested. Any theory or model is provisional and subject to revision in the light of new data even though it may have led to predictions in accord with data in the past. Every model has its strengths and limitations in accounting for observations. *(Harlen 2010, p. 23)*

Even more straightforward is the statement that '[s]cientific explanations, theories and models are those that best fit the evidence available at a particular time' (Harlen 2015, p. 17). The word 'truth' is not mentioned: scientists are not trading in truths, but in 'best fits' to the available evidence. Ironically, it seems to me that it may be that RE is more concerned than science is with the role of truth in the curriculum. There are other approaches to science, no doubt. The philosopher Bertrand Russell provides a good description of a more 'traditional' view of science, alongside a 'traditional' view of religion:

> Philosophy ... is something intermediate between theology and science. Like theology, it consists of speculations on matters as to which definite knowledge has, so far, been unascertainable; but like science, it appeals to human reason rather than to authority, whether that of tradition or that of revelation. All *definite* knowledge ... belongs to science; all *dogma* as to what surpasses definite knowledge belongs to theology. But between theology and science there is a No Man's Land, exposed to attack from both sides; this No Man's Land is philosophy. *(Russell 1961, p. 13)*

But Russell's views do not sit well with those of many other writers on science – or with many other writers on religion. (Having met many theologians and many philosophers, I find that the former are no less full of certainties than the latter.)

On science, I should have realized the 'problem' of the lack of truth before Reiss pointed it out, having worked for several years with Alex Sinclair, a UK science educator at St Mary's University, London, who researches the 'messy' nature of real science. Pupils should be taught about 'famous scientists', not least because most of their discoveries and theories have since then been disproven or superseded. As physicist Richard Feynman says, 'I would rather have questions that can't be answered than answers that can't be questioned' (quoted in Sinclair and Strachan 2016, p. 21). Science education therefore seems just as messy as religious education. The similarities are stressed by the philosopher of science Karl Popper.

> My thesis is that what we call 'science' is differentiated from the older myths not by being something distinct from a myth, but by being accompanied by a second-order tradition – that of critically discussing the myth. ... If we understand that, then ... [w]e shall understand that, in a certain sense, science is myth-making just as religion is. *(Popper 2002, pp. 170–171)*

In response, many RE specialists will say that there is also a very strong tradition of 'critical discussion' within religions and within RE.

Is it a comfort to know that science is as messy as RE? For me, it is, as – from within the RE community – it is easy to feel that our subject is the awkward child of the curriculum, much loved but with a range of additional needs. Instead, RE can be seen as having all kinds of needs, but with most of those needs shared with other subjects on the curriculum. This chapter will explore the relationships between philosophy and truth in RE and how philosophical methods can be used in RE. I hope that this chapter, and this whole book, will meet some of RE's needs – and help RE teachers see themselves as central to pupils' lives and their education.

Where is philosophy and truth in RE?

RE tackles topics common to philosophy – issues of what might exist (ontology), how we can know things (epistemology), and how to live good lives (ethics). And one of the first and still one of the liveliest arguments in RE is the argument over truth. Truth-troubling in RE became particularly lively in the UK with the development of multi-religious RE. It is Ninian Smart who is most often credited with developing this approach, both in school-based RE and in supporting the growth of 'religious studies', in contrast to traditional theology, in universities. Smart was certainly not the first academic to value teaching about a range of the world's religions. In the early nineteenth century, the German philosopher Hegel lectured on world religions, as did his contemporary the theologian Schleiermacher, and his lecture notes (Hegel 1988) stand up surprisingly well when compared to current RE texts. (Hegel had been a schoolteacher, and had taught RE, in his earlier years.) But Smart was a hugely influential figure in the late twentieth century and developed what is now known as a 'phenomenological' approach to RE. This tried to understand religious traditions from the insider's perspective, developing an empathic approach that required a temporary suspension of the enquirer's own beliefs, a suspension of disbelief or 'epoché'. If the suspension of disbelief became permanent, then this might lead to a relativist position, in which no particular truths were ever held to, and all had equal weight. The fear of such an outcome has led some to reject Smart's approach, and certainly some practices in RE – a sort of 'tour of religions' in the style of a travelogue – might indeed lead to such outcomes.

Smart himself did not intend any of this weak relativism. As described in Chapter 2, he saw openness to dialogues as central to a commitment to truth. For Smart, learning about a range of religions – and non-religious ways of life – is a way of keeping truth alive. A similar point is made by Jeff Astley when talking about confessional religious nurture within a particular tradition: 'in my experience it is helpful for members of a particular religion to gain some sense of how another faith might also seem to be salvific, because discovering more about the commitments of others can help you to understand better your own embraces' (Astley, in Astley et al. 2012, p. 257). If the epoché is permanent, then relativism becomes a problem, but this would mean only following the first half of what Smart recommends. In the introduction to his account of religions around the world, he says,

> The intention is to describe, rather than to pass judgment, on the phenomena of religion. The intention is not to speak on behalf of one faith or to argue for the truth of one or all religions or of none. Our first need is to understand. The result, I hope, will be that the reader will be in a better position to judge wisely about religious truth. *(Smart 1969, p. 12)*

If the first task is a suspension of disbelief, the second task is to make wise judgements. One of his final books was an account of 'world philosophies' (Smart 1999). This put different religious, cultural, and recognized academic philosophies into a single account. South Asian philosophies, Islamic philosophies, and Jewish philosophies sit alongside European and North American philosophies. It is the latter two groups that form what most students of philosophy (in the UK and perhaps around the world) think of as 'philosophy'. For me it was shocking to see 'Western philosophy' being accounted for in just two out of sixteen chapters, in this account of the world's philosophies. A good shock, though, as I realized how parochial the professional philosophy I had studied at university had been. Another good reason to see 'how to understand things' as embracing both (professional, 'Western') philosophy and religion and other traditions around the world.

This is not to underestimate the challenge of teaching RE in such a way that truth retains a place in the curriculum. Andrew Wright has argued for a long time that RE should be centred on wrestling with truth claims of religions, in order to be enabled to live more 'truthfully' and in harmony with the ultimate order of things. Like Smart, Wright is hoping for more 'wise judgements' – or, as he describes it, 'judgemental rationality' – with respect to religion. This is the 'religious literacy' that he promotes through 'critical realism' – the idea that there is a reality 'out there' to be explored, that we have limited understanding of it, and that we should argue well about it. Enjoying the process of arguing as I do (and that is what drew me to study philosophy in the first place), I appreciate Wright's promotion of rational argument as important to pupils. It links his views to those promoting 'philosophy for children' (addressed later in this chapter), and provides a good counter-balance to the RE which involves little more than lighting a candle and telling stories with a moral. But seeing RE – or seeing religions – as dominated by the former, rather than balancing cognitive and 'philosophical' elements with experience and empathy and what Astley (himself a critical realist) describes as the 'embrace' of religion (Astley, in Astley et al. 2012), may risk impoverishing RE.

A second problem with centring RE on the 'ultimate truths' within religion is identifying what ultimate truths are associated with what religion. This is not a problem of finding a good enough encyclopaedia of religion, but of finding sufficient agreement within any religious tradition. The history of religions has been the history of arguments over 'truths', which elements are more literally or figuratively true, how those truths are to be interpreted, and so on. Arguments over the inerrancy of religious texts, the authority of interpretations, the implications of truths – all are lively and continuing, in theology and religious studies departments and, even more importantly, in churches, mosques, synagogues, temples, and communities around the world. This is not saying that we should give up on truth, as though the 'religious truth' committee has simply not reported back yet. It is saying that RE teachers can no more supply pupils with a set of authoritative religious truths to argue over than they can supply a set of inerrant scientific truths. Truth is bigger than the people arguing about it (and in this I certainly agree with Wright) and is being argued over (again, we agree). As Wright says,

> [I]n all but the most fundamentalist of environments – and I include here both religious and secular fundamentalisms – the learning community will tend to accept some degree of human fallibility, and hence be driven by a desire to establish a deeper and more truthful understanding of reality. One of the tasks of religious education, whether confessional or liberal, is to provide the time, space and resources necessary to guide pupils as they embark on their own pursuit of truth and striving for spiritual authenticity. (Wright 2005, p. 11)

Going back to Smart's early book: Is this a matter of rational argument alone, or is the importance of being able to be in *dialogue* important? Rupert Wegerif (2008) writes of the difference between *dialectical* and *dialogic* approaches to education. In a dialectical approach, there is a movement towards a conclusion, like the vote at the end of a debate or the verdict at the end of a trial. In a more dialogic approach, the participants talk and listen and different positions may emerge, but there may be no final point of decision or conclusion. 'Truth', says Friedman, 'is not born from dialectic in the head of an individual person but 'between people collectively searching for truth, in the process of their dialogic interaction' (Friedman, quoting

Bakhtin, Friedman 2002, p. 361). Smart's approach is, I think, more dialogical, and Wright's more dialectical. I would hesitate to decide between living in dialogue and living truthfully as an educational aim for RE, but I would probably say that there is more need for genuine dialogue (with or without a definite conclusion) than there is for a set of conclusions (with or without dialogue).

That's the problem with Wright: he makes people want to argue for or against his views! He has certainly worked in recent years to implement a critical realist approach to RE in schools. One of his research students, Angela Goodman, has researched the implementation of this work for pupils aged 11–12 (Goodman 2016), and she suggests that 'CRE [critical RE] is being implemented in RE departments, albeit gradually, and that this is producing some very fruitful results' (Goodman 2016, p. 9). Other approaches, more dialogic in the style of Smart's dialogue, include those based on hospitality. Luke Bretherton, writing as a Christian theologian, talks of hospitality as a way of achieving 'commensurability' across religious and other divisions, and as being more important than simply being confident in your own truth (Bretherton 2006). He bases his approach on that of the philosopher Alasdair MacIntyre, and his approach – welcoming people from other religious positions and attempting to talk intelligently with them – is not dissimilar to the position of Jonathan Sacks, former chief rabbi. Sacks writes of the *dignity of difference*, in his account of how people can live together with all their differences:

> Often, when religious leaders meet and talk, the emphasis is on similarities and commonalities, as if the differences between faiths were superficial and trivial. . . . [But w]e need . . . not only a theology of commonality – of the universals of mankind – but also a theology of difference: why no one civilization has the right to impose itself on others by force: why God asks us to respect the freedom and dignity of those not like us.
>
> The dignity of difference is more than a religious idea. . . . The world is not a single machine. It is a complex, interactive ecology in which diversity – biological, personal, cultural and religious – is of the essence. Any proposed reduction of that diversity through the many forms of fundamentalism that exist today – market, scientific or religious – would result in a diminution of the rich texture of our shared life, a potentially disastrous narrowing of the horizons of possibility.
> *(Sacks 2003, pp. 21–22)*

For Bretherton and Sacks, both confident in the ultimate truths of their own religious traditions, the important quality is that of being able to communicate with dignity with people who are themselves more or less confident in their own, different, ultimate truths. Applying this to RE, Durka gives an eloquent account of hospitality in practice:

> When we regard teaching as a 'dance' between the knowers and the material, it is easier to rethink our own roles. First, it becomes clearer that we are to create a space in which truth is neither suppressed nor merely accepted. The focus is not

on instant answers but rather on adventure, wrestling with untruth, silence and listening. Palmer calls this atmosphere *hospitality*. *(Durka 2002, p. 18.)*

If truth is already 'out there' to be described and memorized by the pupils, then there is a danger that schools would be living in the past. If truth emerges over time, in dialogue, then schools are living in the present – and preparing for the future. John Hick says that 'religion is concerned, not primarily with ideas and propositions, but with life itself – with the concrete character and quality of our experience and activity' (Hick, in Hick 1974, p. 144). His is certainly a dynamic, future-directed, view of a 'dialogue into truth': '[w]e live amidst unfinished business; but we must trust that continuing dialogue will prove to be dialogue into truth, and that in a fuller grasp of truth our present conflicting doctrines will ultimately be transcended' (Hick, in Hick 1974, pp. 140 and 155).

How can teachers and pupils be researching such big topics as 'the truth' in RE? Here is an activity that can be collectively, dialogically, researched.

Activity 10.1: Truly, madly, deeply

RE cannot avoid topics common to philosophy – issues of what might exist (ontology) and how we can know things (epistemology). It certainly cannot avoid controversies over truth, and every RE teacher will have been asked, many times, 'Yes, but is it *true*?' Researchers argue about these issues, and the arguments are good for RE lessons, too.

If people are in love, they may describe themselves as 'truly, madly, deeply' in love. (The words also form the title of a 1990 film, and a song by Savage Garden.) The 'truly' in the phrase indicates the idea that this is genuine, not fake, love; 'madly' in this context means passionately, with great feeling; 'deeply' means that there is something comprehensive about the love – it is complete and not temporary or partial. True love may have all of these characteristics. Much of what has been said about truth (including in the quotations earlier in this chapter) indicates that 'truth' may be more than the absence of falsity or fakeness. Those three ideas, of genuineness, of feeling, and of completeness, are worth exploring as aspects of truth – and worth exploring, especially, in religious contexts.

Whatever topic is being explored in RE, choose one event or object or person. It might be a religious artefact, a festival, a narrative from a sacred text, a revered or divine figure. The best way of choosing a topic is to wait for someone to say, 'Yes, but is it *true*?' But any topic can be chosen.

The task is not to work out whether or not it is 'true', but to work out how to discuss the different dimensions of truth.

Working in pairs, a third of the pupils will discuss (within their pairs) what evidence or other criteria may be used to explore how 'genuine' this event/object/person is: what sort of evidence would be needed and how could it be 'proven' to be genuine and not fake. (It can help if one of each pair is acting as a 'believer' and the other acting as a 'sceptic', but pupils shouldn't be forced into these roles if they are uncomfortable with them.)

Meanwhile, a third of the pupils will discuss (within their pairs) what it would mean to really *feel* like this is important: how would they know if this was really a 'passion' of theirs.

And the third group of pupils will discuss (in pairs) how this event/object/person fits with the rest of the religion or non-religious way of life, how does it 'complete' the rest of the system, and why might it be needed to make sense of the rest of the beliefs.

Now, create groups in which there are representatives of the 'truly', the 'madly', and the 'deeply' groups. Each group should provide an account of how this event/object/person might be thought to be true, overall, and what sort of ideas, feelings, and arguments are relevant to its truth.

What the groups should be able to produce are accounts of how to explore what might be called the 'full truth' of what they are studying, and the experience of discussing and sharing ideas on the nature of truth. It is the long answer to the question, 'Yes, but is it *true?*' Like love, the truth in RE is something more than just a factual thing; it is also felt and fits in a larger or more permanent (or perhaps eternal) system.

Making use of philosophical methods in RE

In addition to trying to understand the nature of truth and the relationship between philosophy and religion, teachers can use philosophical methods in RE. Most famous of these is Matthew Lipman's *Philosophy for Children* or P4C (Lipman 2003), supported in the UK by organizations such as SAPERE (the *Society for the Advancement of Philosophical Enquiry and Reflection in Education, www.sapere.org.uk/*, and see Fisher 2013) and in the United States by organizations such as the IAPC (the *Institute for the Advancement of Philosophy for Children, www.montclair.edu/cehs/ academics/centers-and-institutes/iapc/index.html*). Typically, a group of children will be given a key question or stimulus, and will be asked to discuss it as a 'community of inquiry', supported by the teacher or another facilitator to work together towards an understanding of the issue – with the teacher as an inquirer alongside the children. These are not, in general, lessons *about* philosophy, but lessons that use philosophical techniques to explore an issue. Sometimes the issue is a 'typical' philosophical issue, a thought experiment such as the account by Plutarch of the *Ship of Theseus*: Is a ship the same ship, if every bit of it has been replaced over time, plank by plank? Sometimes the issue is from a current newspaper, or from a modern or traditional children's story. In RE lessons, the use of dilemmas and narratives from religious traditions would be obvious starting points for a 'community of inquiry' activity.

Two things should be said about the various initiatives related to philosophy for children. One is that thoughtful, inquiry-based, carefully argued, and dialogic learning was going on in schools long before it was named 'philosophy for children'.

Even though I trained as a philosopher – well, *because* I trained as a philosopher – I know that philosophers didn't invent, and don't have a monopoly on, thoughtful learning in schools. This means that teachers – especially RE teachers, who can draw on just as long a history of thoughtfulness in religious traditions as philosophers can draw on in philosophical traditions – should not think of philosophy for children as a shiny new 'gimmick' that will, uniquely, transform learning in their schools. Many philosophers involved in philosophy for children say this themselves: the pedagogy is based on Dewey's approach to pragmatic, engaged, learning in schools. It is not, philosophically speaking, something that is particularly new or unusual. A second thing that should be said is that thoughtful inquiry-based, carefully argued, and dialogic learning can happen at any time, in any subject, in school. It should not be a 'party piece' for those odd occasions when everyone can sit around in a circle and do 'one of those puzzles'. Again, this is stressed by philosophers: the idea is to help schools become more thoughtful, and to introduce some techniques that might help. So teachers should not worry about doing a 'patented method' once a week or once a term, and think that is enough to make their schools thoughtful.

Having said all of that, there are many really useful philosophical approaches to teaching difficult issues in RE, and RE teachers who haven't tried them will be missing out. Lat Blaylock, in a Westhill seminar, recommended a set of questions such as 'what is really real, what is the nature of the world around us, what is a human being, what happens when you die, why is it possible to know anything, how do we know what is right or wrong, and what is the purpose of human life?' The teacher could provide pupils with six example answers for each question, and get the pupils to work out which is closest, and which is furthest, from what the pupil thinks. Of the example answers, number 1 answers might be broadly rational agnostic, number 2 might be nihilist, number 3 theistic, 4 humanist optimists, 5 spiritual post-moderns, and 6 Buddhist worldviews. (The example answers can be adapted to the religions and non-religious ways of life being studied in RE.) Using the same questions, the pupils could, instead, work out – and role-play – what the answers to those questions might be from well-known figures from modern life (celebrities? politicians?) or from history (religious or 'religiously engaged' figures, such as Henry VIII, George Washington, or Joan of Arc). They might also role-play as fictional figures. These would be good, thought-provoking, activities for all ages.

Blaylock also recommends a version of Plato's cave (Plato's description of how and what we experience may be merely a shadow-show of the 'reality' beyond the cave), converted to a world in which children's only reality is that of television or computer screens. If children are brought up only experiencing screen-life and thinking it the whole of reality, how would they get to know the 'real world' beyond those screens? (A great lesson, and one that looks more and more realistic as the years go by.) Vivienne Baumfield, also in a Westhill seminar, recommended a simple 'odd one out' activity. This starts with three items, the questions being 'What is the odd one out?' and 'Why?' A smiley sun, a light bulb, and a candle: which is the odd one out? (The sun because it is natural, the light bulb because it doesn't have flames, the candle because it is not coloured?) Or pope, priest, bishop? (Begins with a P, six letters, only in Roman Catholicism?) This method came in part from George Kelly (1955) on personal construct psychology, on how children construct meanings, and is a very good diagnostic activity, helping understand how people think, as well as getting people to think. The method creates positive dissonance. As a teacher said, 'I've learned a lot from listening to some of these kids: I'm thinking, wow, I never figured it out that way.' Philosophical techniques are about teachers', as well as pupils', thinking.

Amongst the many advantages of using philosophical approaches to important questions in RE is that philosophy can provide a set of common techniques that can tackle issues in many religious and non-religious traditions. It is not that philosophy is 'neutral', but it is, still, a discipline with techniques that can be widely used. There is a disadvantage if philosophy becomes merely a set of techniques, though, and without any substantial purpose. Professional philosophy has, at various times, been a discipline helping people lead good, flourishing, lives (the view of philosophers such as Aristotle), and has at other times been a very cerebral technique for solving particular problems that, once solved, leave philosophy with nothing else to do (the view of Wittgenstein, early in his philosophical career). That second type of philosophy is criticized by the eminent contemporary philosopher Nel Noddings. She says that a lot of philosophical thought experiments are too 'ideal': she, instead, tries to develop 'non-ideal' theories, 'where we insist upon talking about the real world'. 'Real world' issues, she says, 'can be difficult and horrific enough, instead of making up these wild things' (Noddings, quoted in Stern 2016, p. 32). Well, RE has plenty of real-world issues to keep philosophy from drifting into made-up, ideal, and 'wild' thought experiments.

Another huge advantage of using philosophical techniques in RE is that, where the aim is to create a 'community of enquiry', the pupils and teachers alike are doing research. Research-driven RE is the theme of this whole book, so an approach that makes pupils into enquirers, in this way, is a fine example of what I would want to promote in all RE. Teachers, too, are pushed to think about issues that are (still) open for debate and discussion, rather than seeing the curriculum as a set of knowledge to be 'delivered'. The tendency of some philosophers to separate themselves from religion can even be turned to RE's advantage, as there are many wonderfully articulate philosophers who can represent various atheist and humanist positions – important for pupils who, if they only hear of religious people tackling deep questions, may think that there are no 'non-religious' views other than 'I disagree'. Jacqueline Watson (2007) writes well about including non-religious philosophical viewpoints. She talked, in one of the Westhill seminars, of Jean-Paul Sartre's existentialism, with 'man' being 'condemned' to be free, and Bertrand Russell's complex views on love and on knowledge. Both Sartre and Russell have been described as atheists, but it is important to note that 'atheism' is not a single belief system: Russell is reported as having said to the Indian leader Jawaharlal Nehru that what they had in common was that they were both atheists, to which Nehru is reported as replying, 'Yes, but never forget, Russell, that you are a *Christian* atheist and I am a *Hindu* one' (Priestley 2000, and see Madge et al. 2014 on varieties of 'non-faith' stances of young people).

Catriona Card, an RE specialist working with young pupils (aged 4–5), talks about the importance of the 'big questions' that children will themselves ask and the value of discussing them even at that age. She suggests getting children to compose the biggest questions they can think of – and then working together (in a community of enquiry) to explore some of the possible answers.

Bob Bowie (in a Westhill seminar and in Bowie 2012, 2017) suggested teaching about ethics and morality in RE using thoughtful and communal techniques common to philosophy for children. There are the well-established techniques such as comparing and contrasting two different religious/ethical viewpoints on a topic, and getting all members of the class to position themselves on a 'continuum' line from one strong view to another (e.g. 'war is always wrong' to 'war is a good way of settling fundamental disputes') and justifying their position. And there are activities such as getting the pupils to create a 'photostory' or 'storyboard' (as in activity 9.2), to illustrate an important ethical issue – and then use the finished product to teach others in the group about that issue. He notes that pupils need to be aware that there are different religious and non-religious ways of thinking ethically, and that they can apply an ethical theory to a situation. Bowie is also concerned that ethics should not be a 'philosophically professionalised' subject: ethics are embedded in religious and non-religious ways of life. Integrating some of the P4C principles into RE, Sue Hookway provides a whole range of ways of tackling truth and critical thinking in good RE lessons (Hookway 2004). Pat Hannam, an enthusiastic and skilled proponent of philosophy for children as central to RE, described in a Westhill seminar the typical P4C process as involving a presentation of a stimulus, generating philosophical questions from students, working with the questions, and choosing the question (e.g. by voting), dialogue (not discussion or debate), a closing activity (e.g. Based on what you heard, have you changed your mind?). The teacher plays a facilitator role, deepening the philosophical content. Principles include everyone agreeing to accept reasonable criticism, and everyone addressing their comments to others in the class, sitting in a circle. The types of thinking in such situations, Hannam continues, are variously creative, critical, caring, and collaborative (see also Biesta and Hannam 2016). Helpfully, she situates P4C clearly in the American pragmatist philosophical tradition: Charles Peirce (weaving together the cognitive and affective), John Dewey (advancing democracy), and William James. James' contribution is informed by his interest in 'varieties of religious experience' (James 1983) and how we change. Real change, James says, is a 'project in our hearts'.

Hannam outlined a P4C session starting with Martin Luther King's 'I have a dream' speech. Discussing the speech and what it means, the group is asked what philosophical questions emerge. What do we mean by 'dream'? What do we mean by being 'like sisters and brothers'? What contributes to the beauty and passion and power of the words? Why do we hate? What is equality? Are all humans of equal value? Why do we have to fight for our dreams? Are dreams agents for change? Is there any point in dreaming? Do we still dream? What dream do we need for today? Can one person make a difference? Why does difference lead to conflict? We can get involved in these questions, such as what exactly equality might mean. The question that was chosen was 'Why do we hate?', inspired by the quotation about the world being ruined by the passions of hatred. The facilitator's job is helping the community of enquiry, and not giving the group, for example, a dictionary definition of hatred. In another situation – also using the Martin Luther King speech – the outcomes were respect, persistence, courage, thoughtfulness, and how we know when to tolerate. Hannam finished her presentation with a quotation from Bertrand Russell. I would like to present a longer version of that quotation, as it says interesting things about philosophy (with which I agree) and science (about which I am uncertain) and theology (with which I disagree). It continues from the end of a previous Russell quotation (earlier in this chapter):

> Science tells us what we can know, but what we can know is little, and if we forget how much we cannot know we become insensitive to many things of very great importance. Theology, on the other hand, induces a dogmatic belief that we have knowledge where in fact we have ignorance, and by doing so generates a kind of impertinent insolence towards the universe. Uncertainty, in the presence of vivid hopes and fears, is painful, but must be endured if we wish to live without the support of comforting fairy tales. It is not good either to forget the questions that philosophy asks, or to persuade ourselves that we have found indubitable answers to them. To teach how to live without certainty, and yet without being paralysed by hesitation, is perhaps the chief thing that philosophy, in our age, can still do for those who study it. *(Russell 1961, p. 14)*

I might add to this view of philosophy that in addition to living in uncertainty, teachers should also, themselves and for their pupils, live in a world where there are 'conflicting certainties'. Two people with different views, both of whom are uncertain, may find it easy to be in dialogue. Two people who are both equally certain, but who believe different things: that is where dialogue is most important. Whatever we think about school pupils, it is clear that many have very strongly held views. Education is not – should not be – a process of undermining certainties. It should be about bringing certainties together in dialogue. Sometimes, certainties will indeed be undermined; sometimes, they will remain – but with a greater understanding of the value of another person's certainties. As Richard Nisbett says, there is a Buddhist dictum that 'the opposite of a great truth is also true' (Nisbett 2003, p. 176). I have written of the rich ambiguity that RE teachers may display, in Chapter 3 of this book. But I would like to end with an example of what Nisbett says, taken from a sacred text. The closing text of the Hindu scriptural account of the Creation (from the Rig-Veda X, cxxix, in Zaehner 1992, p. 14) is this:

> Whence this emanation hath arisen,
> Whether God created it, or whether he did not, –
> Only he who is its overseer in highest heaven knows.
> He only knows,
> or perhaps he does not know!

Activity 10.2: Community of inquiry

I enjoy the book *When I Was Born* (Martins and Matoso 2010). The narrator (a boy) tells a simple story of how little he knew when he was born, and what sort of things he has learned since then. It is enjoyed by the youngest of school pupils, but – like many of the best books for children – it is also enjoyed by older pupils and by adults. It starts,

– 'When I was born I had never seen anything. Only the darkness of my mother's tummy.'

I suggest it can be used to create and explore the creation of a community of inquiry (Lipman 2003, p. 20). The teachers should read the story once, and ask if there are any questions. See if other pupils can answer the questions. Those that are unanswered can be saved for later. Remind the pupils that the narrator has learned a lot since being born. How did he learn all those things, do you think? Here is a list of some of the ways he learned, which may help:

Eyes
Meeting people
Travelling
Meeting animals
Playing on my own
Playing with other children
Touching things
Seeing different colours
Tasting things
Speaking
Breathing
Smelling
Hearing things
Running, dancing, and jumping
Being with a grown-up
Towards the end of the book, the narrator says

– 'Now I know that there is a whole world to discover: millions and millions of things my hands haven't yet reached; millions and millions of lands my feet haven't yet taken me to. And new smells and sounds and tastes.'

As a group, work out the best ways in which we can learn new things. I suggest starting with three bits of learning: how we can best learn how things work, how we can best learn how to get on with other people, and how we can best learn what happened a long time ago or a long way away. For young children, these are the kinds of phrases to be used; the older the children, the more the statements could be tied to RE topics, so they might be: how we can best learn how religious artefact is used, how we can best learn how to get on with people who have different beliefs to our beliefs, and how we can best learn about ancient sacred texts.

For each topic, a child can make a suggestion, and other children should listen. (The talker could be given an object which 'allows' them to talk.) Other children can indicate whether they agree (thumbs up) or disagree (thumbs down) or have something else to say (thumbs to the side). The teacher chooses who gets the 'talking object'. The discussion goes on, to create a community of inquiry.

Create a 'how we learn' list for the classroom, made up of what has been said in the discussion. Most statements will begin 'Some of us learn best by . . . .' If there is something that everyone agrees on, the statements can begin 'All of us learn best by . . . .'

After creating this 'how we learn' list, it can be used in the future to remind us all – including the teacher – how different people learn.

Conclusion

Religion and philosophy are strange bedfellows, but they are – despite their protestations – bedfellows. And both have a troubled relationship with truth and with uncertainty. The philosopher and writer on religion Martin Buber brings together some of these tensions in his novel *Gog and Magog* (Buber 1999). Written during the Second World War, a couple of years after Buber left Germany (where he had been the head of the Centre for Jewish Adult Education until 1938) to live in Jerusalem, the novel was set during the Napoleonic Wars – another apocalyptic period in history. At the centre of the novel is a rabbi who is a 'seer', someone who understands not only religion but also knows what will happen. But he is a reluctant seer, as the truth is so painful. Much of the world was living with painful truth, as Buber was writing, and his account of what being able to see the whole truth was like is touching – and shocking. Early in the novel, Jaacob Yitzchak is introduced:

> Jaacob Yitzchak was called the "Seer" because in truth he "saw." It was told that, when he was born, he had been able to see from world's end to world's end. Thus had man been destined to see when on that first day of Creation, ere yet a constellation was in the firmament, God's Word caused to arise the Original Light. . . . The child who "saw," however, was so dismayed by the flood of evil which he beheld engulfing the earth, that he besought the gift to be taken from him and his vision to be restricted to a narrower span. *(Buber 1999, p. 4)*

There are pupils in school – teachers, too – who find the big questions in life too difficult to ask and answers to those questions too shocking to contemplate. I'm afraid that RE cannot really avoid some such questions, some such answers. That is our lot. What we can do, though, is use more communal and dialogic approaches to tackling the questions and the answers. This makes for good philosophy and for good RE. As the poet Emily Dickinson says, we should tell children the truth, but tell it 'slant': the truth should 'dazzle gradually', she say, '[o]r every man be blind' (Dickinson 1970, pp. 506–507).

One of the biggest areas of philosophical inquiry is ethics, and it is central to all religious traditions too. It is worth a chapter of its own, then.

Chapter 11
Ethics, Rights, Morality, and Virtues

*Bravest thing about people, Miss Joan, is how they go on loving mortal
beings after finding out there's such a thing as dying.*
(Anne Tyler, *The Tin Can Tree*)

Introduction

A colleague once sent an article to a journal dedicated to 'applied philosophy', and
it was sent back, rejected, with the message 'this is just *too applied*'. Professional
philosophy may sometimes seem to cut itself off from 'real life' and to risk sinking
into 'self-referring technical virtuosity' (Stern 2016, p. 22). But the history of
philosophy is one of deep engagement with social and political issues and, perhaps
even more, with issues of ethics, rights, morality, and virtues. Religious traditions
can be seen as just as remote from real life – and are sometimes encouraged to stay
away from 'real life', as when senior member of religious communities criticize
governments and are told to stick to 'spiritual' issues and leave political issues to
politicians. On ethics, rights, morality, and virtues, religions have been accused
of generating lists of unquestionable and outdated rules in batches of ten, or 613,
or four, or seven. Both philosophers and religious leaders may be accused of
deceiving themselves and deceiving others, by describing a morality that is merely
a 'front' for a power game – as in Nietzsche's claim that 'preachers of equality' had
'secret tyrant-longings' which 'disguise themselves … in virtue-words!' (Nietzsche
1993, p. 145). RE teachers may want to avoid all such problems by leaving ethics,
morality, and virtues at the classroom door or only teaching the 'facts' about ethical
systems and not trying to 'apply' them to the lives of pupils. One of the leading
proponents of RE in the United States, Stephen Prothero, is a good positive example
of this, saying that, 'unlike others who have advanced civic arguments for the study
of religion in our schools, I focus on spreading knowledge rather than inculcating
virtues' (Prothero 2007, p. 21).

For myself, I don't think we have a choice, as teachers, 'to teach' or 'not to teach' ethics. Every moment of every lesson, teachers are teaching ethics by how they behave in the lesson (Are they modelling fairness? Are they demonstrating kindness? Are they promoting curiosity?) and by what they value in the curriculum (Which people are studied and how does this represent society to the pupils? Whose stories are told? What approaches to understanding are promoted?). A wise claim by two educational psychologists, one that I would like emblazoned on every school staffroom wall, is that '[u]nhappy, stressed workaholics are not good role models for young people' (Newton and Tarrant 1992, p. 194). Indeed. And by implication, reasonably happy, reasonably unstressed, adults with a reasonably balanced life *are* good role models. That would be a good start to teaching pupils about 'the good life', I think. And if RE teachers only teach 'about' ethics in religious and non-religious traditions, whilst modelling 'bad' or unjust ways of life, it is not difficult to imagine what lesson the pupils are more likely to learn. Some of the lessons learned are simple ones, including the lesson that it is good to talk about difficult issues. Anne Tyler's novel *The Tin Can Tree* starts with a child's funeral. Later, a group of women discuss what to do about the child's mother. It is a long discussion. Finally, the character Missouri tells Joan: 'Bravest thing about people, Miss Joan, is how they go on loving mortal beings after finding out there's such a thing as dying.' After this exchange, Charleen says, 'Was *that* what you did all this talking to say?' 'It was', replies Missouri (Tyler 1965, pp. 76–77). May RE teachers be as brave, carrying on teaching about matters of life and death.

This chapter looks at some of the ways in which ethics, rights, morality, and virtues are taught within RE lessons (an 'integrated approach'), and some of the ways in which they might be taught *apart* from RE. Understanding how ethical education could work outside RE enables RE teachers to see what alternatives there are to an integrated approach and to use examples of good practice to inform RE lessons. In the UK, as in many countries, ethically rich subjects such as personal and social education or sex and relationships education are often taught by RE teachers (perhaps because they are used to dealing with difficult personal issues), and the boundaries between subjects are blurred by many schools that timetable a whole range of 'E' subjects together. 'E' subjects are a group of personally engaging subjects: physical education, religious education, personal and social education, citizenship education, sex and relationships education, driver education, moral education, and more. They are, as Moran says, characterized by having an expected 'practical' result and by being somewhat distanced from the practice of a university-based academic discipline.

> When we are doubtful that there is an academic subject and especially when we want a practical result, the word 'education' shows up in the curriculum subject itself. Thus, we sometimes have such things as physical education, driver education, music education, moral education, sex education as the names of what is taught. ... The implication here might be that in England, for all the talk about phenomenology and objectivity, the British public (and their politicians)

think that religious education ought to have some personal and practical effect.
(Moran 1989, p. 101)

Moran is absolutely right that RE in the UK is expected to have a personal influence on pupils, although I would say that every subject of the curriculum, with or without the 'E', is expected to have such an influence – none, I think, are simply junior versions of university academic disciplines. But that argument is for another book (Stern 2018). Moral education is one of Moran's concerns, and he describes the interesting balance between integration and separation that this chapter attempts to address:

Moral education ought to be a distinct field of its own. It should not be dictated to by any religion or by religious officials. But … [m]oral education's attempt to cut all ties with all religion is suicidal. It cuts itself off from most of the practical side of morality, leaving moral education to be the ethical discussion of hypothetical dilemmas or the clarifying of subjective viewpoints. Moral education needs religious education neither as lord nor servant but as thoughtful colleague.
(Moran 1989, p. 189)

This chapter explores research on some different approaches to teaching these themes and ways in which teachers and pupils can themselves research what might be done in RE. Before that, it may be worth separating out 'ethics', 'rights', 'morality', and 'virtue', even if there are plenty of philosophy texts that will provide fuller descriptions. Broadly, 'ethics' and 'morality' are often used interchangeably, referring to what is right and wrong, good and bad. Ethics can refer to a system of rules for a particular system, such as the 'professional ethics' of doctors or teachers and 'research ethics' of researchers, whereas morality nearly always refers to what is right or wrong for a person to do in any circumstances. 'Rights' are usually formalized, agreed, systems of rules or principles (such as agreed declarations of human rights). Occasionally, 'ethics' refers to what is in line with the order of the universe, without any particular moral claim: Spinoza's book, *The Ethics* (Spinoza 1955), is usually seen as a good example of this. Rights may also be of this form, as in theories of 'natural rights'. Whereas ethics and morality are descriptions of what is right or wrong, good or bad, 'virtues' are personal characteristics of individual people, sometimes also referred to as their 'values'. A person possessing the virtue of courage is prepared to face danger; a person possessing the virtue of kindness has a tendency to help people. Because virtues are *characteristics* of a person, the process of developing virtues may also be called '*character* education'. For some reason – beyond my understanding – 'moral education' has a tradition of being promoted by more liberal or progressive educational writers, whilst 'virtue development' or 'character education' has a tradition of being promoted by more traditionalist or conservative educational writers. (The traditions may swap over at some point in the future.) However, in this chapter I will use the various terms rather loosely, reflecting the different approaches of writers on these matters.

Integrated approaches: Swedish and English examples

In Sweden, ethics education forms a distinct strand within RE in the national curriculum. The implementation of the curriculum is being researched, and this provides an interesting case study. The 2011 curriculum (Skolverket 2011) is a comprehensive document that outlines the purposes of schooling, the nature of each subject, and assessment levels and expectations in every subject. The history of RE in Sweden has been of a broadly 'social scientific' subject since the 1960s, described as an 'objective and neutral non-confessional' subject, without any church influence (Larsson, in Kuyk et al. 2007). In the national curriculum document of 2011, RE incorporates ethics education – rather than, as in a number of German *Länder*, being an *alternative* to ethics education. Where ethics and moral education are taught apart from RE, they are often treated as more universal and are often connected to more-or-less universal philosophical theories (such as utilitarianism and duty-based theories) and/or to theories of universal human rights (such as the UN's Universal Declaration of Human Rights of 1948). Where they are taught within RE, ethics are more often tied to particular religious or national traditions. In Sweden, there has been a mixture of both traditions, but in the 2011 curriculum, a big role is given to the 'basic values of Swedish society' (Skolverket 2011, p. 14). This may sound familiar to UK teachers who have recently been expected to promote 'fundamental British values' (DfE 2011, p. 14). An emphasis on national values may be a reaction against some globalizing tendencies, although many are uncomfortable with the move towards narrower nationalisms in recent years. The UK's 'fundamental British values' include 'democracy, the rule of law, individual liberty and mutual respect and tolerance of different faiths and beliefs' (DfE 2011, p. 9). Sweden's 'basic values' are worth quoting in more detail, because, as I say, they retain universal as well as national elements.

> The inviolability of human life, individual freedom and integrity, the equal value of all people, equality between women and men, and solidarity with the weak and vulnerable are the values that the school should represent and impart. In accordance with the ethics borne by Christian tradition and Western humanism, this is achieved by fostering in the individual a sense of justice, generosity of spirit, tolerance and responsibility. *(Skolverket 2011, p. 9)*

One of the interesting features of Swedish education, however, is that the curriculum also states that there are *other* values that should be discussed besides these. Teachers should 'clarify and discuss with the pupils the basic values of Swedish society and their consequences in terms of individual actions', but they should also 'openly communicate and discuss *different* values, views and problems' (Skolverket 2011, p. 14, emphasis added). The openness is critical here; otherwise, the 'different' values would simply be presented in order to dismiss them as 'incorrect' or 'inappropriate' (this is the argument put forward about the British situation in Elton-Chalcraft et al. 2017). Here is the Swedish explanation:

> The internationalisation of Swedish society and increasing cross-border mobility place high demands on the ability of people to live with and appreciate the values inherent in cultural diversity. Awareness of one's own cultural origins and sharing in a common cultural heritage provides a secure identity which it is important to develop, together with the ability to understand and empathise with the values and conditions of others. The school is a social and cultural meeting place with both the opportunity and the responsibility to strengthen this ability among all who work there. *(Skolverket 2011, p. 9)*

It is not intended merely that values are taught, they should be *lived*. Discussing democracy, the curriculum document says this:

> It is not in itself sufficient that teaching only imparts knowledge about fundamental democratic values. Democratic working forms should also be applied in practice and prepare pupils for active participation in the life of society. This should develop their ability to take personal responsibility. By taking part in the planning and evaluation of their daily teaching, and being able to choose courses, subjects, themes and activities, pupils will develop their ability to exercise influence and take responsibility. *(Skolverket 2011, p. 10–11)*

Such value education is particularly important in RE, as '[r]eligions and other outlooks on life are ... central elements of human culture' and '[t]eaching should ... provide knowledge about and understanding of how Christian traditions have affected Swedish society and its values' (Skolverket 2011, p. 176). 'Teaching in religion should essentially give pupils the opportunities to develop their ability to ... search for information about religions and other outlooks on life and evaluate the relevance and credibility of sources' (Skolverket 2011, pp. 176–177). Within RE, ethics will include 'daily moral dilemmas', 'views of the good life and the good person ... linked to different kinds of ethical reasoning, such as virtue ethics', 'ethical questions', and 'ethical concepts' (Skolverket 2011, p. 180).

By the age of 16, Swedish pupils should have a 'very good knowledge of Christianity and the other world religions' and 'other outlooks on life', and pupils should be able to 'reason and argue about moral issues and values by applying well developed and well informed reasoning, and use ethical concepts and models in a well functioning way' (Skolverket 2011, p. 184). The inclusion of international issues is helpful in discussing rights. The last seventy-five years have seen more migration and refuge-seeking than any other period in the history of the world, and claims of citizenship, attempts to block citizenship, withdrawal of citizenship, and so on, have characterized political struggles throughout the period. Many of these issues derive, incidentally (or not so incidentally), from religious conflicts. Just within Europe, Jewish migration, population movements in the former Yugoslavia, political developments in Northern Ireland, and refugee crises related to conflicts in Afghanistan, Syria, and elsewhere have dominated international debates on rights, citizenship, and morality. A debate may be useful.

Activity 11.1: Worldwide debate on religion

This activity has been developed with pupils aged from 14 to 19. It could also be adapted to suit younger pupils.

The teacher allocates countries (or continents) to individual pupils or pairs or groups of pupils. Each pupil (or group) is then to become a representative of that country. The task is to write a script for a United Nations speech on the significance (or lack of significance) of religion on their country, using information from one newspaper from that country (or two newspapers, for older pupils), using that day's papers (from *www.onlinenewspapers.com/*). The reports could be word-processed, and the combination of all reports might be made into a big 'world newspaper' for the day, with added reportage on the debate to follow.

Have a UN debate on the motion 'religion is the most important influence on the world today'. Pupils will take part in the debate representing their countries and only are to speak 'in role', with a choice of 'for' or 'against' the motion, depending on their initial research on how important religion is in 'their' country. (For more on the UN itself, look at *www.un.org/en/*)

Teaching ethics as part of RE means that ethics education can draw on the richness of religious as well as non-religious traditions. It also means that ethics is assessed as part of RE. The assessment of RE is tricky at the best of times, but when it includes ethics, it becomes even trickier. Are we to assess pupils' understanding of ethics (e.g. their ability to argue well about ethics), their ability to act ethically (according to their own ethical code), or their ability to act according to a particular (school-based, religious, or national) ethical code? Should we assess pupils' levels of moral development, as in the work of psychologists such as Kohlberg (1981)? The Swedish approach to assessment in ethics tends to emphasize the cognitive skills of pupils, which fits better with Kohlberg's approach – providing pupils with moral dilemmas and assessing the complexity and universality of their responses. However, teachers in Sweden recognize that the actual behaviour of pupils is of greater importance (as noted by contributors to Franck 2017), and the curriculum does aim for behaviour outcomes for pupils. As with so many aspects of schooling, if an 'aim' isn't assessed, there is, sadly, a chance that it will remain only in the policy document and will not be implemented in schools. How this works in practice is being researched in Sweden, and the first major publication from that research project (Franck 2017) is a good example of how to tackle assessment of such a challenging aspect of the curriculum.

A second example of an attempt to integrate RE and ethical education comes from the UK, where RE is determined at local level. The English city of Birmingham has a long history of contributing to developments in RE. Stephen Parker and Rob

Freathy (2011) have produced an interesting historical account of Birmingham's RE syllabuses, two of which (those of 1975 and 2007) were groundbreaking in different ways. The earlier of the syllabuses, coordinated by Birmingham university theologian John Hick, included representatives of a range of religions on the syllabus-writing committee and also included a representative of humanism. This was a hugely influential approach, taken up by most other syllabus committees over subsequent decades. The syllabus of 2007 was groundbreaking in different ways. It 'did not mention the possibility that children might learn their values from non-religious stances for living ... [and] did not consider secular worldviews as a valuable focus for learning' (Parker and Freathy 2011, p. 259). And, of particular significance for this chapter, the 2007 syllabus had a 'strong linkage between children's moral education and their RE, which had often been deliberately disassociated from the 1960s onwards, and the aim of fostering the conative, dispositional domain, marked [the syllabus] out as distinctive and divergent from existing trends' (Parker and Freathy 2011, p. 258). That is, the RE curriculum looked to religions to develop children's virtues: '[t]he dispositions of pupils will be developed using the treasury of faith' (Birmingham City Council 2007, p. 5). There are twenty-four dispositions – or virtues – that pupils should develop through RE:

Being imaginative and explorative
Appreciating Beauty
Expressing Joy
Being Thankful
Caring for Others, Animals and the Environment
Sharing and Being Generous
Being Regardful of Suffering
Being Merciful and Forgiving
Being Fair and Just
Living by Rules
Being Accountable and Living with Integrity
Being Temperate, Exercising Self-Discipline and Cultivating Serene Contentment
Being Modest and Listening to Others
Cultivating Inclusion, Identity and Belonging
Creating Unity and Harmony
Participating and Willing to Lead
Remembering roots
Being Loyal and Steadfast
Being Hopeful and Visionary
Being Courageous and Confident
Being Curious and Valuing Knowledge
Being Open, Honest and Truthful
Being Reflective and Self-Critical
Being Silent and Attentive to, and Cultivating a Sense for, the Sacred and
Transcendence (Birmingham City Council 2007, p. 29)

The document includes descriptions of several religions, with particular virtues targeted to be developed. Being imaginative and explorative is associated with, amongst other things, the Bahá'í worldview, the Buddhist Eightfold Noble Path, the Christian view of the world, the Hindu *Aum*, the Islamic view of the world, the Jain worldview, the Jewish approach to living well, the Rastafarian worldview, and the life of Guru Gobind Singh. Each of the other virtues is similarly associated with a range of religious traditions. Unlike the Swedish RE curriculum, there is no required assessment process or levels described for the 2007 Birmingham syllabus, although some (non-statutory) guidance on assessment is available on a website. Research on how effective RE is at developing pupils' ethics or virtues is easier to complete if there is a standardized assessment system – as in Sweden. (That is the basis of the research reported in Franck 2017.) It may be a little harder to carry out in Birmingham, but such research will be fascinating – not only seeing if the pupils of Birmingham are distinctly virtuous but also seeing what the influence on those virtues is of RE and of other aspects of schooling.

While theologian John Hick was most influential on the 1975 Birmingham syllabus, it was theologian Marius Felderhof who was the biggest influence on the 2007 syllabus. In the UK, it is relatively unusual to have RE syllabuses so directly influenced by senior theologians, and this might help explain why these two examples were so different from other contemporaneous syllabuses. Felderhof explains his position in this way:

> One creates confusions about what it means to educate religiously by including secular philosophies in RE as 'alternatives' to religious faith. RE is about the endeavour to learn what religious life has to contribute by seeing oneself as a responsible self rather than as a spectator devising theories about human nature and the world. By all means criticise religious life but do not misrepresent it as if it were a theory. *(Felderhof, in Barnes 2012, p. 155, and see also Felderhof et al. 2007; Felderhof and Thompson 2014)*

Activity 11.2: Assessing RE-based ethics or virtue development

It would be helpful if research into ethical development started with the pupils themselves. As a class, choose a virtue (e.g. courage or kindness) or an ethical rule (e.g. tell the truth or avoid stealing) and choose a religious topic from forthcoming RE lessons that might be relevant to the virtue or ethical rule.

Before the RE topic is studied, the pupils should write, briefly (perhaps for homework), what they know about the virtue/rule (including why they think it important), and an example of how they have demonstrated that virtue or obeyed the rule.

After the RE topic has been studied, the pupils should write again, about what they have learned that is new about the virtue/rule (including why they think the new knowledge is important), and how – if at all – they may behave differently, following the lesson.

Share the findings of this individual research with the whole class. As a class, come to agreement on what influence the RE lesson seems to have had on the pupils' beliefs and what influence it might have on the pupils' behaviour.

Ethics and virtues are not – or should not be – temporary or short-term characteristics. So for the final element of this research, leave at least two or three months before 'assessing' the virtue/ethics learning. At that time, the pupils should assess themselves (justifying their assessments), describing how their behaviour has changed – if at all – following the RE lesson.

The Birmingham syllabus incorporates virtue development into an RE curriculum that excludes non-religious ways of life. So how might virtue development be taught *outside* such RE? That is the subject of the following section of this chapter.

Separate character/virtue education: The US example

In the United States, character or virtues education has a place in schools where there is no RE. (It has also grown in the UK in recent years, as in Arthur 2010; Arthur and Carr 2013; Arthur et al. 2015.) Research on this development therefore makes for another interesting case study. Virtues have been seen as central to education since before Aristotle's work on the topic more than two millennia ago. In the United States, as in all countries, pupils have been taught how to live well – or to live as adults want them to live – for as long as schools have existed. It is sometimes a surprise to Americans that up until the twentieth century, the 'texts' for this kind of learning were often taken from the Bible. But the kind of character education familiar to modern schools really developed in the 1920s, according to William Chapman's history of the subject (Chapman 1977). Chapman worked in the Character Research Project at Union College, Schenectady, New York. That research unit included the psychologist John Peatling, who, recognizing the similar interests of those researching character and values and those researching RE, worked with John Hull in Birmingham to co-found in 1978 ISREV, the International Seminar on Religious Education and Values (*www.isrev.org*) (as described in Chapter 4). Character education in the 1970s and 1980s was further boosted in the 1990s by the emergence of what became known as positive psychology. The history of psychology has – according to positive psychologists – focused rather too much on things going wrong, looking at people's limitations, their neuroses and psychoses, their mental illnesses and personality disorders. Positive psychologists decided to look at apithological (healthy, wellness-related) rather than pathological (unhealthy, illness-related) aspects of people.

Positive psychology is the scientific study of what goes right in life, from birth to death and at all stops in between. It is a newly christened approach within psychology that takes seriously as a subject matter those things that make life most worth living. *(Peterson 2006, p. 4)*

This is from Chris Peterson's *Primer in Positive Psychology*, an excellent textbook to understand the whole range of issues raised by these writers. It has chapters on 'character strengths' and 'values' that are of particular interest to RE teachers. And, working with Martin Seligman, Peterson has also produced a major handbook of 'character strengths and virtues' (Peterson and Seligman 2004). Anyone wanting to go into detail of character education and virtue development will benefit from these books. Their 'core virtues' are courage, justice, humanity (renamed 'love' in a later classification by Peterson), temperance, transcendence, and wisdom. RE teachers are likely to be intrigued by 'transcendence':

Transcendence – strengths that forge connections to the larger universe and provide meaning, [including] *appreciation of beauty and excellence (awe, wonder, elevation), gratitude, hope (optimism, future-mindedness, future orientation), humor (playfulness),* [and] *spirituality (religiousness, faith, purpose)*: having coherent beliefs about the higher purpose and meaning of the universe; knowing where one fits within the larger scheme; having beliefs about the meaning of life that shape conduct and provide comfort. *(Peterson and Seligman 2004, p. 30, formatting and punctuation simplified.)*

That description looks like a combination of descriptions of spiritual development (as required of UK schools) and a simplified version of some types of religious belief and practice. The questions determining how spiritual or religious you are suggest more of the latter than the former:

- What is your current religious preference?
- Are you a member of a church or religious institution?
- How often do you attend religious or worship services?
- How religious would you say you are?
- How important is religion in your life today?
- How spiritual would you say you are?
- How often do you pray?
- How often do you meditate?
- How often do you read religious materials or watch or listen to religious programs?
- I believe there is a sacred force in all living things and that this force connects us to each other.
- I believe in life after death.

- I believe that every life has a purpose.
- I feel God's presence.
- I look to God/a Higher Power for support, guidance, and strength.
- My belief in God/a Higher Power helps me to understand my purpose in life.
- My belief in God/a Higher Power helps me to understand the meaning of the things that I experience. (Peterson and Seligman 2004, pp. 600–601.)

Adults and young people (aged 10–17) may want to complete a questionnaire of their 'values in action' covering the whole range of strengths, virtues, and values. There are example questions in Peterson and Seligman (2004), and there is a complete online version (at *www.viasurvey.org*), which is free but for which you have to register. That will report what your distinctive character strengths are and, by implication, what your not-so-strong bits are. It may annoy you, but it is quite a good way to see how the values-virtues-strengths are seen in practice.

What might this mean for schools? Well, there are many US-based programmes for developing strengths, and the rest of the world is catching up. One high-profile approach is that of Tom Lickona and colleagues at the *Center for the 4th and 5th Rs*. After the 'three Rs' (usually described as reading, writing, and arithmetic), Lickona adds 'respect' and 'responsibility' as the next two Rs. In Lickona and Davidson (2005, freely available to download), there is a guide to 'smart and good' high schools which describes two types of school-related virtues or character: 'performance' character and 'moral' character, both set in a school regarded as an 'ethical learning community'.

> By **performance character**, we mean those qualities needed to realize one's potential for excellence – to develop one's talents, work hard, and achieve goals in school, work, and beyond. By **moral character**, we mean those qualities needed to be ethical – to develop just and caring relationships, contribute to community, and assume the responsibilities of democratic citizenship. By an **ethical learning community**, we mean staff, students, parents, and the wider community working together to model and develop performance character and moral character. (Lickona and Davidson 2005, p. xxi)

Lickona describes eight strengths of character that 'offer a vision of human flourishing over a lifetime':

1. Lifelong learner and critical thinker
2. Diligent and capable performer
3. Socially and emotionally skilled person
4. Ethical thinker
5. Respectful and responsible moral agent
6. Self-disciplined person who pursues a healthy lifestyle
7. Contributing community member and democratic citizen
8. Spiritual person engaged in crafting a life of noble purpose. (Lickona and Davidson 2005, p. xxi)

At the heart of positive psychology is a belief in human well-being, happiness, or flourishing (sometimes using the Ancient Greek word *eudaimonia*, as also used by Aristotle). Happiness has become something of an education 'fashion' in recent years, not least as a compensation for some of the unhappiness created by other aspects of schooling. The approach of positive psychology looks mostly at individual characteristics, albeit within a model that prioritizes sociable virtues. (Those who work most comfortably alone, and those who might be described as 'loners', are not well recognized in the positive psychology literature.) There are other approaches that focus more on the caring relationships themselves, and the philosopher Nel Noddings is prominent amongst those. She writes of the problem of character education as being in the tradition of getting children to take part in a ready-made historical conversation, as also happens in many religious traditions. She says that 'it is assumed that there are values to be transmitted, virtues to be encouraged, a character to be established' (Noddings 1994, p. 112). But happiness is of value, and in her book *Happiness in Education*, Noddings notes that '[t]o be happy, ... children must learn to exercise virtues in ways that help to maintain positive relations with others, especially with those others who share the aim of establishing caring relations' (Noddings 2003, p. 160). It is care that is central to her view of happiness and of ethics in generally – and her position in philosophy is as a 'care ethicist'. Exploring how teachers care for pupils (and for each other), and how pupils – despite being the people regarded as being 'cared for' in school – may also care for teachers, is an important topic. 'Care' is itself missed off most lists of virtues, and yet might – as in Noddings – be the most important one. And that, in turn, highlights the challenge of virtue-based education. Simply listing the virtues is a controversial and contestable exercise.

A second, and no less significant, challenge for research-oriented teachers is to see whether virtue development 'works'. Do pupils think or behave differently as a result of virtue-based courses or moral education? In the United States, a major study has been carried out into a range of social and character development (SACD) programmes for pupils aged 8–11. They found that '[o]n average, the seven programs [researched] did not improve students' social and emotional competence, behavior, academic achievement, and student and teacher perceptions of school climate', and 'although the numbers of schools and students in each program were not always sufficient to support firm conclusions at the program level, the patterns of estimated impacts for each program were largely similar: students' outcomes were not affected' (SCDRC 2010, p. liii). In other words, for all the efforts of these programmes to help develop character, there was no evidence that they developed character. That is a bit of a problem, but I should point out that it is difficult to find good evidence for the sort of behavioural, attitudinal, and ethical characteristics that are central to this whole chapter. Looking back at yourself, when did you learn to be kind? When did you learn to be generous, or caring, or connected, or ...? Some of us may have an easy answer to those questions: a person (usually in the family) may be the person from whom we think we learned a virtue. But such learning is generally hard to pin down, and the idea that a course about virtue would have startling and immediate effects on pupils' virtues is probably too much to ask.

Education may have short-term effects, but the short-term effects are usually the more knowledge-based things, the new facts learned or the new words understood. Virtue or character development, along with moral education and – I would add – spiritual development, is a lifelong process, sometimes moving quickly, sometimes stalling or moving backwards, but rarely able to be pinned down to a series of lessons, however wonderful those lessons are. So please don't be put off by the lack of evidence of the impact of character education in this study. Try some research for yourself, anyway.

Activity 11.3: The value of virtues and vices

One of the leading researchers in positive psychology, Chris Peterson, has produced a list of virtues and vices. Or, rather, a list of virtues, their opposites, exaggerations, and absences. Psychologists and psychiatrists have for many years used the DSM (the *Diagnostic and Statistical Manual of Mental Disorders*, APA 2013), but as Peterson's work starts from strengths, rather than illnesses, he calls his list the 'unDSM' (Peterson, in Csikszentmihalyi and Csikszentmihalyi 2006, p. 29, with the table below adapted from p. 39).

Using the table below, work out what strengths you think you have (you could print off the table and circle the characteristics that apply to you), and how you deal with the strengths (and their absence) during your work as a teacher.

Now, work with your pupils. Ask them, in pairs, to choose one positive quality from the table that they *both* feel they have. Work out what bits of RE (or, if necessary, what bits of other subjects on the curriculum) have helped support this strength.

Then, also working in pairs, choose one 'negative' quality (an 'exaggeration', 'absence', or 'opposite' quality to a strength) that they both feel they have. Work out what bits of RE (or, if necessary, what bits of other subjects on the curriculum) have helped either overcome or at least make good use of this quality.

(Younger pupils may work in pairs to pick a word from anywhere on the list and find – or invent – a story that illustrates the quality described by that word, and tell that story to the rest of the class.)

It is important to say that some 'negative' qualities may be used positively: someone's boredom may be the stimulus to turning their life around, someone's foolishness or alienation may lead them to do something completely original (because they do not stick to conventions), and so on.

Having completed these activities, discuss what you have learned about character strengths (or virtues) and their relationship to RE.

Strength	Absence	Opposite	Exaggeration
Wisdom and Knowledge			
Creativity	Conformity	Triteness	Eccentricity
Curiosity/Interest	Disinterest	Boredom	Morbid curiosity/ Nosiness

Strength	Absence	Opposite	Exaggeration
Wisdom and Knowledge			
Judgement/Critical thinking	Unreflectiveness	Gullibility	Cynicism
Love of learning	Complacency	Orthodoxy	Know-it-all-ism
Perspective	Shallowness	Foolishness	None (it is impossible to have too much perspective)
Courage			
Bravery	Fright/Chicken Little-ism	Cowardice	Foolhardiness
Persistence	Laziness	Helplessness	Obsessiveness
Authenticity/Honesty	Phoniness	Deceit	Righteousness
Vitality	Restraint	Lifelessness	Hyperactivity
Love			
Intimacy	Isolation/Autism	Loneliness/Avoidance of commitment	Emotional promiscuity
Kindness	Indifference	Cruelty/Mean-spiritedness	Intrusiveness
Social intelligence	Obtuseness/Cluelessness	Self-deception	Psychobabble
Justice			
Citizenship	Selfishness	Narcissism	Chauvinism
Fairness	Partisanship	Prejudice	Detachment
Leadership	Compliance	Disruptiveness/Sabotage	Despotism
Temperance			
Forgiveness/Mercy	Mercilessness	Vengefulness	Permissiveness
Humility/Modesty	Footless self-esteem	Arrogance	Self-deprecation
Prudence	Sensation seeking	Recklessness	Prudishness/Stuffiness
Self-regulation	Self-indulgence	Impulsivity	Inhibition

Strength	Absence	Opposite	Exaggeration
Transcendence			
Appreciation of beauty/Excellence	Oblivion	*Schadenfreude-ism*	Snobbery
Gratitude	Rugged individualism	Entitlement	Ingratiation
Hope	Present orientism	Pessimism/Despair	Pollyannaism
Humour	Humourlessness	Dourness	Buffoonery
Spirituality	Anomie	Alienation	Fanaticism

Conclusion

If you have completed Activity 11.3, then you or your pupils may have asked about qualities that are not in the list. In discussing the table with other researchers (with the conversations published in Stern 2016), they – and I – agreed to add several qualities. There was 'care' (absence: carelessness; opposite: uncaring; exaggeration: worrying), and 'enstasy/comfortable solitude' (absence: loneliness or unable to be in solitude; opposite: over-dependent on others; exaggeration: anti-social), and one or two other qualities. What qualities would you add to the list that are important to you or your pupils? When I used the list, useful as it is, I came to realize how complicated it can be to pin virtues down or agree what virtues are important. And in my conversations on the topic (in Stern 2016), I found all people had their own 'hierarchy' of virtues. Each person had one or two (or three, or more – in one case, 26) 'really important' virtues, but no two people had the same list of important virtues.

This complexity is one of the reasons that Noddings concentrates on 'care' as the overarching virtue, in order to avoid questions about '[w]hen is a "virtue" not a "virtue"?' (Noddings 2015, p. 64). She also stresses caring as 'best construed as a quality of relation, not primarily as a virtue belonging to an individual' (Noddings 2015, p. 121). Other writers on ethics and morality use other 'singular' virtues, as John Stuart Mill uses happiness (Mill 1910), and Kant uses 'duty' (Kant 1964). And each religious tradition has its own hierarchy of virtues. For example, the virtue of 'humility' is often described as a characteristic Christian virtue. (I am less sure about this myself, as all the Biblical examples I can find of 'humility' refer to being humble when in the presence of God – there is little I can find about being humble with other *people*.) This whole topic makes for plenty of interesting and very 'applied' lessons – whether taught within RE or as a separate subject.

Chapter 12
Creativity and RE

Human beings are spiritually cut off from one another by too many walls, walls that must first be broken down in our hearts before they can be dismantled by peaceful means in the world around us.
(Savall)

Introduction

Any subject of the curriculum can be taught and learned more or less creatively. What RE has at its disposal is the incomparable archive of creative activities within religious traditions. Religious music, art, poetry, and architecture are central to just about all religious traditions, and RE as a school subject can not only make use of such resources but also make use of various creative arts as pedagogic approaches. Here, research on art and music in the teaching of RE is provided. (There are many opportunities for further expansion of these activities by specialist art therapists and music therapists, too.) But we should not run too quickly to the paint pots. One of the leading lights in RE counsels against promoting creativity as if it were always good. In a Westhill seminar on creativity, Andrew Wright warned of 'creative accountancy', or the creativity needed to develop atomic bombs, and went on to say that creativity in theology can be bad, especially if theology is seen as *essentially* creative, as essentially *fictional*. Phillip Pullman's *The Good Man Jesus and the Scoundrel Christ* (Pullman 2010) and Dan Brown's *The Da Vinci Code* (Brown 2004) are, wrongly, treated as theologies. Every human being can be a theologian, in the sense of talking about God, but theology should not lose touch with reality – which can lead to Wright's version of 'constructivism', or 'creating our own world views'. Theology is, he says, properly talk about (the reality of) God. When the discipline was attacked for the lack of intellectual rational proof, theology was transformed by writers such as Ninian Smart into religious studies, described by Wright as the study of religious communities. This found its way into RE in the UK in the early 1970s, which had up until that time been broadly theological. RE became a study of ways of living, and not about the ultimate order of things. RE was directed towards creating a tolerant harmonious moral society, rather than towards exploring ultimate realities. For Andrew Wright, theology should return to RE.

Wright developed critical RE, identifying theology as a – as *the* – critical feature of it, exploring truth. Truth is disputed, so we need to engage with the disputes, exploring truths in a plural setting. Wright believes that saying all religions are 'true' in their own ways is 'Protestant liberalism', and that RE in the UK is promoting such Protestant liberalism. Wright calls this a kind of confessionalism and wants to 'bring truth back' with 'critical realism'. Where does creativity fit in Wright's approach to RE? He rejects the 'dominant view' of creativity as involving the exercise of freedom, tolerance, self-expression, and originality, which all leads – he says – to non-realism. Wright, in contrast, promotes creating the new *within* traditions, *within* communities – with creative constraints and creative opportunities. This is not passive, but it is not simply 'self-expression'. Pupils must be involved in active construction, and interactive engagement, in the pursuit of truth and truthfulness and truthful living. It is like master builders and apprentices (or master painters or musicians), learning within a discipline. Wright's creativity is communal, therefore, and 'disciplined' – working within communal, religious, and also academic disciplines.

I include this account of Wright's position because it is all too easy to put creativity alongside motherhood and apple pie as 'a good thing', without unpicking the implications of different forms of creativity. For myself, I am not sure that liberal Protestants believe all religions to be true in their own ways, or that constructivism means we can just make up any old truth for ourselves. (And although I agree that Phillip Pullman is not a theologian by Wright's definition, I do think he is an interesting example of philosophically informed intelligent and creative atheism, including in the book to which Wright refers.) But the insight into how creativity can work within a system, within a community, within a discipline is important. And I am as uncomfortable as Wright is with the kind of RE that says, 'Let's re-write the ten commandments' without any thought to the significance of the 'original' Ten Commandments to Jewish and Christian traditions. That is why I tend to focus, in this chapter, on creativity in RE that, at the very least, allows for and, if possible, incorporates the creativity from within the religious and non-religious traditions being studied.

Using art to teach RE

The early childhood specialist Kathy Ring (Anning and Ring 2004; Ring 2013) notes that when young children 'make marks', their mark-making does not differentiate 'drawing' and 'writing'. It often does not separate out 'acting out' either. Anyone who has seen a young children draw a wheel, and do it with a repeated circular motion with a pencil, will see that the child is 'wheeling' as much as 'drawing a wheel'. This insight into how children write/draw is important in understanding the development of creativity. Separating writing from drawing, literacy from art, is a somewhat artificial and certainly rather difficult process, and is not universal. Calligraphy traditions in Arab nations, and in China and Japan, bridge literacy and art – and spiritual development, too. Writing verses from the Qur'an and copying the calligraphy of ancient masters (Wong 2006a) can be described as spiritual experiences in themselves. And there is such a long history, in religious traditions, of using art to express important truths. Why would we not see art as central to RE? In the Westhill seminar on creativity, Deborah Weston talked about using art to describe your beliefs and values. Pupils can create collages of symbols, visual signs of identity. From this starting point, they could go on to write about the factors leading to their current identity, and the source and meaning of those factors. Emma McVittie extended this with a consideration of what is and isn't creative. Quoting a poem about a boy who drew a beautiful picture, but was 'taught' by his teacher to draw 'like everyone else', the boy, like his desk, became 'square inside and brown, and his hands were stiff, and he was like anyone else' (*bit.ly/2negurV*). Creativity can be stifled, in other words, and RE should be able to host creative work.

Lat Blaylock set up and continues to support *Spirited Arts* (*www.natre.org. uk/about-natre/projects/spirited-arts/* and see Blaylock 2004b, 2004c), in which thousands of pupils contribute their art on a specific theme each year. Twenty-five thousand contributed on the theme of 'art in heaven', for example. This work can promote the understanding of religious and non-religious traditions ('learning about religion'), and it can also promote learning *from* those traditions. In addition to the more obvious religious art of past centuries, Blaylock suggests exploring contemporary art. Damien Hirst's *A Thousand Years* (*www.damienhirst.com/a-thousand-years*), for example, is a study in mortality that references Psalm 90:4 ('A thousand years in your sight are like a day that has just gone by'). And Hirst's *For the love of God* (*www.damienhirst.com/for-the-love-of-god*) is on a similar theme of mortality – featuring a diamond-encrusted skull, and challenging us on the value or lack of value of diamonds to the dead. Blaylock also recommends the work of Yasmin Kathrada (*www.ykartist.com/gallery/*), a British Muslim whose work often treats religious themes.

Margaret Cooling has for many years used art to teach RE (Cooling 1998, 2000a, 2000b, 2009). She recommends choosing a painting on a religious subject and getting a group of children to create a story, as a group, to explain a particular painting. What message is the painting communicating? She suggests using paintings by John August Swanson (*www.johnaugustswanson.com/*), whose religious paintings are rich with narrative and detail. Cooling counsels against creativity that is 'decorative': following Michael Grimmitt, she believes RE is in part a process of construction, with creativity instrumental in pupils' meaning-making. However, she also recognizes Wright's arguments and sees the use of art in RE as a form of 'responsible hermeneutics' (Thistleton 2009). The encounter between a text and a reader is dialogic, which then implies constrained creativity – not unconstrained and 'free' but constrained by the nature of the material being investigated. Exegesis and interpretation are added to by hermeneutics, which asks critically what we are doing when we read, understand, or apply texts. In these ways, Margaret Cooling – also working with Trevor Cooling – draws away from what might be thought of as an open-ended use of art, towards an approach that would suit the approach of Wright. Not creativity as loose 'free expression', but creative work *within* traditions. Maria James talked at the same Westhill seminar about how art could be used to understand some of the most complex issues within a religion. Paintings by Lewis Lavoie (*www.muralmosaic.com/*), with a large painting made up of many smaller paintings, are good to stimulate pupils' thoughts about vital topics in RE. His *Adam*, a version of Michelangelo's Sistine Chapel Adam, is made up of people of the world, and references the United Nations. The idea of the Biblical Adam being a person of and for the whole world is explored through this work of art. Pupils are entranced by watching the video on the artist's website of him painting the elements that go to make up *Adam*. It is not difficult to see how pupils would follow this up with a theme of their own.

So from young children's 'mark-making' through to older pupils working on the interpretation of medieval sacred art, the processes of making art and the 'products' of art provide important insights into religious and non-religious ways of living. I completed some research as part of a project on solitude and loneliness in education (Stern 2014b). Pupils aged 7–8 were presented with several paintings and were asked to write down what they thought the characters in the paintings were thinking. The Caspar David Friedrich picture, *Woman before the Rising Sun* (or *Woman before the Setting Sun*), elicited some of the most complex responses.

> 'She is thinking of good things in her live and happy things', says Carol (aged 8), but several others are thinking of her as on the edge of exploration. 'I don't want to stay in a very small palsce of the world I want to expolore the world', says Dominic (aged 7), whilst Tanya (aged 8) attributes to the woman 'Why am I staying here, I need to explore the world – Sun you see all of the world why can't I'. That last comment is indicative of a set of what might be called more poetic or philosophical responses. 'Sun rise to the sky may I travele by and die and may I fly', says Amina (aged 7). Leonard (aged 7) suggests 'let the sun risi with the glory of god', whilst Andrew (aged 7) has the woman asking 'Am I lighting the sun?' (Stern 2015, pp. 81–82)

This was – to me – a surprising set of responses from such young children. What they were able to do, without any guidance on how to interpret pictures, and with a very simple task (i.e. 'What do you think this person is thinking?'), was a deeply touching analysis of the painting. Their analyses overlapped with their own personal feelings, with Amina's rather sad, alienated, situation, and with Andrew's religious commitment. But the analysis of the picture itself surpasses the typical analyses written by adults – and I have tried the same activity with many adults since completing it with the pupils. High-quality art can be researched by children, using such simple techniques, and their research can generate perceptive accounts of religious and other traditions.

Activity 12.1: Concept collage and caption

This activity builds on some of the activities described above. It is designed to work well with those pupils (and teachers) who would not think of themselves as 'artistic'.

Start with a stimulus from a sacred text. Here, I am suggesting a Sikh text, but of course it could be adapted to sacred texts from any tradition. To introduce some variety into the task, I suggest the teacher looks up that day's *Hukamnama* (www.sikhnet.com/hukam). Each day, in every gurdwara, the Sikh holy book, the Guru Granth Sahib, is opened – humanly 'at random'. The page at which the book falls open provides what is regarded as God's 'instruction' (*hukam*) for the day. The Golden Temple at Amritsar puts their *Hukamnama* online – and this is the one available at the website (and also able to be emailed each day to the teacher). When studying Sikhism, I recommend that the teacher and pupils work on that day's *Hukamnama*, to see what the implications would be for Sikhs who understood this as an instruction from God. The language of the Guru Granth Sahib is poetic – like that of many sacred texts – and is written to be sung. But I suggest taking an extract from that day's text and using it as the title of a collage to be produced by small groups of pupils.

Here are some examples of extracts from various daily *Hukamnama*:

- As rain is dear to the earth, and the flower's fragrance is dear to the bumble bee, and the mango is dear to the cuckoo, so is the Lord to my mind. As the husband is dear to his wife, so is the Lord to my mind. As milk is dear to the baby, and the raindrop is dear to the mouth of the sparrow-hawk, as water is dear to the fish, so is the Lord to my mind. All the seekers, Siddhas and silent sages seek Him, but only a rare few behold Him.
- That man, who in the midst of pain, does not feel pain, who is not affected by pleasure, affection or fear, and who looks alike upon gold and dust; that man, blessed by Guru's Grace, understands this way, he merges with the Lord of the Universe, like water with water.
- O Lord, my thirst for the Water of Your Name will not go away. The fire of my thirst burns even more brightly in that Water. You are the Ocean of Water, and I am just a fish in that Water. You are the cage, and I am Your parrot. So what can the cat of death do to me?

If the pupils are to create a collage, they might do this by cutting out relevant pictures from magazines or papers (the 'old-fashioned' way!) or by clipping pictures from the internet. The idea of the collage is to illustrate a key concept in the text. What are the most important meanings in the text, and what pictures can best represent these? That is why it is good to have a group of pupils working on a text, to bounce ideas off each other. In putting a collage together – either on paper or on a computer – the cumulative effect of the many pictures should be more than just a list. That is the idea of the pictures by Lavoie, described above: they 'add' an overall effect to the various elements that make up the picture.

A complete collage can carry the title taken from the sacred text, but it should also come with an explanation as to how it illustrated the text. Effective collages (either on paper or on computers) can be saved and used to help support the learning of future students of those topics.

Using music to teach RE

Research on what music means to young people can inspire RE teachers to use music as far more than a source of entertainment. In this section, I have made use of responses from research with a number of RE teachers and advisers who attended the Westhill seminar on creativity, along with pupils in their schools. The music described in this section, and other music available to schools, includes what might be called controversial and challenging music – whether in its words or the music itself. Music can therefore have a distinctive role in multi-religious and multicultural contexts, and can include a recognition of sub-cultural music. This is not the same as teachers attempting to use the music popular with young people to ingratiate themselves to their students. As de Waal says, 'I'm worried about this idea that in order to make teaching interesting and to engage pupils you have to get down to their level' (quoted in Paton 2010). In any case, the music actually liked by young people is not always what their teachers think they will like. Research in 2010 with young people aged 13–14 (and therefore born in 1996 or 1997) asked them for a piece of music that each could describe as 'my own music'. The young people's 'positive' choices included tracks from the 1970s (Meat Loaf's *Bat Out of Hell*), from the 1950s (Elvis, Chuck Berry), and from the eighteenth century (Mozart), as well as more predictably fashionable and recent pop music. There is a plurality to the tastes of young people. Teachers who either try to second-guess youthful tastes or try to say what 'should' be liked are unlikely to succeed.

Plurality is important in many ways, of course. On 'What difference does plurality make?' one suggestion of Rüppell and Schreiner relates to music, albeit with a significant and proper qualification: '[m]ost people find music as an easier way of entering into religious traditions other than their own', but '[w]hile the melody may bring people together, the words could stand in the way of community building', so 'a Christian or Muslim may resist singing praise to Hindu divine forms such as Siva and Vishnu, and a Jew may find it difficult to join in the words or a music which include the name of Jesus Christ' (Rüppell and Schreiner 2003, p. 165). But as well as expressing plurality, music can also express a unity and a resolution of conflict. Community cohesion is often taken to mean the creation of unity. Although it would be a mistake to assume that that was all community cohesion meant, still, unity can happen. So community cohesion may be a combination of diversity, conflict, and unity and the resolution of conflict. If that seems like a strange and ineffable combination, then, well, schools need to deal with the ineffable. And as Aldous Huxley said, 'after silence that which comes nearest to expressing the inexpressible is music' (Huxley 1950, p. 19, quoted in Chapter 8).

Music can be a source of inclusion (Stern 2004) and a form of personal and political dialogue (Stern 2009a). As the philosopher John Macmurray says, music can be seen as 'an instrument for the exploration of all possible worlds' (Macmurray, quoted in Warren 1989). Music can explore this world – and the next. Some songs popular with children are about what happens after death. A good example *is In the Big Rock Candy Mountains* (in Burnett 2000, and online at *www.youtube.com/ watch?v=KSGuBNopzBw*). Like most accounts of heaven, this song tells us as much about life before death as life after death. It is a delightful view that was very positively described by respondents to my research ('toe tapping, jolly, humorous', 'my son introduced me to it – he loves it'), a view of the future beyond death, even as it implies the suffering before death ('life after death is better than life on earth for the people it was written for'), that captures a sense of political liberation for the poor and impoverished ('reaction against industrialisation, mechanism which led to war'). It is perhaps closer to the early Christian church views on poverty and the afterlife than later images of harp-playing angels. But that is a delicate Christian theological matter. One respondent referred to 'Pharisee & Publican – outcast'.

The biggest reaction to any of the music used in this research was provided by an example of probably the most famous UK Muslim musician. Yusuf Islam (also known as Cat Stevens) writes with shockingly raw emotion about the war in Bosnia, and he links this with the murder of children and adults in Dunblane in Scotland, in *The Little Ones* (Islam et al. 1997, with a performance at *www.youtube.com/ watch?v=EHcnlq5Oh1w*). It starts 'Oh, they've killed all the Little Ones/While their faces still smiled', and goes on to explain how the killers will have to face the 'little ones' on the Day (i.e. the Day of Judgement). The sin-free little ones will go to Heaven, '[w]here playtime lasts forever'. But where will the killers, the 'devils' go? The performance, described as 'haunting' and 'harrowing' by respondents, matches the words, described as 'shocking' and 'powerful'. It is, said one adult, 'a very powerful and confident statement of belief in Judgement and in eternal reward'. Young people aged 14–15 encountered this piece of music in a topic on evil and suffering. The teacher describes their reaction:

> I played it initially without telling them the story behind it and then discussed their initial feelings. I then told them the story behind it. The look of shock on their faces when I played it again was amazing. Stunned silence!

As one of the adults said, the shock in part is related to the belief expressed in the song that 'for some, justice demands hell'.

Dialogue is crucial in education, and in life. Musical dialogue need not simply be a duet. Rather, it is a way of communicating what is meant, through music, and a way for the listener to understand, through music. Some approaches to music, and to RE, may suggest that 'in the end', all discord is resolved. However, that is not always the case musically, and it need not be so in religious and social terms either. A good example of 'in the end' is given by the composer Chopin, who died aged only 39. Chopin's last composition (his *Mazurka in F minor Opus 68 No 4*) ends with the haunting instruction 'D.C. al segno senza fine', that is, go back to the sign near the start of the piece and repeat the music over and over, without end. Writing your last piece of music as an endless piece tells us something about incompleteness in music and in life. You might want – yourself, and with your pupils – to choose a piece of music that you would like to last forever, that could be your 'theme tune' forever. Explain your choice. Adult respondents suggested various pieces from the less surprising ('The Death March') to the more surprising ('I can see clearly now the rain has gone (Hothouse flowers version)'), but it is the questions and explanations that prove more interesting. One respondent wrote as follows:

> it would have to be lovely, both capable of deep feeling and … pleasure – no words could do this I think – the music of Bach's passion chorale is possible, but feels to weighty – can I have a whole piano concerto? Grieg, or Tchaikovsky, or Beethoven please?

There is questioning in such responses. In the end, what matters? Chopin was perhaps hoping for his music to be out of time, in something like this way. Or perhaps he was simply playing a game with his audience. Whatever, it is the ambiguity of music, its ability to hold to conflict and its resolution, at the same time, that gives it a special place in the understanding of people and communities.

Another use of music to help understand and resolve religious conflict is bringing religious-musical traditions together. This can be illustrated from one of the most profound of religious conflicts. Music can take a lead in bringing together people in conflict. Daniel Barenboim is a Jewish musician, born in Argentina of Russian Jewish descent, living in Israel since he was ten, and working for many years in Germany. In the early 1990s, he met Edward Said, a Palestinian-born cultural critic from a Christian background living and working in the United States. Together they founded the West-Eastern Divan project 'as a way to bring together musicians from Israel, Palestine and the other Arab countries to make music together, and ultimately – when we realised how much interest there was for the idea – to form an orchestra' (Barenboim 2008, pp. 63–64). They took their name from a collection of poems by Goethe (the *West-Eastern Divan*, published in 1819). Goethe was a German poet inspired by Arabic and the Persian poetry of Hafiz. As Barenboim says,

> The West-Eastern Divan Orchestra is, of course, unable to bring about peace. It can, however, create the conditions for understanding without which it is impossible even to speak of peace. It has the potential to awaken the curiosity of each individual to listen to the narrative of the other and to inspire the courage necessary to hear what one would prefer not to. … People have often called this a wonderful example of tolerance, a term I dislike, because to tolerate something or somebody implies an underlying negativity; one is tolerant in spite of certain negative qualities. … Goethe expressed this succinctly when he said 'To merely tolerate is to insult; true liberalism means acceptance.' True acceptance, I might add, means to acknowledge the difference and dignity of the other. In music, this is represented perfectly by counterpoint or polyphony. Acceptance of the freedom and individuality of the other is one of music's most important lessons.
> *(Barenboim 2008, pp. 73–74)*

It is an orchestra of musicians from many religious groups. Although the example of this orchestra is not explicitly to bring music from different religious traditions together, the inter-religious source of its name, as well as the choice of repertoire, specifically raise religious issues. At one point, a young Israeli Jewish member of the group said he had been discriminated against in an informal musical session, when others would not let him join in a performance.

['T]hey said to me "You can't play Arabic music. Only Arabs can play Arabic music."' It was quite an extraordinary moment. And there was this whole question about who could play Arabic music and who couldn't.

So that was one problem. And then, of course, the next question was, 'Well, what gives you the right to play Beethoven? You're not German.' So that discussion was going nowhere. . . . However, ten days later, the same kid who had claimed that only Arabs can play Arabic music was teaching Yo-Yo Ma how to tune his cello to the Arabic scale. So obviously he thought Chinese people could play Arabic music. Gradually the circle extended and they were all playing the Beethoven Seventh. *(Said, in Barenboim and Said 2002, pp. 8–9)*

The West-Eastern Divan Orchestra is a striking example of intercultural work, exemplified in its performances (as in the CD and DVD documentary, Barenboim 2005, and part of a performance at *www.youtube.com/ watch?v=vGJcQCE7XYw&feature=related*). It illustrates the claim of Illman that inter-religious work is too often 'treated primarily as an intellectual challenge', rather than 'ethical and practical' (Illman 2010, p. 175).

Illman goes on to cite a second, and equally striking, example of music being used to overcome some of conflicts amongst Israelis and Palestinians, in the work of Jordi Savall and colleagues. He brought Catholic and Orthodox Christians, Moroccan and Palestinian Muslims, and Sephardic-Ladino and Ashkenazi Jews together to work on explicitly religious music, in the *Jerusalem* project. The commercial outcome – two CDs and an accompanying booklet – is an example and a warning. It is an example of musical collaboration that did not try to drown out the distinct voices of peoples and traditions. It is also a warning: such work is hard, and the musicians taking part in the project apparently objected, at various points, to working together on particular elements. They argued, and the arguments were sufficiently resolved. The final two sections of music 'refer to one of the etymologies accounting for the name of the city of Jerusalem, according to which the city's Hebrew name is translated as "the city of the two peaces", a clear metaphorical reference to both "heavenly peace" and "earthly peace"' (Savall 2008, p. 108). The final section is 'earthly peace', and Savall himself describes the music well.

By way of conclusion, we evoke 'earthly peace', a peace sought after by the political leaders who have governed the city over the five thousand years and more of its recorded history. We have symbolised that peace through Arab Jewish, (Orthodox) Armenian and (Catholic) Latin 'votive pleas for peace', as

well as a melody handed down by oral tradition that has been kept alive to the present day in almost all Mediterranean cultures. The melody is … finally … sung by all the performers together in a choral version in which the languages are superimposed on one another, in a symbolic demonstration of the fact that, far from being a utopia, union and harmony are a reality that is attainable if we allow ourselves to experience and feel the power of music to the full. Rounding off this optimistic final expression of optimism, the 'trumpets of Jericho' return, but this time they do so to remind us that human beings are still spiritually cut off from one another by too many walls, walls that must first be broken down in our hearts before they can be dismantled by peaceful means in the world around us. *(Savall 2008, p. 108)*

As an illustration of the ability of music to express religious diversity and to overcome religious conflict, this work is of considerable value. As Illman comments, Savall's work suggests that '[m]usic can bring a spiritual element into dialogue, … [which] means to move from aesthetical to ethical, from superficial to profound, from rational to emotional' (Illman 2010, p. 182). Dialogue is a practice, in music or speech, that can flourish in some contexts, and is much needed in those contexts where it has difficulty flourishing. Knauth points out that '*dialogue which includes a dialogical treatment* of conflicts has to fulfil certain pre-requisites: dialogue is dependent on a communicative and unconstrained atmosphere in class, necessary teaching skills and, last but not least, confidence, which cannot be declared, but has to be developed patiently during constant and sustained dialogical practice' (Knauth, in Avest et al. 2009, p. 132). Using music in dialogic ways, in challenging contexts, is well described by Savall and Illman. Similar musical work has been completed within Northern Ireland, working with Protestant and Catholic Christians (Odena 2010), within Germany, looking at German Christian and Muslim Turkish musical traditions back to the eighteenth century (Concerto Köln and Sarband 2004, 2005, online examples at *www.youtube.com/watch?v=DgZtfdgUoZs*), and, with popular music across the world, the *What About Me?* project of Bridgeman and Catto (2008, with a trailer at *www.youtube.com/watch?v=LZbiv3EkkF8*). The relationship of music to 'public theology' is also well described by Gill (2010), who notes how religious music can be used in ways and in social contexts that seem to exclude or diminish the significance of other forms of religious practice and expression.

Music can in these and other ways help express religious as well as other forms of diversity.

Activity 12.2: Playlist the curriculum

Research on what music (of all kinds) means to young people can inspire RE teachers to use music as far more than a source of entertainment. A simple research activity, suitable for a wide age range of pupils, is to create a playlist of a particular element of the RE curriculum. It may be a key concept, an event, or a whole tradition. (Themes I have used myself include liberation, old age, and life and death.) But whatever the concept or theme, the playlist should be able to be justified by the pupils. A set of RE playlists grouped into themes is currently available online (at *old.natre.org.uk/music/themes.php*). That is a good starting point for teachers, but pupils will have their own musical interests and knowledge.

Choosing music from a wide variety of religious and non-religious traditions has never been easier, thanks to sites such as YouTube (*www.youtube.com*). It is helpful if pupils make use of their own musical favourites, as long as they can justify the link to the chosen topic.

Playlists may be put onto phones or other devices, and played in the background of future RE lessons.

Conclusion

Returning to Wright's concerns with a creativity that is 'boundless' and unconnected to communities and traditions, I hope that the suggestions in this chapter allow for creativity to be far more than mere decoration or entertainment, or purely individual self-expression. Whereas it might be an insult to a religion to reduce it to something merely decorative, it would be just as much of an insult to ignore the creative expression common to every religious – and non-religious – tradition. Some of the activities described in this chapter use creative activities, also, to explore and research RE topics. In these ways, creativity becomes a means to understand, as well as a way of generating 'objects' that can help other people understand. Within broader educational research, an approach to research has developed that is known as 'arts-based educational research (*www.abersig.com/* in the United States, and *www. bera.ac.uk/group/arts-based-educational-research* in the UK). These groupings bring together researchers who use arts as a *method* of research: they are not (or not primarily) exploring arts in education, but using arts to explore education. A good example is an opera devised by Nick Owen and colleagues, based on texts from officials and staff and parents involved in a campaign related to a school closure. The opera, called *Closing Schools for the Future*, used quotations as a libretto, and set them to music. All who heard the opera understood the issues better than those who might have only read the documents or heard the debates. I am not suggesting that RE teachers should be composing operas in their spare time – although if someone does, I'll be first in line to come and see it – but, instead, to see creative work as a way to understand, as well as an 'object' to be understood.

Chapter 13
The Future of RE:search

I was scared because I'm a Christian and I thought that when I was there I wouldn't know if I'm a Christian or a Hindu
(A 10-year-old pupil, explaining associating the word 'frightening' with a *mandir*, prior to a visit)

Introduction

The future of RE as a subject and the future of research in RE are closely connected. Those connections are made throughout this book. In this chapter, there is an attempt to see whether there is a single argument running through the various themes in RE and research, based on the identification of problems in need of solutions, or, more positively, questions in need of answers. Within RE, problems or questions have been identified with respect to many issues, including the proper understanding and use of sacred texts, the methods of developing dialogue within and between communities, the nature of and ways of achieving inclusion, the development of coherent pedagogy in RE, and how RE can properly contribute to political issues. Within research, problems or questions have been identified with respect to interpretation and translation, how meaningful dialogue can be stimulated and captured, how to measure inclusion, understanding the relationship between what teachers do and what pupils learn, and understanding and measuring the impact of ethics or character education. Chapter 9, on ethnography, raised the problem or question of how RE can proceed through the use ethnographic research methods. Difficult as it is to reduce such complex problems to a single one, it seems as though there is a relational theme running through them all. How do pupils relate to sacred texts and their use in religious communities, how do pupils relate to each other and to communities within and beyond school, how do pupils and teachers relate to each other, how do pupils and teachers of RE relate to national and international social and political contexts, and how do RE and research relate to each other? There is a single concept that helps illuminate all of these relationships: that of sincerity. Sincerity is not the answer to all the problems of RE or research, but it is a valuable principle rarely addressed in the literature, and one that can help carry RE and research through to a better future, a future making full use of research in RE, a future that might be properly described as one of RE:search.

That approach was exemplified in the Westhill seminars. When I got back in touch with the participants in the seminars, several years later, I explored with them the influence of time spent discussing and thinking about research in RE.

> The influence of the seminars on professionals was perceived by respondents as being mostly on the way they teach (88% agree or strongly agree that 'seminars changed for the better the way I teach'), and their confidence in teaching (85% agree or strongly agree). This was all the more interesting, as most of the respondents were very experienced: 83% had 11 or more years' professional experience in religious education. Professionals based in higher education were as conscious as others of the confidence-building quality of the seminars, with one experienced teacher educator saying in interview that 'it was very helpful for my confidence … reassuring me that I was on the right lines'. *(Stern 2014a, p. 28)*

Not only were the seminars themselves perceived to be influential, somewhat surprisingly, not far behind was the influence of *publications* from the seminars, including the first edition of this book. Seventy-eight per cent of participants agreed or strongly agreed that those 'changed the way I teach', and 75 per cent said the publications 'increased my confidence'. One teacher wrote that '[t]his whole experience raised my confidence in my ability to "think" and be part of the "thinking" world of religious education' (Stern 2014a, p. 28). There was also very significant evidence of the seminars influencing pupils, the greatest influence being on pupil learning (74 per cent agree or strongly agree) and pupil interest in RE (72 per cent agree or strongly agree) (Stern 2014a, p. 32).

Activities that 'bring together education professionals from different sectors, involving not only the presentation of, but discussion of and time to think about, research, and encouraging active participation in that research, are a model of practice-engaged educational, rather than just education, research of significance well beyond religious education' (Stern 2014a, p. 36, and see Bakker and Heimbrock 2007). This is all encouraging. But there is plenty more to be done, as RE, research, and professional practice all move on at a fast pace.

Research and sincerity in phenomenological and positivistic research

Much empirical research in RE (as described, for example, in the excellent Francis et al. 1996) has followed social scientific methodologies, focusing on questioning in a way that avoids confusing (over-complex or unclear) or leading questions.

If confusing questions generate confused answers, and leading questions bias the answers in the direction in which the questioner leads, researchers can simply avoid these types of questions. By avoiding misleading questions, it is thought that lying will be avoided and truth will emerge. But those involved in religion will understand how limited is 'avoiding lying' as an approach to research, and how much more is required for meaningful dialogue about religion. Reaching towards the truth, in RE research or in the rest of life, requires more than 'not lying'. The 'more' that is required may be described as 'sincerity'.

Within social science research, there are two major traditions: phenomenological or interpretive research, which generally makes use of more qualitative research methods, and positivistic research, which generally makes use of more quantitative research methods. Research projects often draw on both traditions, despite those traditions being based on contrasting philosophies. The implications of 'sincerity' are therefore worth working through both traditions. And although sincerity is little studied in mainstream methodology textbooks, it is supported by philosophic heavyweights such as Wittgenstein, Macmurray, and Habermas. Wittgenstein contrasts 'truthfulness' and 'sincerity', so that 'A dog cannot be a hypocrite, but neither can he be sincere' (Wittgenstein 1958, p. 229e). That is, people and dogs can be truthful, but only people can be sincere. Also, attempting to avoid some of the biases associated with particular research tools, then, RE research should try to elicit a form of sincerity from respondents, something more than 'avoiding lying'. Macmurray, similarly, contrasts 'negative untruthfulness' (i.e. lying) and sincerity, with sincerity being 'much more than' avoiding lying:

> [Sincerity] is positively expressing what you do think and believe. To refrain from expressing what you think or believe or know to someone, if it is to his advantage or to someone else's advantage that he should know it, is positive dishonesty. We call it dissimulation – the suppression of the truth. *(Macmurray 1995, p. 76)*

This is similar to Mingers' description of the contrast in Habermas between 'truth' and 'truthfulness'.

> Habermas argues that any communicative utterance aimed at generating understanding and agreement implicitly raises four validity claims – that it is comprehensible, that it is factually correct or in principle possible (truth), that it is acceptable normatively (rightness), and that it is meant sincerely (truthfulness). *(Mingers 1999, p. 4)*

Is this relevant to RE? Geiger notes the 'pervasive ... assumption' in RE 'that students engage in learning sincerely', and so the possibility – even likelihood – of *insincerity* in RE is 'a major blind spot for RE' (Geiger 2016c, p. 505). The value of sincerity and the risk of insincerity are just as great for participants in research.

Phenomenological research approaches focus on 'meaning-making', with the meaning often being seen as made by individuals, and in some circumstances by the researcher and the respondent together. Such research is likely to ignore the systematic measurement of social organizations and the possibility of systematic measured comparison of organizations. Research methods used include participant observation when the researcher joins the group to be studied, the close analysis of conversations or texts, and in-depth interviews sometimes modelled on psychotherapeutic interviewing techniques. Many of which are well described in Silverman 1997, and for studies of religion in McCutcheon (1999). This can lead to more individualistic meaning-making, as in Moustakas' description of heuristic research. 'Heuristics' is a term used in general research methodology for rather open investigation or discovery, sometimes by trial and error, and for Moustakas, heuristic research 'refers to a process of internal search through which one discovers the nature and meaning of experience and develops methods and procedures for further investigation and analysis', and '[t]he self of the researcher is present throughout the process and, while understanding the phenomenon with increasing depth, the researcher also experiences growing self-awareness and self-knowledge' (Moustakas 1994, p. 17).

Moustakas' views will have many echoes for those in RE concerned with the search for truth: 'I must pause and consider what my own life is and means, in conscious awareness, in thought, in reflections', he says, and though I may come to knowledge, 'knowledge does not end with moments of connectedness, understanding, and meaning' as '[s]uch journeys open vistas to new journeys for uncovering meaning, truth, and essence' (Moustakas 1994, p. 65). '[T]he beauty of knowledge and discovery' is that '[i]t keeps us forever awake, alive, and connected with what is and with what matters in life' (Moustakas 1994, p. 65). That is a wonderful picture of research. However, the tendency to more individualistic meaning-making of this kind might yet trouble some researchers of religion and some other phenomenological research. For example, personal involvement can cause difficulties, as described of the meetings with a Vodou priestess noted by MacCarthy Brown (in McCutcheon 1999). Helpfully, the individualistic (and potentially over-personal) approach is contrasted by Silverman with the possibility of systematic analysis in qualitative research. He stresses the need 'to broaden our conception of qualitative research beyond issues of subjective "meaning" and towards issues of language, representation and social organization' (Silverman 1997, p. 1). He also notes his 'belief that a social *science*, which takes seriously the attempt to sort fact from fancy, remains a valid enterprise', as part of the 'search for ways of building links between social science traditions rather than dwelling in "armed camps" fighting internal battles' (Silverman 1997, p. 1). Ethnography can be building that bridge, by following the guidance of Silverman and also that of Moustakas, who himself refers back to Buber's 'explorations of dialogue and mutuality' (Moustakas 1994, p. 17).

It is the return to issues of dialogue that reaffirms the need for sincerity in phenomenological research, and it is dialogue that can also bring back the broader community dynamics, vital in schools and in school-based research in RE. The mutuality of relationships in community is underpinned by Macmurray's concern with schools as communities, affirming the humanity and integrity of pupils and teachers alike. He says that 'the integrity of the personal is to be found more certainly and more securely in the early years of life than is ever likely to be achieved in our maturity', so 'the task of the teacher appears no longer as an effort to achieve an integrity of character that is absent in the young ...; but rather to preserve the integrity of childhood through the process of its growth and maturity' (Macmurray 1964b, pp. 17–18).

Positivist, in contrast to phenomenological, approaches to research can at times be stereotyped as entirely focused on 'scientific counting', creating systematic models of organizations and ignoring all questions of meaning. The stereotype of positivist research may also include an entirely neutral researcher who has no impact on the people being researched. Yet some of the more positivist research does indeed investigate meanings and most certainly recognizes the difficulties of achieving neutrality. It is possible that sincerity can help enhance positivist research, and that is what is attempted here. To develop sincerity in research requires creating contexts in which respondents feel that their answers matter, and that the questioner wants and needs to know what they think for substantive reasons. This may require more dialogue and 'engagement', and less anonymity and pretended neutrality, than is usual in research. It can mean that research should routinely be set in the context of purposes related to the subject of research. For example, introducing research on school effectiveness to pupils, a researcher might ask the pupils whether they would like to help improve their school (the answer is almost inevitably 'yes'), and whether they know better than, say, their teachers, how to improve their school (the answer is generally also 'yes'). In such a context, and if the researcher is committed to reporting the research back to the pupils, the student council, and the staff, the pupils are likely to feel – correctly – an incentive to be sincere. The only people who might be excluded from accepting the assumption that school might be improved would be those who believed school as a whole, or this school in particular, was wholly inadequate – for example, those who might support the 'deschooling' movement (as for example, in Illich 1971, 1974) – and those who believed the school was perfect in every way. Such pupils are rare, and work by Rudduck and colleagues suggests that pupils have many criticisms of schools (including schools with better and worse public 'reputations'), but that they share basic educational goals, so that '[b]ehind the public mask of nonchalance that some pupils wear to hide their anxiety about the future is a concern to succeed and some realisation of the consequences of not making the grade' (Rudduck et al. 1996, p. 3).

Researchers, too, will avoid the 'mask of nonchalance', by admitting their interest in the responses. In that way, sincerity creates a more honest relationship that is likely to involve more sincere responses from pupils. The apparent bias of the research – a bias towards finding out what matters – will itself be likely to enhance, rather than detract from, the value of the responses. 'Sincerity' as an approach to research can also be related to the stress on 'ownership' of research tools, highlighted in the methodology of Dalin and Rust. They say that

[o]rganization development assumes that school personnel should have a maximum degree of ownership in the renewal process. Research on change indicates that

successful implementation is highly correlated with a sense of ownership of the ideas, the process and solutions found. *(Dalin and Rust 1983, p. 175)*

In this way, 'ownership' can be seen as a way of increasing the likelihood of sincerity. Developing the theme of ownership, sincerity can also be demonstrated by valuing the products of research: research results can be given back to those researched, for their own use. The sincerity involved in such approaches to research also has professional implications.

Sincerity in RE research

Sincerity in RE research has an impact on RE classrooms when those classrooms involve pupils and teachers working together as researchers, as in ethnographic, interpretive, constructivist, and various other RE traditions. Classrooms aiming for 'more than not lying' will be learning communities, bound together in a rich dialogue of truths and human development. RE, a subject itself rich in dialogue, truths, and human development, can lead the way to research-rich schooling. The themes identified for the Westhill seminars addressed in this book included current research in RE of relevance to teachers in the UK and across the world. The research tasks – described as 'activities' – spread through the book each illustrate different ways in which RE research, and therefore RE, might exemplify sincerity. It is helpful to give specific examples, explaining the relationship between the task and sincerity.

On sacred text, Activity 7.3 on storytelling from the Bhagavad Gita is helped by the expectation of trying to understand the intentions of those who use the text in a religious context and trying to understand the purposes to which pupils might put the text. The work would demonstrate less sincerity to the extent that pupils were given questions with simple, readymade, right and wrong answers, or were given no time to consider the importance of the texts to their own lives, religious or not. Research on dialogue, like dialogue of all kinds, can be made more likely to be sincere if participants have something of importance to talk about, and Activity 2.1 on what more can be done to promote religious harmony provides such a topic, a topic of especial significance in those periods when disharmony is all too common. Inclusion is investigated by inspection bodies (such as Ofsted in the UK), and some inspection guidance suggested inspectors should talk to pupils about their feelings on inclusion (Ofsted 2000a). The involvement of pupils is to be welcomed, and research on inclusion in RE should go even further. Activity 6.1 asks pupils and teachers to investigate in detail how inclusive the RE curriculum is, with sincerity promoted by the self-reflective nature of the research. It can be further enhanced by explicitly framing the research as part of improvement planning for the RE department. In a similar way, on pedagogy, pupils are asked in Activity 5.2 about their own subjects, and the responses are not guesses at the 'right answers', but genuinely meant questions about how teachers and pupils typically speak in lessons. Making research more sincere can be about making the questions and answers current and relevant to the lives of the pupils, as in the debate in Activity 11.1. Ethnographic research in RE is likely to be based in a tradition where sincerity might be expected, and Activity 9.2 looks at clarifying the process of ethnography, in order to enable more sincere research to take place. It illuminates ethnography by transposing it: by drawing *with* people rather than drawing/writing *about* people.

The more sincerity there is in RE research, the more value that research is likely to have, in itself and for RE, schools, and the wider communities in which they are set. There are many who will joke about sincerity and trivialize its significance. There is a well-known quotation from Jean Giraudoux, a French diplomat and writer of the early twentieth century: 'The secret of success is sincerity. If you can fake that, you've got it made' (*www.quotationspage.com/quote/481.html*). Joking apart, an approach to RE and research that embodies sincerity is one that could help enrich and enliven an already-rich and vibrant subject. Teaching RE, with teachers and pupils as researchers in the classroom, can bring people and communities together. Now, just as in every other period of history, this is a worthwhile and much needed task.

It is helpful to end the chapter (and the book) with a task that has a long religious history and a shorter history as a research tool: Moksha Chitram (adapted from Mackley 2002; Stern 2003b). The Moksha Chitram game originated in Hindu communities in India, helping players think about how to achieve the ultimate goal of *moksha*: release from the cycle of births and rebirths. The game was adapted by British Christians in India in the nineteenth century, based around the 'seven deadly sins' and corresponding virtues, but continuing to use the original Indian symbolism of snakes and ladders. Commercial, secularized, versions of the game became popular under the title 'snakes and ladders'.

Activity 13.1: Moksha Chitram

The activity could help pupils reflect on any 'goal', but for these purposes, the ultimate end in life is probably the most appropriate one.

- Each pair of pupils should be provided with an empty grid (as below) with 100 squares, numbered from 1 to 100, and a way of drawing snakes and ladders. (The grid works well as a word-processed document, with the snakes and ladders as 'stretchable' clip art items, able to be hyperlinked to other pictures or documents or websites.)
- In pairs, pupils should consider what they want to achieve in life and represent that in a drawing or piece of writing in square 100.
- Now they will think about some of the things that might hinder them from achieving their goal, the 'snakes', with the length of the snake representing the degree of hindrance. Each pair might produce four or five snakes, each labelled according to what they represent.

- Now they will think about some of the things that might help them to achieve their goal, the 'ladders', with the length of the ladder representing the degree of help. Each pair might produce four or five ladders, again labelled according to what they represent.
- Now, play the game, using a die.
- The completed Moksha Chitram games can be used as a display, and the pupils are likely to be keen to discuss how the games work and what they tell them about what helps and hinders them in life. The connections to inclusion are clear: pupils are investigating barriers and the overcoming of barriers.

100	99	98	97	96	95	94	93	92	91
81	82	83	84	85	86	87	88	89	90
80	79	78	77	76	75	74	73	72	71
61	62	63	64	65	66	67	68	69	70
60	59	58	57	56	55	54	53	52	51
41	42				46	47	48	49	50
40	39				35	34	33	32	31
21	22			25	26	27	28	29	30
20	19	18	17		15	14	13	12	11
1	2	3	4	5	6	7	8	9	10

Conclusion

All the staff and all the pupils in school are living and working together. The idea of workers having a 'work-life balance' is, rightly, popular with human resource departments as much as with trade unions and professional associations. For me, the problem with the phrase is simply its implication that when we are at 'work', we are not 'living'. Martin Buber wrote of the modern world's artificial division between the institutions in which we work (thought to be efficient places without emotion) and the homes in which live (thought to be emotional places of 'feelings', and without any useful activity). He said neither was fully human:

> the separated *It* of institutions is an animated clod without soul, and the separated *I* of feelings an uneasily-fluttering soul-bird. Neither of them knows man: institutions know only the specimen, feelings only the 'object'; neither knows the person, or mutual life. *(Buber 1958, p. 63)*

For Buber, schools should be *living* places, places where we are leading meaningful mutual lives. The mutuality of schools, in turn, means that teachers and other adults working in the school are important, just as the pupils are important. Many would recognize the comment from Macmurray, that '[t]he tendency to sacrifice the adults to the children [in school] is as disastrous as it is widespread' (Macmurray 1946c, p. 6). What the Moksha Chritram activity can do – for teachers and pupils alike – is to see how schools can contribute to living well. RE is – in my view – central to this task, as it helps us all explore the various ways in which different people have answered life's big questions. The more we can be curious, as teachers and as pupils, the better. That has been the purpose of this book.

Bibliography

Almirzanah, S (2014) 'Celebrating Differences through Dialogue in Indonesia', *Religious Education*, 109:3, pp. 234–245.

American Psychiatric Association (APA) (2013) *Diagnostic and Statistical Manual of Mental Disorders*: Fifth Edition (DSM-5); Arlington, VI: American Psychiatric Association Publishing.

Anczyk, A and Grzymała-Moszczyńska, J (2016) 'Religious Discrimination Discourse in the Mono-Cultural School: The Case of Poland', *British Journal of Religious Education*, pp. 1–11.

Anning, A and Ring, K (2004) *Making Sense of Children's Drawings*; Maidenhead: Open University Press.

Aristotle (1984) *The Complete Works of Aristotle*; Princeton, NJ: Princeton University Press.

Arthur, J (2010) *Of Good Character: Exploration of Virtues and Values in 3–25 Year-Olds*; Exeter: Imprint Academic.

Arthur, J and Carr, D (2013) 'Character in Learning for Life: A Virtue-Ethical Rationale for Recent Research on Moral and Values Education', *Journal of Beliefs & Values*, 34:1, pp. 26–35.

Arthur, J and Lovat, T (eds) (2013) *The Routledge International Handbook of Education, Religion and Values*; Abingdon: Routledge.

Arthur, J, Kristjánsson, K, Walker, D, Sanderse, W, Jones, C, Thoma, S, Curren, R, and Roberts, M (2015) *Character Education in UK Schools: Research Report*; Birmingham: Jubilee Centre for Character and Virtues.

Assessment Reform Group (1999) *Assessment for Learning: Beyond the Black Box*; Cambridge: University of Cambridge School of Education.

Astley, J, Francis, L J, Robbins, M, and Selçuk, M (eds) (2012) *Teaching Religion, Teaching Truth: Theoretical and Empirical Perspectives*; Bern: Peter Lang.

Avest, I ter, Bakker, C, and Miedema, S (2008) 'Different Schools as Narrative Communities: Identity Narratives in Threefold', *Religious Education*, 103:3, pp. 307–322.

Avest, I ter, Jozsa, D-P, Knauth, T, Rosón, J, and Skeie, G (eds) (2009) *Dialogue and Conflict on Religion: Studies of Classroom Interaction in European Countries*; Münster: Waxmann.

Back, S (2012) *Ways of Learning to Teach: A Philosophically Inspired Analysis of Teacher Education Programs*; Rotterdam: Sense.

Bakker, C and Heimbrock, H-G (eds) (2007) *Research RE Teachers. RE Teachers as Researchers*; München: Waxmann.

Ball, S J (1981) *Beachside Comprehensive: A Case Study of Secondary Schooling*; Cambridge: Cambridge University Press.

Ballard, R (ed) (1994) *Desh Pradesh: South Asian Experience in Britain*; London: C Hurst & Co.

Barenboim, D (conductor) (2005) *Barenboim: West-Eastern Divan Orchestra: Tchaikovsky Symphony No 5, Verdi Overture the Force of Destiny, Sibelius Valse Triste*; Warner Classics CD and DVD 2564 62190–2.

Barenboim, D (2008) *Everything Is Connected: The Power of Music*; London: Phoenix.

Barenboim, D and Said, E W (2002) *Parallels and Paradoxes: Explorations in Music and Society: Edited with a Preface by Ara Guzelimian*; London: Bloomsbury.

Barić, D and Burušić, J (2015) 'Quality of Religious Education in Croatia Assessed from Teachers' Perspective', *British Journal of Religious Education*, 37:3, pp. 293–310.

Barker, E (ed) (1982) *New Religious Movements: A Perspective for Understanding Society*; New York: Edwin Mellen Press.

Barker, E (1984) *The Making of a Moonie: Brainwashing or Choice?*; Oxford: Blackwell.

Barker, E (1989) *New Religious Movements: A Practical Introduction*; London: HMSO.

Barker, E (ed) (2013) *Revisionism and Diversification in New Religious Movements*; London: Routledge.

Barnes, L P (ed) (2012) *Debates in Religious Education*; London: Routledge.

Barratt, M (1994a) *Bridges to Religions: Lucy's Sunday*; London: Heinemann.

Barratt, M (1994b) *Bridges to Religions: The Buddha's Birthday*; London: Heinemann.

Barratt, M (1994c) *Bridges to Religions: An Egg for Babcha*; London: Heinemann.

Baumann, G (1996) *Contesting Culture: Discourses of Identity in Multi-Ethnic London*; Cambridge: Cambridge University Press.

Baumann, G (1999) *The Multicultural Riddle: Rethinking National, Ethnic and Religious Identities*; London: Routledge.

Baumfield, V (2002) *Thinking through Religious Education*; Cambridge: Chris Kington.

Baumfield, V (2003) 'Democratic RE: Preparing Young People for Citizenship', *British Journal of Religious Education*, 25:3, pp. 173–184.

Baumfield, V (2014) 'To Teach Is To Learn', *British Journal of Religious Education*, 36:1, pp. 1–3.

Baumfield, V (2016) 'Making a Difference in the Religious Education Classroom: Integrating Theory and Practice in Teachers' Professional Learning', *British Journal of Religious Education*, 38:2, pp. 141–151.

Baumfield, V M (2017) 'Between a Rock and a Hard Place? The Dilemma of the Religious Educator', *British Journal of Religious Education*, 39:2, pp. 119–121.

Baumfield, V, Bowness, C, Cush, D, and Miller, J (1994) *A Third Perspective*; privately published.

Beadle, L (ed) (2006) *Steps in RE Onwards and Upwards: Addressing the Additional Support Needs of Students in Key Stage 3 (11–14 year olds) in RE*; Birmingham: RE Today Services.

Beane, J A (1995) 'Curriculum Integration and the Disciplines of Knowledge', *Phi Delta Kappan*, 76:8, pp. 616–622.

Beckerlegge, G (ed) (2001a) *The World Religions Reader*: Second Edition; London: Routledge and the Open University Press.

Beckerlegge, G (ed) (2001b) *From Sacred Text to Internet*; Aldershot: Ashgate and the Open University Press.

Bell, J (1999) *Curriculum and Professional Development in RE: Syllabus Implementation Studies 1996–99: Research Report on the Implementation of the New Syllabus in LEA 1*; Norwich: University of East Anglia.

Benjamin, S (2002) *The Micropolitics of Inclusive Education: An Ethnography*; Buckingham: Open University Press.

Berglund, J, Shanneik, Y, and Bocking, B (eds) (2016) *Religious Education in a Global-Local World*; Cham: Springer.

Bernstein, B (1975) *Class, Codes and Control, Volume III: Towards and Theory of Educational Transmission*; London: Routledge and Kegan Paul.

Berryman, J W (1999) 'Silence Is Stranger Than It Used To Be: Teaching Silence and the Future of Humankind', *Religious Education*, 94:3, pp. 256–272.

Biesta, G and Hannam, P (2016) 'Religious Education and the Return of the Teacher', *Religious Education*, 111:3, pp. 239–243.

Birmingham City Council (2007) *The Birmingham Agreed Syllabus for Religious Education*; Birmingham: Birmingham City Council.

Black, P and Wiliam, D (1998a) 'Assessment and Classroom Learning' *Assessment in Education: Principles, Policy & Practice*, 5:1, pp. 7–74.

Black, P and Wiliam, D (1998b) 'Inside the Black Box: Raising Standards through Classroom Assessment', *Phi Delta Kappan*, 89:2, pp. 139–148.

Blaylock, L (2000a) 'Teachers with Others Specialisms in RE: The 'TWOS' Project', *REsource*, 22:2, pp. 6–10.

Blaylock, L (2000b) 'Issues in Achievement and Assessment in Religious Education in England: Which Way Should We Turn?', *British Journal of Religious Education*, 23:1, pp. 45–58.

Blaylock, L (ed) (2001a) *Listening to Children in Primary Religious Education*; Birmingham: PCfRE.

Blaylock, L (ed) (2001b) *Listening to Young People in Secondary Education*; Birmingham: PCfRE.

Blaylock, L (2004a) 'Six Schools of Thought in RE', *REsource*, 27:1, pp. 13–16.

Blaylock, L (2004b) *Picturing Jesus: Worldwide Contemporary Artists: Powerful Contemporary Visual Images of Some Gospel Stories of Jesus from Artists in Every Continent of the World*; Birmingham: Christian Education Publications.

Blaylock, L (2004c) *Picturing Jesus: Worldwide Contemporary Artists: Powerful Contemporary Visual Images of Some of Jesus' Gospel Stories from Artists in Every Continent of the World*; Birmingham: Christian Education Publications.

Blinkova, A and Vermeer, P (2016) 'Religious Education in Russia: A Comparative and Critical Analysis', *British Journal of Religious Education*, 2016, pp. 1–13.

Bowie, B (2012) 'Human Rights Education and the Post Secular Turn', *Journal of Beliefs & Values*, 33:2, pp. 195–205.

Bowie, R A (2017) *Dignity and Human Rights Education: Exploring Ultimate Worth in a Post-Secular World*; Oxford: Peter Lang.

Bowker, J (ed) (1997) *The Oxford Dictionary of World Religions*; Oxford: Oxford University Press.

Bretherton, L (2006) *Hospitality as Holiness: Christian Witness Amid Moral Diversity*; Aldershot: Ashgate.

Bridgeman, D and Catto, J [1 Giant Leap] (2008) *What about Me?*; 4DVD C4DVD10235.

British Humanist Association (BHA) (2002) *Spiritual Development in Schools – Some Issues for Humanists*; London: BHA.

Brown, D (2004) *The Da Vinci Code*; London: Transworld.

Brown, E (1996) *Religious Education for All*; London: David Fulton.

Bruner, J S (1996) *The Culture of Education*; Cambridge, MA: Harvard University Press.

Bryan, H and Revell, L (2011) 'Performativity, Faith and Professional Identity: Student RE Teachers and the Ambiguities of Objectivity', *British Journal of Educational Studies*, 59:4, pp. 403–419.

Buber, M (1958) *I and Thou: Second Edition with a Postscript by the Author*; Edinburgh: T&T Clark.

Buber, M (1999 [1941]) *Gog and Magog: A Novel*; Syracuse, NY: Syracuse University Press.

Buber, M (2002 [1965]) *Between Man and Man*; London: Routledge.

Buchanan, M T (ed) (2013) *Leadership and Religious Schools: International Perspectives and Challenges*; New York: Continuum.

Buchanan, M T and Engebretson, K (2009) 'The Significance of Theory in the Implementation of Curriculum Change in Religious Education', *British Journal of Religious Education*, 31:2, pp. 141–152.

Buchanan, M T and Gellel, A (eds) (2015) *Global Perspectives on Catholic Religious Education in Schools*; Cham: Springer.

Al-Buraidi, J A (2006) *An Empirical Study of the Perceptions of Male Teachers and Students of the Islamic Education Curriculum in Secondary Schools in the Kingdom of Saudi Arabia*, PhD Thesis, University of Hull: Hull.

Burke, C and Grosvenor, I (2003) *The School I'd Like: Children and Young People's Reflections on an Education for the 21st Century*; Abingdon: RoutledgeFalmer.

Burnett, T B (producer) (2000) *Music from the Motion Picture O Brother, Where Art Thou?*; Mercury 170 069-2(11).

Bustion, O (2017) 'Autism and Christianity: An Ethnographic Intervention', *Journal of the American Academy of Religion*, pp. 1–29.

Carrington, B and Troyna, B (eds) (1988) *Children and Controversial Issues: Strategies for the Early and Middle Years of Schooling*; London: Falmer.

Chapman, W E (1977) *Roots of Character Education: An Exploration of the American Heritage from the Decade of the 1920s*; Schenectady, NY: Character Research Press.

Chater, M and Erricker, C (2013) *Does Religious Education Have a Future?: Pedagogical and Policy Prospects*; London: Routledge.

Chichester Diocesan Board of Education (2006) *Educating the Whole Child: Spiritual, Moral, Social and Cultural Development*; Hove: Chichester Diocesan Board of Education.

Chödzin, S and Kohn, A (illustrations by Marie Cameron) (1997) *The Barefoot Book of Buddhist Tales*; Bath: Barefoot Books.

Chrisafis, A (2015) 'Pork or Nothing: How School Dinners Are Dividing France', *Guardian*, 13 October 2015.

Chryssides, G (1999) *Exploring New Religions*; London: Cassell.

Chryssides, G (2003) 'Books on New Religious Movements', *REsource*, 26:1, pp. 4–7.

Chryssides, G D and Wilkins, M Z (ed) (2006) *A Reader in New Religious Movements*; London: Continuum.

Cohen, L, Manion, L and Morrison, K (2011) *Research Methods in Education*: Seventh Edition; Abingdon: Routledge.

Concerto Köln and Sarband (2004) *Dream of the Orient*; Deutsche Grammophon B0001J04HE.

Concerto Köln and Sarband (2005) *The Walz: Ecstasy and Mysticism*; Archiv B0009AM5H2.

Conroy, J C, Lundie, D, Davis, R A, Baumfield, V, Barnes, L P, Gallagher, T, Lowden, K, Bourque, N, and Wennell, K (2013) *Does Religious Education Work?: A Multi-Dimensional Investigation*; London: Bloomsbury.

Cooling, M (1998) *Jesus through Art*; Norwich: RMEP.

Cooling, M (2000a) *Assemblies from the Gallery*; Norwich: RMEP.

Cooling, M (2000b) *The Bible through Art: From Genesis to Esther*; Norwich: RMEP.

Cooling, M (2009) *Christianity through Art: A Resource for Teaching Religious Education through Art*; Norwich: RMEP.

Cooling, T (1994a) *A Christian Vision for State Education: Reflections on the Theology of Education*; London: SPCK.

Cooling, T (1994b) *Concept Cracking: Exploring Christian Beliefs in School*; Stapleford: The Stapleford Centre.

Copley, T (1998a) *Echo of Angels: The First Report of the Biblos Project*; Exeter: Biblos Project, School of Education University of Exeter.

Copley, T (2005) *Indoctrination, Education and God: The Struggle for the Mind*; London: SPCK.

Copley, T and Walshe, K (2002) *The Figure of Jesus in Religious Education*; Exeter: University of Exeter.

Copley, T, Freathy, R, and Walshe, K (2004) *Teaching Biblical Narrative: A Summary of the Main Findings of the Biblos Project, 1996–2004*; Exeter: University of Exeter.

Copley, T, Lane, S, Savini, H and Walshe, K (2001) *Where Angels Fear to Tread: The Second Report of the Biblos Project*; Exeter: University of Exeter.

Council of Europe (1996) *Children's Rights and Childhood Policies in Europe: New Approaches?*; Strasbourg: Council of Europe Publishing.

Council of Europe Committee of Ministers (2008) *Recommendation CM/Rec(2008)12 of the Committee of Ministers to Member States on the Dimension of Religions and Non-Religious Convictions within Intercultural Education*; Strasbourg: Council of Europe.

Croché, S (2015) 'Science and Religion on the Blackboard: Exploring Schoolmasters' Beliefs and Practices in Senegal', *British Journal of Religious Education*, 37:1, pp. 37–52.

Csikszentmihalyi, M and Csikszentmihalyi, I S (eds) (2006) *A Life Worth Living: Contributions to Positive Psychology*; Oxford: Oxford University Press.

Cupitt, D (1991) *What Is a Story?*; Norwich: SCM Press.

Cush, D (1994) 'RE Does Not Equal Worship', *Times Educational Supplement*, 23 September 1994.

Cush, D (1999) 'The Relationships between Religious Studies, Religious Education and Theology: Big Brother, Little Sister and the Clerical Uncle?', *British Journal of Religious Education*, 21:3, pp. 137–146.

Dalin, P, and Rust, V D (1983) *Can Schools Learn?*; Windsor: NFER-Nelson.

Daniels, H (2001) *Vygotsky and Pedagogy*; London: RoutledgeFalmer.

Daniels, H and Edwards, A (eds) (2004) *The RoutledgeFalmer Reader in Psychology of Education*; London: RoutledgeFalmer.

Davie, G (1994) *Religion in Britain since 1945: Believing without Belonging*; Oxford: Blackwell.

Davie, G (2015) *Religion in Britain: A Persistent Paradox*: Second Edition; Chichester: Wiley Blackwell.

Davis, D H and Miroshnikova, E (2013) *The Routledge International Handbook of Religious Education*; London: Routledge.

Department for Education (DfE) (1994a) *Religious Education and Collective Worship: Circular number 1/94*; London: DFE.

Department for Education (DfE), Welsh Office (1994b) *Code of Practice on the Identification and Assessment of Special Educational Needs*; London: DFE.

Department for Education (DfE) (2011) *Teachers' Standards: Guidance for School Leaders, School Staff and Governing Bodies*; London: Department for Education.

Department for Education (DfE) (2013) *The National Curriculum in England: Framework Document: December 2014*; London: Department for Education.

Department for Education and Employment and the Qualifications and Curriculum Authority (DfEE and QCA) (1999) *The National Curriculum for England*; London: HMSO.

Dickinson, E (1970) *The Complete Poems*; London: Faber and Faber.

Dodd, T, Hartshorn, B, Due, B, Gunnarsson, G, Vedelsby, M, MacAdam, R (2002) *Intercultural Matters: Islam and European Education: Issues of Relevance for Teachers*; Castelo Branco: Escola Superior de Educaçã, Instituto Politécnico de Castelo Branco.

Donald, J and Rattansi, A (eds) (1992) *Race, Culture and Difference*; London: Sage.

D'Souza, M O (2000) 'Religious Particularism and Cultural Pluralism: The Possible Contribution of Religious Education to Canadian Political Identity', *Religious Education* 95:3, pp. 233–249.

D'Souza, M O (2016) *A Catholic Philosophy of Education: The Church and Two Philosophers*; Montreal, QC: McGill-Queen's University Press.

Durka, G (2002) *The Teacher's Calling: A Spirituality for Those Who Teach*; New York: Paulist Press.

Elton-Chalcraft, S, Lander, V, Revell, L, Warner, D, and Whitworth, L (2017) 'To Promote, or Not to Promote Fundamental British Values? Teachers' Standards, Diversity and Teacher Education', *British Educational Research Journal*, 43:1, pp. 29–48.

Erricker, C and Erricker, J (2000) *Reconstructing Religious, Spiritual and Moral Education*; London: RoutledgeFarmer.

Erricker, C and Erricker, J (eds) main contributor Levete, G (2001) *Meditation in Schools: A Practical Guide to Calmer Classrooms*; London: Continuum.

Estivalèzes, M (2017) 'The Professional Stance of Ethics and Religious Culture Teachers in Québec', *British Journal of Religious Education*, 39:1, pp. 55–74.

Everington, J (2012) '"We're All in This Together, The Kids and Me": Beginning Teachers' Use of Their Personal Life Knowledge in the Religious Education Classroom', *Journal of Beliefs & Values*, 33:3, pp. 343–355.

Everington, J (2014) 'Hindu, Muslim and Sikh Religious Education Teachers' Use of Personal Life Knowledge: The Relationship between Biographies, Professional Beliefs and Practice', *British Journal of Religious Education*, 36:2, pp. 155–173.

Everington, J (2016) '"Being Professional": RE Teachers' Understandings of Professionalism 1997–2014', *British Journal of Religious Education*, 38:2, pp. 177–188.

Feinberg, W (2014) 'An Assessment of Arguments for Teaching Religion in Public Schools in the United States', *Religious Education*, 109:4, pp. 394–405.

Felderhof, M C and Thompson, P (eds) (2014) *Teaching Virtue: The Contribution of Religious Education*; London: Bloomsbury.

Felderhof, M C, Thompson, P, and Torevell, D (eds) (2007) *Inspiring Faith in Schools: Studies in Religious Education*; London: Routledge.

Ferrara, C (2012) 'Religious Tolerance and Understanding in the French Education System', *Religious Education*, 107:5, pp. 514–530.

Fisher, R (2013) *Teaching Thinking: Philosophical Enquiry in the Classroom*: Fourth Edition; London: Bloomsbury.

Flutter, J and Rudduck, J (2004) *Consulting Pupils: What's in it for Schools?*; London: RoutledgeFalmer.

Fowler, J W (1981) *Stages of Faith: The Psychology of Human Development and the Quest for Meaning*; San Francisco: Harper.

Francis, L J, Kay, W K, and Campbell, W S (eds) (1996) *Research in Religious Education*; Leominster: Gracewing.

Franck, O (ed) (2017) *Assessment in Ethics Education: A Case of National Tests in Religious Education*; New York: Springer.

Freathy, G (2016) *The RE-searchers Approach: A Quick Start Guide with Exemplar Units of Work and Activities*; Exeter: University of Exeter.

Freathy, G, Freathy, R, Doney, J, Walshe, K, and Teece, G (2015) *The RE-searchers: A New Approach to Religious Education in Primary Schools*; Exeter: University of Exeter.

Friedman, M S (2002) *Martin Buber: The Life of Dialogue*: Fourth Edition; London: Routledge.

Friso, V and Caldin, R (2014) 'Religious and Spiritual Education in Disability Situations in Italy', *Journal of Beliefs & Values*, 35:2, pp. 222–224.

Gates, B (1989) *RE: Supply of Teachers for the 1990s*; Lancaster: RE Council.

Gates, B (1991) *What Conspired against RE Teacher Supply?*; Lancaster: RE Council.

Gates, B (1994) *Time for Religious Education and Teachers to Match: A Digest of Under-Provision*; Lancaster: RE Council.

Gaudin, P (2017) 'Neutrality and Impartiality in Public Education: The French Investment in Philosophy, Teaching about Religions, and Moral and Civic Education', *British Journal of Religious Education*, 39:1, pp. 93–106.

Gearon, L (ed) (2002a) *Human Rights & Religion: A Reader*; Brighton: Sussex Academic Press.

Gearon, L (2002b) 'Human Rights and Religious Education: Some Postcolonial Perspectives', *British Journal of Religious Education*, 24:2, pp. 140–151.

Gearon, L (ed) (2003a) *Learning to Teach Citizenship in the Secondary School*; London: Routledge.

Gearon, L (2003b) *The Human Rights Handbook: A Global Perspective for Education*; London: Trentham.

Gearon, L (2004) *Citizenship through Secondary Religious Education*; London: RoutledgeFalmer.

Gearon, L (2005) 'The Teaching of Human Rights in Religious Education: The Case of Genocide', in Bates, D (ed) *Education, Religion and Society: Essays in Honour of John M Hull*; London: Routledge.

Gearon, L (2013) 'The Counter Terrorist Classroom: Religion, Education, and Security', *Religious Education*, 108:2, pp. 129–147.

Geaves, R. (1998) 'The Borders between Religions: A Challenge to the World Religions Approach to Religious Education', *British Journal of Religious Education*, 21:1, pp. 20–31.

Geaves, R, Gabriel, T, Haddad, Y, and Idleman Smith, J (2004) *Islam and the West Post September 11th*; Aldershot: Ashgate.

Geiger, M W (2015) 'Religious Education Person to Person: Attending to Relationality', *Religious Education*, 110:2, pp. 162–180.

Geiger, M W (2016a) 'Emerging Responsibilities, Emerging Persons: Reflective and Relational Religious Education in Three Episcopal High Schools', *Religious Education*, 111:1, pp. 10–29.

Geiger, M W (2016b) 'Locating Intersubjectivity in Religious Education Praxis: A Safe Relational Space for Developing Self-Conscious Agency', *British Journal of Religious Education*, 2016, pp. 1–11.

Geiger, M W (2016c) 'Personae, Persons, and Intersubjectivity: A Relief for Understanding Roles, Deception, and Communion in Religious Education', *Religious Education*, 111:5, pp. 504–520.

Gent, B (2011) 'The World of the British *Hifz* Class Student: Observations, Findings and Implications for Education and Further Research', *British Journal of Religious Education*, 33:1, pp. 3–15.

Gill, R (2010) 'Public Theology and Music', *International Journal of Public Theology*, 4:4, pp. 410–425.

Gillibrand, J (2010) *Disabled Church – Disabled Society: The Implications of Autism for Philosophy, Theology and Politics*; London: Jessica Kingsley.

Goodman, A (2016) 'Critical Religious Education (CRE) in Practice: Evaluating the Reception of an Introductory Scheme of Work', *British Journal of Religious Education*, 2016, pp. 1–10.

Grimmitt, M (1987) *Religious Education and Human Development*; Great Wakering: McCrimmon.

Grimmitt, M (ed) (2000) *Pedagogies of Religious Education: Case Studies in the Development of Good Pedagogic Practice*; Great Wakering: McCrimmon.

Grove, J and Smalley, S (2003) *Diversity and Inclusion and Religious Education: A Good Practice Guide*; AREIAC.

Hammond, J, Hay, D, Leech, A, Moxon, J, Netto, B, Robson, K, and Straughier, G (1990) *New Methods in RE Teaching: An Experiential Approach*; London: Oliver & Boyd.

Haralambos, M, Holborn, M, Chapman, S, and Moore, S (2013) *Sociology: Themes and Perspectives*: Eighth Edition; London: Collins.

Harlen, W (ed) (2010) *Principles and Big Ideas of Science Education*; Hatfield, Hertfordshire: The Association of Science Education.

Harlen, W (ed) (2015) *Working with Big Ideas of Science Education*; Trieste: IAP: The Global Network of Science Academies.

Hatfield, E (2004) *Feeling included? A critical analysis of the impact of pedagogy on inclusion in a primary school*; Hull: unpublished MA dissertation, University of Hull.

Haurant, S (2011) 'French Government "Banning Vegetarianism" in School Canteens', *Guardian*, 26 October 2011.

Hay, D (2006) *Something There: The Biology of the Human Spirit*; London: Darton, Longman and Todd.

Hay, D (2007a) 'On Music as Revelation', *RE Today* 25:1, pp. 4–5.

Hay, D (2007b) *Why Spirituality Is Difficult for Westerners*; Exeter: Societas Essays in Political & Cultural Criticism.

Hay, D and Nye, R (2006) *The Spirit of the Child*: Revised Edition; London: Jessica Kingsley.

Haynes, C C (2012) 'First Amendment Column: Paying the Price for Religious Illiteracy', *Green Bay Press Gazette*, 9 October 2012.

Hegel, G W F (1988 [1832]) *Lectures on the Philosophy of Religion*; Berkeley, CA: University of California Press.

Hess, M E (2017) 'White Religious Educators Resisting White Fragility: Lessons from Mystics', *Religious Education*, 112:1, pp. 46–57.

Hick, J (ed) (1974) *Truth and Dialogue: The Relationship between World Religions*; London: Sheldon.

Hick, J (1989) *An Interpretation of Religion*; London: Macmillan.

Higher Education Funding Council for England (Hefce), Scottish Funding Council, Higher Education Funding Council for Wales, Department for Employment and Learning (2011) *REF2014: Research Excellence Framework: Assessment Framework and Guidance on Submissions*; Bristol: Hefce.

Hofstadter, D (1980) *Gödel, Escher, Bach: An Eternal Golden Braid: A Metaphorical Fugue on Minds and Machines in the Spirit of Lewis Carroll*; Harmondsworth: Penguin.

Hofstadter, D (2007) *I Am a Strange Loop*; New York: Basic.

Holland, J (2001) *Understanding Children's Experiences of Parental Bereavement*; London: Jessica Kingsley.

Holland, J (2016) *Responding to Loss and Bereavement in Schools: A Training Resource to Assess, Evaluate and Improve the School Response*; London: Jessica Kingsley.

Holt, J D (2002) 'The Church of Jesus Christ of Latter-day Saints in the RE Classroom', *REsource*, 24:3, pp. 6–8.

Holt, J D (2004) 'Jehovah's Witnesses in the RE Classroom', *REsource*, 26:2, pp. 617–619.

Hookway, S R (2004) *Questions of Truth: Developing Critical Thinking Skills in Secondary Religious Education*; Norwich: RMEP.

Hoppers, C O and Richards, H (2012) *Rethinking Thinking: Modernity's 'Other' and the Transformation of the University*; Pretoria: University of South Africa.

Hornby, G (2001) Promoting Responsible Inclusion: Quality Education for All, in O'Brien, T (ed) *Enabling Inclusion: Blue Skies – Dark Clouds*; London: HMSO.

Hull, J M (1998) *Utopian Whispers: Moral, Religious and Spiritual Values in Schools*; Norwich: RMEP.

Hull, J M (2003) *Many Religions – One World: An Educational Response to Religious Violence*; Birmingham: University of Birmingham School of Education Research Seminar.

Hull, J M (2004) 'Teaching as a Trans-world Activity', *Support for Learning*, 19:3, pp. 103–106.

Hull, J M (2005) 'Religious Education in Germany and England: The Recent Work of Hans-Georg Ziebertz', *British Journal of Religious Education*, 27:1, pp. 5–17.

Huxley, A (1950 [1931]) *Music at Night and Other Essays*; Edinburgh: Penguin in Association with Chatto & Windus.

Hyde, B (2006) "You Can't Buy Love': Trivialising and the Challenge for Religious Education', *Journal of Beliefs & Values*, 27:2, pp. 165–176.

Hyde, B (2008a) *Children and Spirituality: Searching for Meaning and Connectedness*; London: Jessica Kingsley.

Hyde, B (2008b) 'Weaving the Threads of Meaning: A Characteristic of Children's Spirituality and Its Implications for Religious Education', *British Journal of Religious Education*, 30:3, pp. 235–245.

Hyde, B (2013) 'A Category Mistake: Why Contemporary Australian Religious Education in Catholic Schools May Be Doomed to Failure', *Journal of Beliefs & Values*, 34:1, pp. 36–45.

I'Anson, J (2004) 'Mapping the Subject: Student Teachers, Location and the Understanding of Religion', *British Journal of Religious Education*, 26:1, pp. 45–60.

Illich, I D (1971) *Deschooling Society*; London: Calder & Boyers.

Illich, I D (1974) *After Deschooling, What?*; London: Writers' and Readers' Publishing Cooperative.

Illman, R (2010) 'Plurality and Peace: Inter-Religious Dialogue in a Creative Perspective', *International Journal of Public Theology*, 4:2, pp. 175–193.

Ipgrave, J (1999) 'Issues in the Delivery of Religious Education to Muslim Pupils: Perspectives from the Classroom', *British Journal of Religious Education*, 21:3, pp. 146–157.

Ipgrave, J (2001) *Pupil-to-Pupil Dialogue in the Classroom as a Tool for Religious Education: Warwick Religions and Education Research Unit Occasional Papers II*; Coventry: WRERU

Ipgrave, J (2003) *Building e-Bridges: Inter-Faith Dialogue by E-Mail*; Birmingham: REToday Services.

Ipgrave, J (2004) 'Including Pupils' Faith Background in Primary Religious Education', *Support for Learning*, 19:3, pp. 114–118.

Ipgrave, J (2009) 'The Language of Friendship and Identity: Children's Communication Choices in an Interfaith Exchange', *British Journal of Religious Education*, 31:3, pp. 213–225.

Ipgrave, J (2012) 'Conversations between the Religious and Secular in English Schools', *Religious Education*, 107:1, pp. 30–48.

Ishak, M S b H and Abdullah, O C (2013) 'Islamic Education in Malaysia: A Study of History and Development', *Religious Education*, 108:3, pp. 298–311.

Islam, Y, Merlin, D, Alili, A, Podojak, S, Šaban, B, and Whiteman, A L (1997) *I Have No Cannons That Roar*; Jamal Records J70003CD.

Jackson, R (1990) 'Children as Ethnographers', in Jackson, R and Starkings, D (eds) *The Junior RE Handbook*; Cheltenham: Stanley Thornes.

Jackson, R (1997) *Religious Education: An Interpretative Approach*; London: Hodder.

Jackson, R (ed) (2003) *International Perspectives on Citizenship, Education and Religious Diversity*; London: RoutledgeFalmer.

Jackson, R (2004) *Rethinking Religious Education and Plurality: Issues in Diversity and Pedagogy*; London: RoutledgeFalmer.

Jackson, R (2006) 'New European Union Research on Religious Education', *Editorial, British Journal of Religious Education*, 28:2, pp. 111–113.

Jackson, R (2015) 'The Politicisation and Securitisation of Religious Education? A Rejoinder', *British Journal of Educational Studies*, 63:3, pp. 345–366.

Jackson, R, Miedema, R, Weisse, W, and Willaime, J-P (eds) (2007) *Religion and Education in Europe: Developments, Contexts and Debates*; Münster: Waxmann.

Jackson, R and Nesbitt, E (1993) *Hindu Children in Britain*; Stoke-on-Trent: Trentham.

James, W (1983 [1902]) *The Varieties of Religious Experience: A Study in Human Nature*; Harmondsworth: Penguin.

Jasper, A and I'Anson, J (2017) *Schooling Indifference: Reimagining RE in Multi-Cultural and Gendered Spaces*; London: Routledge.

Johnson, C and Stern, L J (2005) 'Westhill Seminar 6: Ethnography, Pluralism and Religious Education', *Resource*, 28:1, pp. 3–6.

Kant, I (1964 [1795]) *Groundwork of the Metaphysic of Morals*; New York: Harper.

Kay, W K and Francis, L J (eds) (2000) *Religion in Education: Distance Learning: Volume 3*; Leominster: Gracewing.

Keast, J (ed) (2007) *Religious Diversity and Intercultural Education: A Reference Book for Schools*; Strasbourg, France: Council of Europe Publishing.

Keats, J (1947 [1848, 1878]) *The Letters of John Keats*; London: Oxford University Press.

Kelly, G A (1955) *The Psychology of Personal Constructs*; New York: Norton.

Kenngott, E-M (2017) 'Life Design-Ethics-Religion Studies: Nonconfessional RE in Brandenburg (Germany)', *British Journal of Religious Education*, 39:18, pp. 40–54.

Kessler, R (2000) *The Soul of Education: Helping Students Find Connection, Compassion, and Character at School*; Alexandria, VI: ASCD.

Kessler, R (2002) 'Nurturing Deep Connections: Five Principles for Welcoming Soul into School Leadership', *The School Administrator*, 59:8, pp. 22–26, September 2002.

Klass, D (1999) *The Spiritual Lives of Bereaved Parents*; Philadelphia: Brunner/Mazel.

Klass, D, Silverman, P R, and Nickman, S L (eds) (1996) *Continuing Bonds: New Understandings of Grief*; Philadelphia: Taylor and Francis.

Kohlberg, L (1981) *The Philosophy of Moral Development*; San Francisco: Harper & Row.

Kozyrev, F (2011) 'Russian REDCo Findings in Support of Dialogue and Hermeneutics', *British Journal of Religious Education*, 33:2, pp. 257–270.

Krisman, A (2001) 'The Yin and Yang of RE and Special Needs: Teaching RE to Pupils with Special Needs within a Multi-Faith Community', *SHAP: World Religions in Education: 2000/2001: Living Community*, pp. 83–84.

Krumboltz, J D (2009) 'The Happenstance Learning Theory', *Journal of Career Assessment*, 17:2, pp. 135–154.

Krumboltz, J D and Levin, A S (2010) *Luck Is No Accident: Making the Most of Happenstance in Your Life and Career*: Second Edition; Atascadero, CA: Impact Publishers.

Künkler, M and Lerner, H (2016) 'A Private Matter? Religious Education and Democracy in Indonesia and Israel', *British Journal of Religious Education*, 38:3, pp. 279–307.

Kuyk, E, Jensen, R, Lankshear, D, Manna, E L, and Schreiner, P (eds) (2007) *Religious Education in Europe: Situation and Current Trends in Schools*; Oslo: IKO.

Lantieri, L (ed) (2001) *Schools with Spirit: Nurturing the Inner Lives of Children and Teachers*; Boston, MA: Beacon.

Latsone, L (2013a) 'Socially Intelligent Intercultural Education', *Educational Research Journal*, 28:1&2, pp. 145–162.

Latsone, L (2013b) 'The Role of Religious Education in Creating Participative and Inclusive Parish Communities: Challenges for Adult Religious Educators of Latvia', *Religious Education Journal of Australia*, 29:1, pp. 22–27.

Lave, J (2011) *Apprenticeship in Critical Ethnographic Practice*; Chicago: University of Chicago Press.

Lave, J and Wenger, E (1991) *Situated Learning: Legitimate Peripheral Participation*; Cambridge: Cambridge University Press.

Lees, H E (2012) *Silence in Schools*; Stoke on Trent: Trentham.

Leicester, M (1992) 'Antiracism versus the New Multiculturalism: Moving beyond the Interminable Debate', in Lynch, J, Modgil, C, and Modgil, S (eds) *Cultural Diversity and the Schools: Equity or Excellence? Education and Cultural Reproduction*; London: Falmer.

Li, J and Moore, D (2014) 'Reconsideration of the Coexistence of Buddhist Temple Education and State Education in Xishuangbanna, China', *British Journal of Religious Education*, 36:2, pp. 139–154.

Liagkis, M K (2015) 'Religious Education in Greece: A New Curriculum, an Old Issue', *British Journal of Religious Education*, 37:2, pp. 153–169.

Lickona, T and Davidson, M (2005) *Smart & Good High Schools: Integrating Excellence and Ethics for Success in School, Work, and Beyond*; Cortland, NY: Center for the 4th and 5th Rs.

Liedgren, P (2016) 'Minorities with Different Values at School – The Case of Jehovah's Witnesses', *British Journal of Religious Education*, pp. 1–13.

Lipman, M (2003) *Thinking in Education*: Second Edition; Cambridge: Cambridge University Press.

Lovelace, A (2001) *Speaking for Ourselves: A REaSE Project Video*; Norwich: RMEP.

Lowndes, J (2001) *Effective Staff Development: Improving Pupils' Achievement*; Havant: Hampshire County Council and Brunel University.

MacBeath, J (1999) *Schools Must Speak for Themselves: The Case for School Self-Evaluation*; London: RoutledgeFalmer.

McCutcheon, R T (ed) (1999) *The Insider/Outsider Problem in the Study of Religion: A Reader*; London: Cassell.

McDonald, J P (1989) 'When Outsiders Try to Change Schools from the Inside', *Phi Delta Kappan*, 71:3, pp. 206–212.

Mackley, J (project director) (1997) *Looking Inwards – Looking Outwards: Exploring Life's Possibilities*; Derby: CEM.

Mackley, J (ed) (2002) *Evil & Goodness*; Birmingham: Christian Education Publications.

McLaughlin, T H (2008) *Liberalism, Education and Schooling*; Exeter: Imprint.

Macmurray, J (1946a) 'The Integrity of the Personal', *Joseph Payne Memorial Lectures, King's College, London*, 1 November 1946.

Macmurray, J (1946b) 'Culture and Function', *Joseph Payne Memorial Lectures, King's College, London*, 15 November 1946.

Macmurray, J (1946c) 'Freedom in Community', *Joseph Payne Memorial Lectures, King's College, London*, 29 November 1946.

Macmurray, J (1992) *Freedom in the Modern World*; Atlantic Highlands, NJ: Humanities Press.

Macmurray, J (1995) *Reason and Emotion*; London: Faber.

Macmurray, J (1996) *The Personal World: John Macmurray on Self and Society*; Edinburgh: Floris.

Madge, N, Hemming, PJ and Stenson, K with Allum, N, Calestani, M, Goodman, A, King, K, Kingston, S, and Webster, C (2014) *Youth on Religion: The Development, Negotiation and Impact of Faith and Non-Faith Identity*; Hove: Routledge.

Marshall, P (ed) (2000) *Religious Freedom in the World: A Global Report on Freedom and Persecution*; London: Broadman and Holman.

Martins, I M and Matoso, M (2010) *When I Was Born*; London: Tate.

Mason, M (2000) 'Spirituality – What on Earth Is It?', *International Conference of Children's Spirituality at Roehampton Institute* (available online at humanism.org.uk/wp-content/uploads/SpiritualitywhatonEarthisit.pdf) (accessed 12 August 2004).

May, S (ed) (1999) *Critical Multiculturalism: Rethinking Multicultural and Antiracist Education*; London: Falmer.

Mill, J S (1910 [1861, 1859, 1861]) *Utilitarianism, Liberty, and Representative Government*; London: Dent.

Miller, J P, Karsten, S, Denton, D, Orr, D, and Kates, I C (eds) (2005) *Holistic Learning and Spirituality in Education: Breaking New Ground*; Albany: State University of New York Press.

Mingers, J (1999) *Critical Management Education: A Critical Issue*; UK Systems Society Conference.

Montreal Gazette (2008) 'Que. Parents Protest Mandatory Religious Course', *Montreal Gazette*, 18 October 2008.

Montreal Gazette (2010) 'Quebec Couple Brings Fight against Mandatory Ethics Course to Canada's Top Court', *Montreal Gazette*, 28 April 2010.

Moore, D L (Chair of the Task Force) (2010) *Guidelines for Teaching about Religion in K-12 Public Schools in the United States*; Atlanta, GA: American Academy of Religion: Religion in the Schools Task Force.

Moran, G (1989) *Religious Education as a Second Language*; Birmingham: Religious Education Press.

Moustakas, C (1994) *Phenomenological Research Methods*; Beverley Hills, CA: Sage.

Nanbu, H (2008) 'Religion in Chinese Education: From Denial to Cooperation', *British Journal of Religious Education*, 30:3, pp. 223–234.

Nash, R J and Bishop, P A (2010) *Teaching Adolescents Religious Literacy in a Post-9/11 World*; Charlotte, NC: IAP.

Ndlovu, L (2014) 'Religion Education Teaching in Zimbabwe Secondary Schools: The Search for an Authentic Values-Oriented Multi-Faith Religion Education Pedagogical Model', *British Journal of Religious Education*, 36:2, pp. 174–201.

Nesbitt, E (2001) 'Ethnographic Research at Warwick: Some Methodological Issues', *British Journal of Religious Education*, 23:3, pp. 144–155.

Nesbitt, E (2003) *Interfaith Pilgrims: Living Truths and Truthful Living*; London: Quaker Home Service.

Nesbitt, E (2004) *Intercultural Education: Ethnographic and Religious Approaches*; Brighton: Sussex Academic Press.

Nesbitt, E (2005) *Sikhism: A Very Short Introduction*; Oxford: Oxford University Press.

Nesbitt, E and Kaur, G (1998) *Guru Nanak*; Calgary, AB: Bayeux Arts.

Newton, C, and Tarrant, T (1992) *Managing Change in Schools: A Practical Handbook*; London: Routledge.

Ng, Y-L (2012) 'Spiritual Development in the Classroom: Pupils' and Educators' Learning Reflections', *International Journal of Children's Spirituality*, 17:2, pp. 167–185.

Nietzsche, F W (1993 [1891]) *Thus Spake Zarathustra*; Garden Grove, CA: World Library: Library of the Future.

Nisbett, R E (2003) *The Geography of Thought: How Asians and Westerners Think Differently ... and Why*; London: Nicholas Brealey Publishing.

Noddings, N (1994) 'Conversation as Moral Education', *Journal of Moral Education*, 23:2, pp. 107–118.

Noddings, N (2003) *Happiness and Education*; Cambridge: Cambridge University Press.

Noddings, N (2015) *A Richer, Brighter Vision for American High Schools*; New York: Cambridge University Press.

Nogueira-Godsey, E (2016) 'Recent Observations on Religion Education in South Africa', *British Journal of Religious Education*, 38:3, pp. 229–235.

Nord, W A (1995) *Religion & American Education: Rethinking a National Dilemma*; Chapel Hill: University of North Carolina Press.

Nye, R (2009) *Children's Spirituality: What It Is and Why It Matters*; London: Church House Publishing.

O'Brien, L (2002) *Connecting with RE*; London: National Society.

Oczkus, L D (2003) *Reciprocal Teaching at Work: Strategies for Improving Reading Comprehension*; Newark, DE: International Reading Association.

Odena, O (2010) 'Practitioners' Views on Cross-Community Music Education Projects in Northern Ireland: Alienation, Socio-Economic Factors and Educational Potential', *British Educational Research Journal*, 36:1, pp. 83–105.

Office for Democratic Institutions and Human Rights (ODIHR) (2007) *Toledo Guiding Principles on Teaching about Religions and Beliefs in Public Schools*; Warsaw: ODIHR/OSCE (available online at www.osce.org/odihr/29154) (accessed 31 March 2017).

Office for Standards in Education (Ofsted) (1993) *Handbook for the Inspection of Schools*; London: HMSO.

Office for Standards in Education (Ofsted) (2000a) *Evaluating Educational Inclusion: Guidance for Inspectors and Schools*; London: Stationery Office.

Office for Standards in Education (Ofsted) (2000b) *The Annual Report of Her Majesty's Chief Inspector of Schools: Standards and Quality in Education 1998/99*; London: Stationery Office.

Office for Standards in Education (Ofsted) (2004) *Promoting and Evaluating Pupils' Spiritual, Moral, Social and Cultural Development*; London: Stationery Office.

Office for Standards in Education (Ofsted) (2016) *School Inspection Handbook: Handbook for Inspecting Schools in England under Section 5 of the Education Act 2005*; Manchester: Ofsted.

O'Hanlon, C (2003) *Educational Inclusion as Action Research: An Interpretive Discourse*; Maidenhead: Open University Press.

Omori, H (2013) 'Religious Education Leading to Higher Education for Women: Historical Insights on Modern Japan', *Religious Education*, 108:5, pp. 529–541.

Orchard, J (2001) *Raising the Standard, Flying the Flag – Challenging Activities for all in RE at Key Stage 3*; London: National Society.

Oswin, M (1991) *Am I Allowed to Cry?: A Study of Bereavement amongst People Who Have Learning Difficulties*; London: Souvenir Press.

Ota, C and Chater, M (eds) (2007) *Spiritual Education in a Divided World: Social, Environmental & Pedagogical Perspectives on the Spirituality of Children and Young People*; Abingdon: Routledge.

Palmer, P J (1993) *To Know as We Are Known: Education as a Spiritual Journey: A Master Teacher Offers a New Model for Authentic Teaching and Learning*; San Francisco: Harper.

Palmer, P J (2007) *The Courage to Teach: Exploring the Inner Landscape of a Teacher's Life: 10th Anniversary Edition*; San Francisco: Jossey-Bass.

Parker, S G and Freathy, R J K (2011) 'Context, Complexity and Contestation: Birmingham's Agreed Syllabuses for Religious Education since the 1970s', *Journal of Beliefs & Values*, 32:2, pp. 247–263.

Parker, S G, Freathy, R, and Francis, L J (eds) (2012) *Religious Education and Freedom of Religion and Belief*; Oxford: Peter Lang.

Parker, S G, Freathy, R, and Francis, L J (eds) (2015) *History, Remembrance and Religious Education*; Oxford: Peter Lang.

Parmar, N (2001) *Using the Bhagavad Gita to Improve the Teaching of Hinduism at Key Stage 2*; Oxford: Farmington Institute.

Paton, G (2010) 'Schools using dance and fashion to get bored pupils interested in maths: Schools are resorting to drama, role-play, music and dance to get children interested in subjects such as maths and science, according to Ofsted', *Daily Telegraph*, 15 January 2010.

Paul-Binyamin, I and Gindi, S (2017) 'Autonomy and Religious Education: Lessons from a Six-Year Evaluation of an Educational Reform in an Israeli School Network', *British Journal of Religious Education*, 39:2, pp. 149–171.

Peterson, A (2017) 'The Contested Place of Religion in the Australian Civics and Citizenship Curriculum: Exploring the Secular in a Multi-Faith Society', *British Journal of Religious Education*, 39:2, pp. 207–222.

Peterson, C (2006) *A Primer in Positive Psychology*; Oxford: Oxford University Press.

Peterson, C and Seligman, M E P (2004) *Character Strengths and Virtues: A Handbook and Classification*; Oxford: Oxford University Press.

Popper, K (2002 [1963]) *Conjectures and Refutations: The Growth of Scientific Knowledge*; London: Routledge.

Priestley, J (1997) 'Spirituality, Curriculum and Education', *International Journal of Children's Spirituality*, 2:1, pp. 23–34.

Priestley, J (2000) 'So This Is Christmas …', *Guardian*, 23 December 2000 (available online at www.theguardian.com/theguardian/2000/dec/23/guardianletters7).

Prothero, S (2007) *Religious Literacy: What Every American Needs to Know – And Doesn't*; New York: HarperCollins.

Pullman, P (2010) *The Good Man Jesus and the Scoundrel Christ*; Edinburgh: Canongate.

Purpel, D E and McLaurin Jr, W M (2004) *Reflections on the Moral & Spiritual Crisis in Education*; New York: Peter Lang.

Qualifications and Curriculum Authority (QCA) (2004) *Religious Education: The Non-Statutory National Framework*; London: QCA.

Ranson, S (2000) 'Recognizing the Pedagogy of Voice in a Learning Community', *Educational Management & Administration*, 28:3, pp. 263–279.

Ravenette, T (1999) *Personal Construct Theory in Educational Psychology: A Practitioner's View*; London: Whurr.

Read, G, Rudge, J, Teece, G, and Howarth, R B (1988) *How Do I Teach RE?: The Westhill Project RE 5–16*: Second Edition; Cheltenham: Stanley Thornes.

Religious Education Council of England and Wales (REC) (2013) *A Review of Religious Education in England*; London: The Religious Education Council of England and Wales.

Ricucci, R (2015) 'Religious Education in the Facebook Era in the Moroccan Diaspora: Muslims On Line, Young People Off Line', *ECER 2015, Budapest* (available online at www.eera-ecer.de/ecer-programmes/conference/20/contribution/35160/) (accessed 31 March 2017).

Ring, K (2013) 'Creative Representation: The Child's Unique Response to Experience', *Early Education*, 69, pp. 6–7.

Rose, J (1995) *Hindu Story & Symbol*; Isleworth: BFSS National RE Centre.

Rosenblatt, L M (1994) *The Reader the Text the Poem: The Transactional Theory of the Literary Work*; Carbondale and Edwardsville, IL: Southern Illinois University Press.

Rosenblatt, L M (1995) *Literature as Exploration*: Fifth Edition; New York: Modern Language Association of America.

Rothgangel, M, Jackson, R, and Jäggle, M (eds) (2014), *Religious Education at Schools in Europe: Part 2: Western Europe*; Göttingen: Vandenhoeck & Ruprecht.

Rothgangel, M, Skeie, G, and Jäggle, M (eds) (2014) *Religious Education at Schools in Europe: Part 3: Northern Europe*; Göttingen: Vandenhoeck & Ruprecht.

Rothgangel, M, Jäggle, M, and Schlag, T (eds) (2016) *Religious Education at Schools in Europe: Part 1: Central Europe*; Göttingen: Vandenhoeck & Ruprecht.

Rudduck, J, Chaplain, R, and Wallace, G (eds) (1996) *School Improvement: What Can Pupils Tell Us?*; London: Fulton.

Rudge, L (1998) '"I Am Nothing" – Does It Matter? A Critique of Current Religious Education Policy and Practice on Behalf of the Silent Majority', *British Journal of Religious Education*, 20:3, pp. 155–165.

Rudge, L (2001) *Making RE Work: Principles to Practice in Curriculum and Professional Development*; Norwich: University of East Anglia.

Rumi (1995) *The Essential Rumi*; Harmondsworth: Penguin.

Rüppell, G and Schreiner, P (eds) (2003) *Shared Learning in a Plural World: Ecumenical Approaches to Inter-Religious Education*; Münster: Comenius Institut.

Russell, B (1961) *The History of Western Philosophy and Its Connection with Political and Social Circumstances from the Earliest Times to the Present Day*: Second Edition; London: George Allen & Unwin.

Sacks, J (2003) *The Dignity of Difference: How to Avoid the Clash of Civilizations*: Second Edition; London: Continuum.

Salmon, P (1994) 'Grids Are All Very Well, but …', *EPCA Newsletter 1994, 2*.

Sauntson, H (2013) 'Sexual Diversity and Illocutionary Silencing in the English National Curriculum', *Sex Education*, 13:4, pp. 395–408.

Savall, J (conductor) (2008) *Hommage: À Jérusalem et Invocation À la Paix [A Homage to Jerusalem and an Invocation to Peace]*; Alia Vox AVSA 9863 A+B.

Scheilke, C T (2011) *12 gute Gründe für einen konfessionellen Religionsundterricht in der Schule der Pluralität*; Stuttgart: Pädagogisch-Theologisches Zentrum Stuttgart.

School Curriculum and Assessment Authority (SCAA) (1994) *Religious Education: Glossary of Terms*; London: SCAA.

School Curriculum and Assessment Authority (SCAA) (1995) *Spiritual and Moral Development: SCAA Discussion Papers: No. 3*; London: SCAA.

Schreiner, P, Kraft, F, and Wright, A (eds) (2007) *Good Practice in Religious Education in Europe: Examples and Perspectives of Primary Schools*; Berlin: Lit for the Comenius-Institut.

Schreiner, P, Spinder, H, Taylor, J, and Westerman, W (eds) (2002) *Committed to Europe's Future: Contributions from Education and Religious Education: A Reader*; Münster: CoGREE (Coordinating Group for Religious Education in Europe) and the Comenius Institut.

Searle-Chatterjee, M (1997) *Community, Description, Debate and Dilemma*; Scaynes Hill: Venture Press.

Searle-Chatterjee, M (2000) '"World Religions" and "Ethnic Groups": Do These Paradigms Lend Themselves to the Cause of Hindu Nationalism?', *Ethnic and Racial Studies*, 23:3, pp. 497–515.

Selçuk, M and Valk, J (2012) 'Knowing Self and Others: A Worldview Model for Religious Education in Turkey, *Religious Education*, 107:5, pp. 443–454.

Sen, A (1981) *Poverty and Famines: An Essay on Entitlement and Deprivation*; Oxford: Oxford University Press.

Sikes, P and Everington, J (2001) 'Becoming an RE Teacher: A Life History Approach', *British Journal of Religious Education*, 24:1, pp. 8–20.

Sikes, P and Everington, J (2004) '"RE Teachers Do Get Drunk You Know': Becoming a Religious Education Teacher in the Twenty-First Century', *Teachers and Teaching*, 10:1, pp. 21–33.

Silverman, D (ed) (1997) *Qualitative Research: Theory, Method and Practice*; London: Sage.

Sinclair, A and Strachan, A (2016) 'The Messy Nature of Science: Famous Scientists Can Help Clear Up', *Primary Science*, 145, pp. 21–23.

Singleton, A (2015) 'Are Religious 'Nones' Secular? The Case of the Nones in Australia', *Journal of Beliefs & Values*, 36:2, pp. 239–243.

Sink, C A and Bultsma, S A (2014) 'Psychometric Analysis of the Life Perspectives Inventory and Implications for Assessing Characteristics of Adolescent Spirituality', *Measurement and Evaluation in Counseling and Development*, 47:2, pp. 150–167.

Sink, C A, Cleveland, R, and Stern, J (2007) 'Spiritual Formation in Christian School Counseling Programs', *Journal of Research on Christian Education*, 16:1, pp. 35–63.

Skeie, G (1995) 'Plurality and Pluralism: A Challenge for Religious Education', *British Journal of Religious Education*, 17:2, pp. 84–91.

Skeie, G (2002) 'The Concept of Plurality and Its Meaning for Religious Education', *British Journal of Religious Education*, 25:1, pp. 47–59.

Skeie, G (2017) 'Impartial Teachers in Religious Education – A Perspective from a Norwegian Context', *British Journal of Religious Education*, 39:1, pp. 25–39.

Skolverket [Swedish National Agency for Education] (2011) *Curriculum for the Compulsory School, Preschool Class and the Recreation Centre 2011*; Stockholm: Ordförrådet AB (also available from www.skolverket.se/publikationen).

Smalley, S (2005) 'Teaching about Islam and Learning about Muslims: Islamophobia in the Classroom', *REsource* 27:2, pp. 4–7.

Smart, N (1960) *A Dialogue of Religions*; London: SCM.

Smart, N (1969) *The Religious Experience of Mankind*; London: Collins.

Smart, N (1983) *Worldviews: Crosscultural Explorations of Human Belief*; New York: Scribner.

Smart, N (1999) *World Philosophies*; London: Routledge.

Smith, G (2005) *Children's Perspectives on Believing and Belonging*; London: National Children's Bureau for the Joseph Rowntree Foundation.

Smith, R (2002) 'Self-Esteem: The Kindly Apocalypse', *Journal of Philosophy of Education*, 36:1, pp. 87–100.

Smith, W C (1978) *The Meaning and End of Religion*; London: SPCK.

Snyder, C R and Lopez, S J (eds) (2005) *Handbook of Positive Psychology*; Oxford: Oxford University Press.

Social and Character Development Research Consortium (SCDRC) (2010) *Efficacy of Schoolwide Programs to Promote Social and Character Development and Reduce Problem Behavior in Elementary School Children*; Washington, DC: National Center for Education Research, Institute of Education Sciences, US Department of Education.

de Souza, M, Engebretson, K, Durka, R, Jackson, R, and McGrady, A (eds) (2006) *International Handbook of the Religious, Moral and Spiritual Dimension of Education*; Dordrecht: Springer Academic Publishers.

Spender, D (1982) *Invisible Women: The Schooling Scandal*; London: Writers' and Readers' Collective.

Spinoza, B (1955 [1677]) *The Ethics*; New York: Dover.

Sporre, K (2012) 'Voices from South and North in Dialogue: On Diversity and Education for the Future', *British Journal of Religious Education*, 34:1, pp. 87–100.

Steiner, R (1965 [1927]) *The Education of the Child in the Light of Anthroposophy*: Second Edition; London: Rudolf Steiner Press.

Steiner, R (1996) *Rudolf Steiner in the Waldorf School: Lectures and Addresses to Children, Parents, and Teachers – 1919–1924*; Hudson, NY: Anthroposophic Press.

Stenhouse, L (1975) *An Introduction to Curriculum Research and Development*; London: Heinemann.

Stern, L J (1999) *Developing as a Teacher of History*; Cambridge: Chris Kington.

Stern, L J (2001) 'Being DIRECT with Primary Religious Education: Linking Primary RE to Local Communities', *REsource* 23:2, pp. 11–15.

Stern, L J (2002) 'EMU Leadership: An Egalitarian Magnanimous Undemocratic Way for Schools', *International Journal of Children's Spirituality*, 7:2, pp. 143–158.

Stern, L J (2003a) *Involving Parents*; London: Continuum.

Stern, L J (2003b) *Progression from Family Learning*; Hull: CityLearning.

Stern, L J (2004) 'Marking Time: Using Music to Create Inclusive Religious Education and Inclusive Schools', *Support for Learning*, 19:3, pp. 107–113.

Stern, L J (2007a) *Schools and Religions: Imagining the Real*; London: Continuum.

Stern, L J (2007b) 'Action Philosophy in Jewish and Christian Traditions', *REsource*, 30:1, pp. 9–12.

Stern, L J (2009a) *The Spirit of the School*; London: Continuum.

Stern, L J (2009b) *Getting the Buggers to Do Their Homework*: Second Edition; London: Continuum.

Stern, L J (2010) 'Research as Pedagogy: Building Learning Communities and Religious Understanding in RE', *British Journal of Religious Education*, 32:2, pp. 133–146.

Stern, L J (2011) 'Expressing Meaning Through Sound: Liberating Music', pp. 18–22 in Pett, S (ed) *Questions: Expressing Meaning*; Birmingham: RE Today Services.

Stern, L J (2012) 'The Personal World of Schooling: John Macmurray and Schools as Households', *Oxford Review of Education*, 38:6, pp. 727–745.

Stern, L J (2014a) 'The Influence of Research within Religious Education: The Westhill Seminars, RE Professionals, Pupils and Schools', *British Journal of Religious Education*, 36:1, pp. 18–38.

Stern, L J (2014b) *Loneliness and Solitude in Education: How to Value Individuality and Create an Enstatic School*; Oxford: Peter Lang.

Stern, L J (2015) 'Children's Voice or Children's Voices: How Educational Research Can Be at the Heart of Schooling', *Forum: For Promoting 3–19 Comprehensive Education*, 57:1, pp. 75–90.

Stern, L J (2016) *Virtuous Educational Research: Conversations on Ethical Practice*; Oxford: Peter Lang.

Stern, L J (2018) *A Philosophy of Schooling: Care and Curiosity in Community*; London: Palgrave.

Stern, L J and James, S (2006) 'Every Person Matters: Enabling Spirituality Education for Nurses', *Journal of Clinical Nursing* 15:7, pp. 897–904.

Stern, L J and Backhouse, A (2011) 'Dialogic Feedback for Children and Teachers: Evaluating the "Spirit of Assessment"', *International Journal of Children's Spirituality*, 16:4, pp. 331–346.

Stoll, L and Myers, K (eds) (1998) *No Quick Fixes: Perspectives on Schools in Difficulty*; London: Falmer.

Sutcliffe, S J (ed) (2004) *Religion: Empirical Studies*; Aldershot: Ashgate.

Teece, G (2004) 'A Perspective from NASACRE: The National Framework for RE – Potential Unleashed', *REsource*, 27:1, pp. 7–8.

Teece, G (2010) 'Is It Learning About & From Religions, Religions or Religious Education? And Is It Any Wonder Some Teachers Don't Get It?', *British Journal of Religious Education*, 32:2, pp. 93–103.

Thistleton, A C (2009) *Hermeneutics: An Introduction*; Grand Rapids, MI: Eerdmans.

Thomas, P (2012) 'Religious Education and the Feminisation of Witchcraft: A Study of Three Secondary Schools in Kumasi, Ghana', *British Journal of Religious Education*, 34:1, pp. 67–86.

Thompson, P (2004a) *Whatever Happened to Religious Education?*; Cambridge: Lutterworth Press.

Thompson, P (2004b) 'Whose Confession? Which Tradition', *British Journal of Religious Education*, 26:1, pp. 61–72.

Townsend, P (1979) *Poverty in the United Kingdom: A Survey of Household Resources and Standards of Living*; Harmondsworth: Viking.

Townsend, P and Gordon, D (eds) (2002) *World Poverty: New Policies to Defeat an Old Enemy*; Bristol: Polity.

Troyna, B (1983) 'Multicultural Education: Just Another Brick in the Wall?', *New Community*, 10, pp. 424–428.

Tyler, A (1965) *The Tin Can Tree*; London: Vintage.

Ubani, M (2015) 'Teaching Religious Education as a Second Choice: The Case of Three Male Student Teachers in Finland', *Journal of Beliefs & Values*; 36:2, pp. 1–14.

Ubani, M (2016) 'RE Student Teachers' Professional Development: Results, Reflections and Implications', *British Journal of Religious Education*, 38:2, pp. 189–199.

United Nations Educational, Scientific and Cultural Organisation (UNESCO) (1994) *The Salamanca Statement and Framework for Action on Special Needs Education*; Paris: UNESCO.

Want, A van der, Bakker, C, Avest, I ter, and Everington, J (eds) (2009) *Teachers Responding to Religious Diversity in Europe: Researching Biography and Pedagogy*; Münster: Waxmann.

Warren, J (1989) *Becoming Real: An Introduction to the Thought of John Macmurray*; York: Sessions Book Trust.

Watson, B (2004) 'Spirituality in British State Education: An Alternative Perspective', *Journal of Beliefs & Values*, 25:1, pp. 55–62.

Watson, J (2007) 'Spiritual Development: Constructing an Inclusive and Progressive Approach', *Journal of Beliefs & Values*, 28:2, pp. 125–136.

Wearmouth, J (ed) (2001) *Special Educational Provision in the Context of Inclusion: Policy and Practice in Schools*; London: Fulton/Open University.

Weeden, P, Winter, J, and Broadfoot, P (2002) *Assessment: What's in It for Schools?*; London: RoutledgeFalmer.

Wegerif, R (2008) 'Dialogic or Dialectic? The Significance of Ontological Assumptions in Research on Educational Dialogue', *British Educational Research Journal*, 34:3, pp. 347–361.

West-Burnham, J and Huws Jones, V (2007) *Spiritual and Moral Development in Schools*; London: Continuum.

Weston, D (2003) 'Children Talking Online', *RE Today*, 21:1, pp. 30–31.

White, J (2000) 'DIRECT: Dialogue, Inclusion, Relevancy, Esteem, Changing Dynamics, Togetherness: Croydon LEA REaSE Report for 1999–2000', *Presented at the REaSE Conference*, May 2000.

White, J (2001), 'BRIDGES – A Way Forward: Draft REaSE Report', BFSS National RE Centre, Brunel University.

Wintersgill, B (1995) 'The Case of the Missing Models: Exploding the Myths', *REsource*, 18:1, pp. 6–11.

Wintersgill, B (ed) (2017) *Big Ideas for Religious Education*; Exeter: University of Exeter.

Wittgenstein, L (1958) *Philosophische Untersuchungen: Philosophical Investigations*: Second Edition; Oxford: Blackwell.

Wong P H (2006a) *A Conceptual Investigation into Spirituality and Conditions for Education in Spirituality, with Application to the Case of Hong Kong*; Hull: University of Hull: PhD thesis.

Wong P H (2006b) 'A Conceptual Investigation into the Possibility of Spiritual Education', *International Journal of Children's Spirituality*, 11:1, pp. 73–85.

Wood, D (1988) *How Children Think and Learn: The Social Contexts of Cognitive Development*; Oxford: Blackwell.

Wright, A (1993) *Religious Education in the Secondary School: Prospects for Religious Literacy*; London: David Fulton.

Wright, A (1997) 'Mishmash, Religionism and Theological Literacy: An Appreciation and Critique of Trevor Cooling's Hermeneutical Programme', *British Journal of Religious Education*, 19:2, pp. 143–156.

Wright, A (2005) 'Spiritual Identity and the Pursuit of Truth', *8th Nordic RE Conference: Religion, Spirituality and Identity*; Helsinki.

Zaehner, R C (ed and trans) (1992) *Hindu Scriptures*; London: Everyman.

Zamorski, B (2000) *Making RE Work: Principles to Practice in Curriculum and Professional Development: Research Report: Implementation of the Agreed Syllabus in LEAs 4, 5 & 6*; Norwich: University of East Anglia.

Index